THE
SECOND CIRCLE

THE
SECOND CIRCLE
TOOLS FOR THE ADVANCING PAGAN

VENECIA RAULS

CITADEL PRESS
Kensington Publishing Corp.
www.kensingtonbooks.com

CITADEL PRESS books are published by

Kensington Publishing Corp.
850 Third Avenue
New York, NY 10022

All Kensington titles, imprints, and distributed lines are available at special quantity discounts
for bulk purchases for sales promotions, premiums, fund-raising, educational, or institutional
use. Special book excerpts or customized printings can also be created to fit specific needs.
For details, write or phone the office of the Kensington special sales manager: Kensington
Publishing Corp., 850 Third Avenue, New York, NY 10022, attn: Special Sales Department;
phone 1-800-221-2647.

First printing, April 2004
10   9   8   7   6   5   4   3   2   1

Printed in the United States of America

Library of Congress Control Number: 2003112310

ISBN 0-8065-2559-2

To Bryn, Anna,
Brigid, and D.

Contents

Acknowledgments   ix

Introduction   xi

1 Apprentice, Journeyman, Master   1

2 Advanced Literacy: The Secret Locations of Occult
       Knowledge   15

3 Changing Your Mind: New Ways of Thinking   34

4 Interconnectivity: Omens, Portents, and Divination   59

5 The Nature of Things: Your Toughest Pagan Teacher   76

6 Magic in the Everyday   95

7 Advanced Ritual   124

8 Altered States of Consciousness   161

9 Specialization   184

Notes   221

Bibliography   223

Resources   227

Index   231

Acknowledgments

SO MANY PEOPLE CONTRIBUTE TO A BOOK LIKE THIS ONE THAT IT CAN be difficult to acknowledge them all. Because this book comes from my own experiences, there are numerous people—friends, family, and authors—who had a hand in the ideas and suggestions described here. So I'd like to start by thanking the universe for the lessons and teachers that it has provided to me.

Above all, I would like to thank: Bryn—my best friend, soul mate, and beloved husband. You are as necessary to me as oxygen. Little Anna—though your "deadline" conflicted nicely with the one for this book, your arrival has opened us to new levels of love and happiness (not to mention lots of laundry). Oakley—you are stoic, loyal, loving, and so patient with the noisy new addition to our household. I am blessed beyond words to have such a wonderful family.

I would also like to thank fellow Witch, closest friend, and talented writer/editor, Elizabeth Vong. Your input made this a much better book. Thank you for your longtime loyalty, unwavering friendship, and willingness to help me figure out where all the commas should go.

I'd like to thank my mother and grandmother for being strong, independent women, and for passing some of that on to me. I'd like to thank my father for his advice on writing ("First tell 'em what you're going to tell 'em, then tell 'em, and then tell 'em what you told 'em").

Many thanks to the wonderful Witches in my life, including: Myra, for your wisdom and commonsense attitude, Robin, for your energy and willpower, and Scott, for your kindness and curiosity. In addition, my thanks to all the authors whose works educated and inspired me, particularly Marion Green, Carl Jung, and Joseph Campbell.

I'd like to thank Bruce Bender and my wonderful editor, Margaret Wolf, and everyone at Kensington for their help and support. It's been a pleasure working with you. I also owe a large debt of gratitude to Patricia Telesco—for her inspired writing as well as her kind advice to this fledgling author. I greatly appreciate all your help and advice regarding publishing Pagan material.

Finally, to those Deities who have taken an interest in me . . . thank you.

Introduction

"WHERE ARE THE BOOKS FOR ADVANCED STUDY?!" SO GOES THE CRY OF Pagans in discussion groups, online chats, and conversations around the country (and perhaps around the world). I understand their frustration. When I visit a bookstore, I'm excited to see so many books for the beginning Pagan. Most weren't available when I was starting out and it made my path much more difficult when I was a beginner. Now I see many books that I wish I'd had when I was a teenager, taking my first tentative steps on the path. Today's new Pagans are spoiled for choice! They can take their pick of any number of books that will gently walk them through their initial training.

But for years I was frustrated at the lack of information for those who had already gotten beyond the beginner stage. I would buy books and be disappointed because they provided no new insights. I felt trapped, as if I'd reached a wall that I couldn't get beyond. "Is this all?" I asked myself. Intuitively, I sensed that the path couldn't really end . . . after all, no matter where we are, we're all still growing and learning. But I couldn't seem to push past the barrier. I was a Cusp Witch (a term I have taken the liberty of inventing). I was standing with my beginning behind me, but without having started the next phase of my journey.

For a long time, I complained and struggled and worked at the problem. I slowly learned to expand my horizons and cast a wider net. Through trial and error, I discovered the mental skills necessary for the type of learning that goes hand in hand with advanced study. I practiced ritual to improve my relationship with the Divine and was rewarded with insights that helped me move forward. I worked at it and worried at it, all the while whining about the lack of guidance, both in writing and in person.

While the influx of new people into what's becoming the most rapidly growing group of religions in the United States was heartening, the "newbie" majority in the Craft didn't help. I was pleased that so many people were discovering the peace and power (as well as self-determinism and responsibility) that had originally attracted me to Witchcraft. But I was disappointed when, again and again, I searched for the elders and experts and found few or none. I found myself becoming bitter and cynical.

Then one day I looked back over the road I walked and realized an amazing thing. I was no longer a frustrated beginner struggling to climb over an insurmountable wall. Instead I had somehow become the person I had been searching for. With 20/20 hindsight I saw that I *had* found the teachers that I thought I'd been missing, many of whom are now my closest friends. I had discovered the knowledge that I thought was unavailable. Much of it was already within me and more was unfolding. Suddenly, my life was filled with books and teachers and inspiration.

I know now that I haven't reached the end of my journey—far from it. The road ahead is still unclear, for we cannot know our lessons before we've learned them. However, I am confident that lessons and insight are still to come. I see the walls that appear before me as challenges—cliffs to be scaled on my trek up the mountain. All of us, people of every faith and creed, are climbing the same peak. We simply walk on different paths.

This knowledge has helped me accept people and their myriad perspectives. I'm no longer frustrated by beginners . . . because I see that I am yet a beginner myself. The road is infinite. The journey is the important part. And if the road goes on forever, then, by definition, we are already halfway there (and by the same token, *only* halfway there).

WHAT THIS BOOK IS

This book is a primer for Cusp Witches and Pagans: people who have passed the beginner stage and need a boost with their advancing study.

If you are standing at the place I was—if the wall looms ahead and you don't know how to begin climbing—this book is for you. No book or teacher can save you the work ahead. My goal is to save you the frustration, cynicism, and anger that I succumbed to.

I don't have all the answers. No one does. That's because in spiritual matters, "all the answers" as a concept simply doesn't exist. But just as the plethora of "Wicca 101" books for beginners help those taking their first steps, I hope to help those who are ready for the next step.

WHAT THIS BOOK IS NOT

This book is *not* complete. It will not spoon-feed you the information you need for advancing study in a step-by-step fashion. You will not be able to read this book and claim that you are ready for adepthood. You will not find all the information you need in this book alone. Why these limitations? Because the road of the advancing Pagan is much more solitary and internally focused than the road of the beginner. You will need to be your own guide down that road.

WHO THIS BOOK IS FOR

How do you know when you're ready to take the next step and begin the next level of training? There's no specific timeline for this type of study. Some people will stay beginners, adjusting to new concepts and modes of thought, for years. Others will move more quickly, having an instinctive grasp of the basics. Finally, some will complete their study as beginners and have no urge to move forward for a time. All of these ways are valid and individual. Your path is different from anyone else's and based solely on your own knowledge, drive, past life experiences, priorities, and needs. There's no right way or right time . . . only your way and your time.

However, some hints that you're ready may include:

- A sense of frustration or being stuck that can't be assuaged with more of the same type of training you've already had. You seem to be *continually repeating yourself and not moving forward.*

• Feeling that you've learned "everything there is to know"—but that it's not enough. Of course you haven't (far from it), but everything seems geared toward a level you've already passed, and you're *wondering if there's anything new under the sun.*

• Suddenly feeling like everything you've learned is somehow pointless or just for show. You are beginning to comprehend the true relativism of spiritual practice and *asking yourself hard questions* like "Do we really need four elements or any elements at all?" or "Do color correspondences really mean anything?" or "What does the circle really do for me?"

• Curiosity about other paths or a sense of boredom with the path you're on. You're *beginning to understand the interconnectivity between all things.* You will need to learn more about those other ways before deciding on your own.

TOOLS FOR LEARNING

This book envisions learning as a four-step process. Basically, to make any lesson "stick," you must read, think, question, and do. First you must assimilate the information. Since this is a book, that means reading. However, this goes for any type of learning, whether from teachers, dreams, divination, or the natural world. This tool corresponds to the element of air.

Next, you have to think about what you've read or learned. When you spend time processing your lessons, you gain a deeper understanding of them. In addition, the information moves from your short-term memory to your long-term memory. Unlike cramming for a test, where you will soon forget everything you learned, taking time to ponder your lessons will integrate them into your memory and into a connected whole. This tool corresponds to the element of water.

In addition, you must question what you've learned. Don't take anything at face value. Even the most respected source of information won't work for everyone. The Pagan paths are based on individual spirituality. What's true and helpful for you may not be at all useful to others. And the knowledge that others find useful may mean nothing to you. You gain wisdom by asking questions such as What does this mean to me? Does it fit into my worldview? Is it useful knowledge? Do I really understand this? This tool corresponds to the element of fire.

The final step in incorporating any knowledge into your life in a meaningful way is to use the knowledge. Take it out into the field and test its usefulness in a real situation. If it works for you, it will become a part of your life and practice. If it doesn't, you can set it aside. It's the difference between reading a book on the Tarot and picking up your deck. This tool corresponds to the element of earth.

OVERVIEW OF THIS BOOK'S CONTENTS

This book attempts to follow a logical progression of the skills and techniques, hints and tips that can help you move into your next stage. Chapters include exercises at the end as well as a conclusion that describes how the information fits into the whole. I highly recommend trying the exercises or inventing your own.

Chapter 1 serves as an introduction to the apprentice/journeyman/master hierarchy that this book is based on. Being an advancing Witch or Pagan equates to your journeyman (or -woman) period and this chapter describes what that means on a physical, spiritual, mental, and emotional level.

Chapter 2 reveals the hidden locations of all those advanced books you've been looking for. You might be surprised at where they can be found. It describes how to read and comprehend these more difficult works as well as how to judge truth and fiction. Finally, it outlines why reading isn't enough. To make the information real, you must manifest the knowledge in both physical and magical aspects of your life.

Chapter 3 may be the most important chapter for the Cusp Witch. It outlines entirely new ways of thinking that you can use to unlock the mysteries. This information can help with reading comprehension as well as knowledge manifestation (including spell casting), and forms the hidden core of the rest of the book.

Chapter 4 dissects the reasoning behind divination and rationally discusses karma, fate, free will, and the nature of time. It can help make your divination more accurate and tune you into omens, psychic powers, and other natural ways of information gathering.

Chapter 5 marks the turning point in the book between internal and external work. This chapter focuses on nature and the Witch's place in the natural world. While the entire book is based on practice instead of theory, the work up to this point is very inwardly focused (reading, thinking, divining). Now we begin to manifest our new ideas and skills into the world.

Chapter 6 covers magic. Far from being another beginner's primer or spell book, this chapter delves into creating your own spells and making real use of magic in your life. It includes a rational and frank discussion of advanced magical ethics as well as the various areas where a spell can manifest.

Chapter 7 can help you exponentially improve your ritual work. It will give you the tools to judge whether a ritual has really been effective and avoid self-delusion. This chapter is the most religious of the book, discussing your responsibilities in dealing with your Deities and the risks and rewards involved.

Chapter 8 describes altered states of consciousness and how to attain them. It will help you determine whether you are ready for this kind of work and under what circumstances. It describes the benefits and pitfalls of some common forms of trance induction and can steer you away from delusionary ego gratification as well as paranoia and mental illness. This is the most advanced work covered in this book.

Chapter 9 is an overview of some of the areas of specialization that you may want to focus on. This period of study is going to involve discovering your strengths and weaknesses and focusing on the type of Master Witch or Pagan you want to become. Many of these roles require years of study and dedication, so you will want to choose your center of attention now.

A PERSONAL ANECDOTE

When I was in grade school I was obsessed with the moon. I would create charts of moon dates with carefully drawn pictures of the various phases. I would study and watch the moon from my window late at night. I read all about the moon in my family's encyclopedia. But the knowledge wasn't enough. I felt that there must be something more to the moon that I was missing. It was a frustrating sensation. Then I discovered Witchcraft and learned that, yes, there was something I'd been missing. There was more to the moon than my encyclopedia had told me . . . worlds more.

This sensation is the key that you are on a cusp, ready for the next step and a new level of knowledge. As a child I was on the cusp of discovering (or, really, rediscovering) Paganism. Years later I felt the same frustration as I stood on the cusp of leaving the beginner stage behind. Do you feel it? The instinct that all you've learned isn't enough? That there must be something more? Hang on, Cusp Witch—because there is!

CHAPTER 1

Apprentice, Journeyman, Master

BEFORE THE DAYS OF MANDATORY SCHOOLING AND ADVANCED DE-grees, most skills were learned through the apprentice system. While this system has fallen out of common use in the United States, in other countries it is still normal for tradespeople to begin their studies with a period of apprenticeship. Even here, some professions require periods of closely supervised study followed by student exploration at increasing levels of independence before the confirmation of master status. Before you decide this is incompatible with high technology and the specialization required by today's careers, remember that physicians use the apprentice system (or residency) to good effect to train all our doctors and surgeons.

One place where this system works well is in religious training. Many formal covens use a variant of this system embodied by three degrees. But there are subtle differences and this book takes them into account. More on covens and solitaries below, but first, here's an overview of the apprentice system:

As an apprentice, you work closely with a teacher to learn the basics. You learn the teacher's system and techniques and you work until the knowledge is intrinsic—until you don't have to even think about it, because it's embedded so deeply within you. You are encouraged to follow more rigid guidelines and rules.

As a journeyman or journeywoman, you take what you've learned and go out into the world with it. You are encouraged to think independently, exploring and analyzing different methods and theories to determine those that work best. You are expected to pick your specialties and focus your research in those areas. Your job is to learn that rules and guidelines, all those do's and don'ts you worked on memorizing, are internal tools to teach discipline; they're not necessarily universal truths. You must learn to look within and rely on your own intuition to determine if there are universal truths, and if so, what those truths are. Finally, you must realize that the system you began with and the tools you use are choices from among many different ways . . . and that no way is necessarily better or worse than any other.

As a master, you gain the right to teach others what you've learned. You know now that, while there are multiple ways of understanding the universe, everyone has to start somewhere. Gaining master status is more that just a matter of being an expert. You must also have the skills necessary to teach and lead. As a journeyman, you must complete a challenging masterwork before you can take on the role of master.

There are also components to these three stages that are specific to Paganism. As a beginning Witch, you are expected to introduce yourself to the Deities of the path you are studying. You must learn to hone your senses so that you can hear Their words of wisdom for you. You have to begin cultivating the inner tools (meditation, energy sensing, dream work) that will put you in touch with the invisible world.

As a journeyman, your job is to learn and commune with a wider world of beings. This is the time to explore history's pantheons of Gods and Goddesses. Even if you never choose to work with Them, you must know of the different paths and their lessons. All things are connected and these connections are a large part of opening a wider world of wisdom. You must also learn to distinguish reality from fantasy . . . the messages of the Divine from your own inner dialog.

The "Shining Ones" will begin asking things of you and giving you tests that you must pass. As a beginner, you rate Their protection. They are gentle with first steps and, if you open your heart to Them with love, They won't let you get into too much trouble. As an advancing Witch or Pagan, you rate Their trust. They will allow you to explore unfettered and may even give you enough proverbial rope to hang yourself with. The challenges become more difficult, but the rewards increase in kind.

THE LESSONS OF THE JOURNEYMAN WITCH

We should all be able to remember times when, as beginner or apprentice Pagans, our enthusiasm for our new path got the better of us. Perhaps there was a time when you were dogmatic about the latest new book or theory or found yourself loudly parroting some Pagan "history"—without the benefit of evidence. Or you remember being enamored of some fancy spell in a book but finding, after weeks of gathering esoteric ingredients, it didn't seem to work. Maybe you got involved in a silly conflict with another group or individual over some perceived slight, only to realize later that most of the trouble was in your own head.

The first lesson you have to learn as you begin advancing into your journeyman stage is forgiveness. Forgive those whom you may have slighted, but also forgive yourself. Learn to look back with fond amusement on your early errors in judgment and perception. Laugh at your youthful follies, and remember that we all started out in the same place. As we move forward, we have to learn to meld our initial enthusiasm for our new path with the discernment and wisdom of our collected experience. But always keep a sense of humor about yourself so that when you've progressed even further, the mistakes you make now will seem just as silly as those you made as a beginner.

As you advance, you begin taking more responsibility for yourself and your actions. For example, the apprentice Pagan relies on others (books, teachers, and so on) for information and trusts that information to be correct. As a journeyman, you will learn to rely only on the information that works for you. Instead of taking all new information at face value, you can judge by seeing whether things fit into your own worldview. And while you may acknowledge the authority of those who know more or have studied longer, you should also learn to question that authority.

Beginners tend to stick to tried and true methods. Moving forward, however, you should strive to incorporate inspiration and creativity into your practice. Why copy spells or rituals verbatim from a book when you can modify them or create your own? When you see your Pagan practice as a creative endeavor, you will rarely feel stuck for fresh material. Your own mind and heart can provide just the solution you need to any problem.

When you're new to Pagan practice, it's easy to see things in a very narrow way: right and wrong, black and white, true and false. Another important lesson for the journeyman is that things are rarely that simple. Every conflict has two sides, and both might have merit. All reality has an element of fantasy, while fantasy is always based in reality. Received truth might be wrong, while fiction is essentially correct. We live in a complex world with complex problems *and* solutions. The advancing Pagan learns to accept and deal with it.

Your journeyman period should manifest in physical, spiritual, mental, and emotional changes. On the physical level, you will learn to integrate your Paganism into your life. As a beginner, you might see this situation as black and white (in the closet / out of the closet). But as you advance, you will discover that these distinctions are illusory. The truth is that you must live as yourself, without hiding who you are *or* broadcasting it from every mountaintop. When you are authentic in this way, you'll find that many of the difficulties you've experienced with other people simply vanish. Of course there will always be people who want to cause trouble, but you will learn to pinpoint them early and avoid their company.

On a spiritual level, your journeyman period is both more expansive and more specialized than before. On the one hand, you will want to learn about different pantheons and make connections between them. On the other, you will also want to focus your religious attention on the few Deities who call to you. Your exploration serves to help you find your path, and while the knowledge you gain will only help your understanding, it's the specific relationship with an individual God or Goddess that really moves you forward. As a beginner you trust your teachers to guide you. As an advancing Pagan you will instinctively understand which Deities you can comfortably call on, which ones you do not want to mix in ritual, and which ones can lay a personal, individual claim to your soul.

Mentally, your journeyman period will sharpen your mind both inwardly and outwardly. You will be reading and learning a great deal of new information as well as practicing critical thinking skills and new ways of comprehending the universe. These skills manifest outward into the world. You will also be really, seriously practicing meditation, trance, and ritual. These mental skills spread their influence inward to the very heart of you. As a beginner you have to trust—trust that the energy is there although you can't sense it, or that the visualization is working although you can't see it. This is an important step, but as you advance you must learn to sense and see clearly as well as clear your mind to honestly judge the effectiveness of your work.

Emotionally, your journeyman period will be focused on finding inner peace. You must come to terms with your path and the responsibilities and rewards it holds for you. You have to learn which opinions are important and which you can safely ignore. You can't let your emotions get the best of you, particularly when it comes to doing magic. To advance, you can't be unbalanced. While you should always endeavor to keep a childlike wonder and joy in your heart, you must also act as an adult. This includes taking responsibility for your life and your actions, facing up to your wrongs, and never apologizing for being right.

Many of these changes come about almost accidentally as part of becoming an advancing Pagan. You shouldn't have to work at being responsible, balanced, discerning, or sensitive. If you simply work at becoming the best Witch or Pagan possible, these things should come as a matter of course.

THE RISKS INVOLVED

Unlike a "traditional" journeyman, you will probably not be set upon by brigands or highway robbers, but there are still risks to be aware of. The primary risk is that of *change*. As you grow and mature, you will be changing and this may affect your life in ways you did not expect. Just as becoming a Pagan may have changed your circle of friends (some people drifting away while others join you), becoming more advanced may change your acquaintances again. This is especially true if your group of Pagan friends consists entirely of beginners. It would be nice if we could all progress together, but this is not the way things work.

It can be hard to feel you're leaving some friends behind spiritually, but at the same time it's important not to acquire a huge ego about it. There are always some people who are going to have a problem with whatever you do. The only way to deal with this is to simply walk your own path honestly, remembering that no one is better or worse for the speed at which he or she walks. As long as you are walking in the same direction, who cares?

Another risk is the acquisition of new friends. For years I operated under the assumption that Pagans would be, by definition, good and honest people. This is, sadly, not true. Despite the fact that the basic premises of Pagan paths include self-responsibility, nondogmatism, honesty, and so on, a Pagan has the same probability of being a jerk as any sampling of the general population.

In addition, because Neo-Pagan paths are still very much minority religions, they call to the dispossessed. People who are different often feel victimized or ostracized. This means that many Pagans are working through issues from their own backgrounds. They might be angry at their old faith or the intolerance of friends and family. They may have been teased or harassed because of their unique interests. While their feelings are certainly legitimate, dealing with them can take time and that means that they may have certain problems they need to work through. These people are fortunate to be Pagan. They will have an opportunity to do their inner work without guilt or judgment, in an environment of acceptance.

However, that doesn't mean that you need to subject yourself to people who are emotional or mental disaster areas. If an encounter with another person leaves you drained or if the chaos of that person's life intrudes itself too far into yours, you may want to consider that your energies are incompatible. You don't necessarily have to be friends with people simply because they are Pagan. Naturally, you will want to be kind and cordial to all members of what is still a small minority, but not necessarily best buddies.

This actually applies to people of all faiths or none. The truth is that the people we surround ourselves with have a huge effect on us. Their influence rubs off on us just as ours rubs off on them. This is why people seek out friends who are like themselves. When two people rub each other the right way, the friendship is a good one. When two people rub each other the wrong way, they will typically not associate at all. However, if associating with someone makes you feel as rubbed down as an overused eraser, you have to act to protect yourself. Certainly, you must make sure you are appropriately shielded and grounded, but the best way to deal with such a situation is much simpler and more normal—simply avoid the person in question.

Another way that change may affect your life is through your relationship to your own environment. You might become aware that your priorities, goals, needs, and interests change. This could precipitate a change in location, employment, or lifestyle. These changes can certainly be startling to the people in your life, but even more so to yourself. While, as a society, we like to think of ourselves as flexible and able to adjust to change, in truth, most people are made deeply uncomfortable by any variation from their own routine. This is true even of "nonconformists" like Pagans. The irony, however, is that the more we accept change in our lives, the more stable our lives will seem.

Another important risk to be aware of as you enter your journey-man period is in distinguishing reality from fantasy. As a beginner you learned to accept things even though you might not have been able to see, hear, or sense them. As you progress, you will be seeing and sensing these things much more frequently. Far from simplifying your practice, this new evidence can make you question your sanity. Questioning whether something really happened or whether you might be a bit nuts is disturbing, but it's also typical of Witches and Pagans who have a solid grounding in reality.

Above all, you must avoid taking your mental fantasies seriously. How? Sane individuals will commonly question their own motivations and sense of the real. Working alone, they have to deal directly with internal questions, conscience, and beliefs. However, in a group (even an informal one) things tend to work very differently. It's quite easy for people to feed off of each other's fantastic ideas or mistaken perceptions to quell their own inner skeptic. This can allow the issue or situation to snowball out of proportion.

The trick in identifying this type of mass hallucination or hysteria is to recognize that it is usually bound up in emotionality and has a strong element of theater or drama. The work of dealing with some unusual, but real, situation (such as an actual magical attack, restless spirit, or the like) is typically very serious and very calm, and would look totally boring to anyone not involved. The people involved also will not tend to advertise the situation around town—they are too busy dealing with their own internal questions as to the validity of the experience to bother.

A final risk that often becomes apparent during intermediate working is that you will be forced to deal with your own emotional and psychological issues (your "baggage," if you will). To progress, you will have to come to know yourself through and through, take responsibility for all your actions, and practice as much honesty as you can manage with yourself as well as others. All of these can bring your childhood issues, neuroses, and repressed traits to the surface.

We all carry some inner "demons" with us. You may be working through only minor anxieties and bad mental habits or dealing with the repercussions of serious past trauma. In any case, part of your healing process includes not being ashamed of this baggage. When you acknowledge the dark parts of yourself honestly, you will be much better equipped to name your problems. This acknowledgment is the first step in healing.

In addition, you should never feel ashamed or guilty for seeking help. We all have a human need to confide our troubles in order to gain some perspective or objectivity. In tribal societies, it's often the medicine man, healer, shaman, or Witch who acts as counselor for the group. You may already have a trusted elder or teacher that you can confide in. But even if you don't, our modern society offers options for accessing this kind of help.

Unfortunately, you may not have the luxury of confiding in a typical psychologist about your spiritual path. After all, the average therapist will probably have difficulties with your spiritual experiences and perhaps even your religious choices. You will need to tread cautiously here. While you don't want to go to someone for help only to find condemnation, you also don't want a therapist who is too radical. The last thing you need is for an overeager analyst to "help" you by discovering a lot of buried memories that never actually happened or engage in some kind of extreme, unproven treatment. From personal experience, however, I can assure you that the right therapist can be hugely beneficial.

My advice here is to find a relatively conventional therapist and simply focus on your issue (fear of commitment or feelings of persecution, for example) as opposed to how your spiritual practices have pushed this issue into the spotlight. Also, unless you are diagnosed with a serious mental illness (in which case you need to work with your physician to determine your best course of action), you will want to avoid thinking of yourself as a patient. Think of your therapist as someone you hire as a sounding board for your issues. The therapist's job is to help you identify the problem and determine a best course of action to solve it.

Although these risks sound serious, I believe that the rewards for the intermediate student of the mysteries are well worth it. In addition, there's a self-correcting mechanism involved. For example, you might lose an old friend, but you will also gain new ones. You will question reality, but those questions will help you strengthen your own sensitivity to the unseen. You may be forced to deal with baggage, but the solution to your issue is often presented to you along with the awareness of the problem. Each of these challenges will make you a stronger, more balanced person and a better Witch or Pagan.

COVENS AND SOLITARIES, BOOKS AND TEACHERS

I have known many coveners and had many human teachers. But I have always been solitary—partly by necessity and partly by choice. Therefore, this book is naturally going to have a bias toward solitaries . . . but not as much as you might think. Your role as journeyman is to explore and discover your own areas of specialty and interest. Even within the coven system, you must do the work yourself. You can be a covener and still face the challenges of the Cusp Witch.

First, although Paganism is typically nondogmatic, each coven has its own way of doing things. Your coven might be very specialized, while you long to branch out and learn many different ways. Alternately, your elders and leaders may not have the time or inclination to explore too broadly. Ideally, they've been through their period of exploration before deciding on their particular path and may leave it up to you to figure it out for yourself.

As a member of a structured coven, you will probably not lack for advanced energy training and inner techniques. However, you may still find advice here for adjusting your perspective and learning to think in the ways that help open you to advanced study. If you've gotten stuck on your group's advanced reading list, there are some tips here that may help. Basically, there's no reason you can't work with this book while working with your coven.

Second, not all coveners are fortunate enough to have elders at their disposal. While their status as "real" covens is debatable (depending on the particular Pagan tradition), I know many groups where every member is still a beginner. They work together with the books they find helpful and make every effort to move forward. But the people in these groups are particularly vulnerable to stagnating. The lack of advanced guidance may run the group aground, with everyone either a beginner or frustrated Cusp Witch.

Note that when I talk about teachers, I am talking about human teachers as well as good books, the Deities, friendly spirits, and your own intuition. You have to learn to grab your lessons where and when you can, particularly if you're solitary. I hope this book will serve as a tool to facilitate your own learning. Take what works and adjust it to your needs. Jettison what doesn't work for you.

CHAPTER ONE EXERCISES

Visualize

Pause for a moment and think about what being a journeyman really means. Close your eyes and picture yourself in another time and place. You are living in a small village in another age. The streets are earth, there are no cars or loud machinery, and electricity is unknown. Most residents are farmers or herders, with only a few people having specialized skills like smithcraft.

Because of your sensitivity, you have been chosen as the apprentice of the village "wise woman." This old lady has been practicing herbal medicine and midwifery, officiating in disputes, leading celebrations, and using magic for the protection of the town and its inhabitants for a number of years. She is a very old woman now and needs to pass on her knowledge before she dies. She picked you as a very young child to learn and follow in her footsteps.

For years you have been her apprentice. You have learned all the knowledge she has accumulated, lived as her child in her hut, and helped her with the chores and tasks—magical and mundane—that she can no longer manage. One day, she wakes you in the middle of the night and leads you to the clearing in the woods behind her home. There she takes you into her sacred order, tracing the mystical symbols on your forehead with oil and imparting the last of her secrets. Then she leaves you to keep vigil in the dark woods until dawn. This is your initiation.

In the morning, she returns with a pack and her old oak staff. She tells you that you must leave her to travel in the wider world. You protest. You have never been out of the woods that surround your little village. It's all you know and all you want to know. But the old woman is insistent. You have to gain knowledge of the wider world; you have to share the knowledge you've gained and collect new information from far afield. You must avoid trouble, fight danger, seek new experiences, and then return home when you know that it is time. You must grow up, and grow in power and wisdom, before you can return to take her place.

This is your journey. You know it may be difficult, even dangerous. You know you will face many challenges and setbacks. You know that you will never be the same. But you embark on the journey nonetheless.

This tale may not ever have been literally true. However, that doesn't change its validity to the Cusp Witch. Whether part of a large craft guild or apprentice to a lone master, at some point the student must embark on a journey—either literal or spiritual—if she is to take her place as a master. This is how guilds have operated for hundreds, perhaps thousands, of years. This is what you must do—if only allegorically—to take the next step in your own journey.

Actualize

If you feel you are ready to enter the next stage of learning and embark on your spiritual journey, you may want to commemorate the event with a ritual or symbolic gesture. If you are already part of a group, this may be a standard initiation that members experience.

If you are solitary, however, you might want to devise something as a symbol of your commitment to a new stage in your development. This will be more powerful if you invent it from scratch, using whatever knowledge you have acquired thus far about magic or ritual structure. Picking a self-dedication from a beginner's book (you will not find one here) will be missing the point.

Do what feels comfortable to you, whether that is a full-blown ritual or a simple blessing. Incorporate whatever symbolism makes sense to you and call on whomever (if anyone) you feel you need to for help. Make the event uniquely your own. If this is difficult for you, consider it a test of your readiness for the material in this book. Easy formulas are not the way of the advancing Pagan.

Conclusion

Like the journeyman (or -woman) of any craft or skill, the advancing Pagan or Witch is entering a time of exploration and growth. Your goals include broadening your knowledge while determining your own specialized skills and interests, expanding your horizons and asking difficult questions, and exercising your abilities inwardly and outwardly. Being an advancing Witch or Pagan is a journey, even if you never leave your home, and like any journey it contains risks and rewards.

The next chapter begins your journey by pointing you to the sources of written material that you will want to explore. While bookshops and libraries are only some of the places where you will be seeking and finding knowledge, they are logical starting points. We are a literate society and you obviously look to books to help you (or you would not be reading this one). Books can be a great source of wisdom and inspiration. But they can also be a real source of frustration when it seems that you're not finding anything new. The following chapter is designed to help you find that wellspring of occult material you've been searching for.

CHAPTER 2

Advanced Literacy:
THE SECRET LOCATIONS OF OCCULT KNOWLEDGE

THE PRIMARY COMPLAINT OF CUSP WITCHES SEEMS TO BE THAT THERE aren't any good books for the intermediate student of the mysteries. This book seeks to help remedy that situation, not by being one of a few, but by pointing you to the mass of advanced information that has already been published. No doubt, you know by now that the word *occult* means "secret" or "hidden." Obviously, from the complaints of Pagans who can't find good reading material, there are a number of valuable volumes that are indeed quite occult.

HIDDEN IN PLAIN SIGHT

A tour of your local library or general interest bookstore will unearth a wealth of knowledge to the trained eye—knowledge as advanced as you are ready for, as sophisticated as you require, and as occult as you could wish. All you need to do is adjust your perspective and broaden your vision.

Are you searching for a pantheon? Do you want to understand your chosen Deities better? Visit the mythology section for scholarly stories of Goddesses and Gods and their attributes. Books on the comparison and analyses of myth will help you understand the subtext of these ancient stories as well as their similarities and differences around the globe. In addition, the traditional religion section of most bookstores will include a global collection of inspired and inspiring writings as well as books on comparative religion and religious practices in history.

Philosophers have been arguing the nature of God for millennia, and you can learn a lot from their work. Women's studies will have something to help you connect with the spirit of the Goddess, and in men's studies you may find a more reasonable masculine role model than that found in mainstream society. Finally, psychology will help you understand the human mind (know thyself) and can only improve your relationship to the Divine.

Do you believe in reconstructing your faith based on the "Old Ways"? History can teach us much about how people actually lived "way back when." Over the past few decades the study of history has begun to focus not simply on kings and conquests but also on the lives and experiences of everyday people. Remove the patina of Christianity and find a wealth of information on Pagan practices based on hard scholarship and not wishful thinking.

Folklore is another area where hints of the past come to us distilled through the lens of tradition as well as changing times. Don't forget to check out collections of fairy tales—just remember to stick to the scholarly, unexpurgated versions or annotated texts. The original tales were very different from the Disney versions we see today. If we go back far enough, history becomes archeology. Nothing beats reports by archeologists in the field to foster understanding of times very long ago. If you have the chance, supplement your reading with a visit to your local museum or arts center to experience ancient artifacts in person.

Are you interested in American Indian or other native spirituality? Modern anthropology attempts to give us cultural information without bias. Better a scholarly account than another book by some self-professed shaman. Naturally, firsthand accounts by native people themselves are the best way to learn about their customs. Even fiction by native authors can open a window into their way of life. Far from a single, unified culture, U.S. native populations practice a broad range of different lifestyles and religions. And because many tribes still exist today, living their spirituality based on direct lineage, they deserve our utmost respect for their heritage.

Curious about animal totems? You will come to a better understanding of animal spirits through an honest appraisal of their everyday habits than by looking in a "What's Your Totem?" book. Start with books on wildlife or zoology, and then supplement your reading with trips to natural settings or the zoo. Or take an additional step and learn about and participate in wildlife rescue.

To connect with your totem, you may need more time in nature, away from the crowds in the local campground. Swing past the outdoor activity section of your local bookstore for information on hiking, camping, orienteering, and woodcraft. This is Paganism at its best! Learn to read topographical and trail maps and you can explore the wildlife where you live directly. Want to know more about where you live or plan to visit? The travel shelf will have everything you need. Another great way of learning more about your hometown is to check out the Chamber of Commerce or historical society. These groups may have publications at the local library or tourist information center.

Are you called to herbalism or healing? The health and gardening sections of the bookstore are a better bet than copies of ancient herbals with dubious information. Remember that the magical and healing properties of herbs are often divided into two areas of study. The best way to learn about herbal healing is to learn directly from someone who's already an expert or a modern book written by such a person. Wilderness survival classes often include a great deal of information regarding edible and medicinal plants from your local geographical area. Going out with an expert is more reliable than squinting at drawings in books. The most accurate way of understanding the magical properties of plants is to grow them yourself and get a sense of their energy. Stick with plants that are native to your area and you'll have better luck getting a good harvest. A basic book on gardening will give you all the information you need to get started.

Need help writing a ritual or spell? Romantic poets will keep you immersed in natural and magical imagery for years. Blake, Wordsworth, and Coleridge are excellent choices. Or take a peek at the poems of other cultures. Haiku spellcasting anyone? Original epic poetry is another great source of material. The bardic or storyteller tradition was an important part of many preliterate Pagan societies. You can learn how to write your own ritual verse with books on meter and rhyme, or take the challenge of learning to play an instrument. If you can't afford instruction, a solid beginner's book and some hard work can give you a good musical foundation. Books on harnessing creativity in general are invaluable. Don't forget to check out the art section for representations of divinity as envisioned by the masters (or find books that show you how to draw or paint your own).

Exploring methods of divination? Researching the history and background behind any type of predictive art will help you become more accurate. To know the Tarot, explore the Western Occult tradition of the Cabala. To understand I Ching, read about the Eastern philosophies that inspired it. The study of astrology can take you back to ancient Egypt and Mesopotamia, while palmistry can open a door to Gypsy culture.

Many of the best books don't stick to one genre, and can best be described as a mix of disciplines. For example, wonderful offerings by the publishing arm of the American Theosophical Society can be found scattered between philosophy, psychology, and religious studies. Books on Feng Shui can be in sections as diverse as metaphysics, Oriental studies, and interior decorating. I found a spectacular book on mazes and labyrinths in the architecture section of a used bookstore. Often, the more difficult it is to classify a book, the more valuable the book. The key is looking beyond the metaphysics section of your local Pagan shop.

You don't have to limit yourself to chain bookstores or public libraries. University libraries often welcome browsers, although you may need a student ID to check items out. I have a wonderful book from the University of Texas Press, a translation of the poetry of the Sumerian High Priestess Enheduanna.[1] You're simply not going to find something like that browsing a commercial bookstore. But armed with the ISBN (International Standard Book Number), you can order just about any book online. You might even be able to get a day pass to browse a university's special collections area. Most have large storehouses of local historical documents as well as rare books and maps.

And remember to visit the campus bookstore. Again, you may need an ID to buy, but that won't stop you from browsing. You may not be in the market for a heavy tome on organic chemistry (and then again you might), but introductory texts on archeology, anthropology, mythology, religious studies, art, or poetry could all be potentially useful.

Finally, if you suffer from a dearth of good bookstores or libraries where you live, the Internet can be a valuable resource. Many works in the public domain are available for reading online or downloading for free. For example Sacred Texts[2] and Bartleby.com[3] both have classical texts available to read. Of course, Amazon is the largest online book retailer and well worth a visit.[4] And for rare or out-of-print volumes, Powells is an excellent choice.[5] You can have any book in print (not to mention out-of-print, collectible, rare, and foreign titles) delivered directly to your home.

No, most of my suggestions aren't for specifically Pagan material. But that doesn't mean we can't take what we need from these books to follow our path. After all, that's the way we learn: by reading, thinking, critiquing, and always trying something new. Pagan paths are holistic, teaching that all things are connected. Why, then, can't we find the will of the Goddess in a cookbook or a new understanding of the Lord and Lady through philosophy? There's divine presence all around us—we only have to open our eyes.

WHY READ THE HARD BOOKS?

I have to admit that I like a straightforward read as much as the next person. But while I enjoy plain, simple writing and clearly presented ideas, I also recognize that not all the information I want is going to be available in that format. The truth is that if you only stick to the books that are easy to read, you will be greatly limiting yourself.

Many of the best books were written some time ago and can be difficult to follow. Language and culture have changed enough to make some books very difficult to understand now—like Shakespeare's plays—even if they weren't at the time they were first published. Agrippa's *Three Books of Occult Philosophy* is an excellent example of this phenomenon.[6] First-source mythology is another area where the rewards will be worth dealing with very different cultural contexts, cryptic imagery, and potentially dubious translation. In addition, the best way to understand ideas or concepts in various scientific disciplines, like psychology or archeology, is to read the academic works directly. But because these works were written for others in the field, they can be complicated for the layperson.

There are also books that are hard to read because the concepts they describe are simply hard to understand. Perhaps they require a very different point of view, or some mind-bending philosophical theory, or believing contradictory ideas simultaneously. When you discover one of these books, consider it a rare gift—worth working on. Perhaps you'll finish the book only to decide the idea doesn't work for you or isn't valid. But you will never know unless you make the effort.

EXTRACTING MEANING FROM MYTH

One of the most common areas of study for Pagans is mythology. What's the first thing we do when we want to learn about a Deity? We take a look at what stories, or *myths*, that Deity appears in. Of course, this is simpler in some cases than others. In the case of literate societies (like ancient Greece and Rome) we can access the myths directly. With nonliterate or minimally literate societies (such as the Celtic and Norse) we sometimes have to interpret the myths through the eyes of an outsider who recorded them. In either case, we can learn a great deal from mythology when we understand the keys to extracting a myth's meaning.

When we strive to understand a mythological story, we shouldn't just be looking for literal understanding but also psychological, personal, archetypal, and spiritual understanding. Some of our comprehension is based in the myth itself and its context, while some is purely personal—based in our own psyches and on the lessons we need to learn.

Sometimes, deconstructing a myth in this manner can pose a real challenge. If you've even read a myth and thought, "Huh?" perhaps you haven't deconstructed the myth enough and are taking it too literally. Should you find your interpretation of the myth at odds with the myth itself, perhaps you've deconstructed too far, projecting your own issues on to the story to the detriment of its integrity (this second problem is harder to spot).

In any case, here are some ideas for extracting the meaning from myth without either missing the point or making one up. I've used the myth of Persephone and Demeter as an example.

First of all, myths are both "true" and "fictional." Did the events in the myth really occur? Perhaps not, but myths contain truths nonetheless. This sounds obvious, but if you see myths only as interesting stories, you won't have the right mind set for digging deeper to extract meaning. You have to expect meaning, symbolism, and archetypes if you are to recognize them. Even myths that are based in history, such as Greek myths of the Trojan war, have this symbolic element. In fact, history becomes myth because it has a larger message to impart.

Second, myths change over time and reflect the societies that tell them. The myth of Persephone and Demeter seems to have a more ancient component in the mother–daughter relationship and a newer component that fits the same story into the Greek pantheon. When you read a myth, you must always keep the culture in mind. The Greeks were patriarchal, and this is reflected in many aspects of the Persephone-Demeter myth. However, you must never dismiss a myth because of its cultural origins because . . .

Third, myths transcend cultural constraints. They do this because their elements are *archetypal*. Archetypes come from our collective unconscious and are therefore not bound to an individual society, age, country, language, and so forth. The truths of a myth are found within their archetypal elements, not the culture-specific patina that they acquire. (More information on archetypes is contained in the next chapter.)

Fourth, myths tend to focus on human behavior in all its complexity—even myths about the Deities. There is always potentially more than one meaning to a myth. In fact, the most enduring myths are often the most complex and filled with meaning. Because they are multifaceted, they can be understood from a number of viewpoints, and this ensures their longevity. Love, parenthood, growing up, eternal life, the turn of the seasons—all these are part of the myth of Persephone's descent to the underworld and Demeter's search for Her.

Fifth, myths can speak to us personally. That is, while it's incorrect to distort the myth based on your own needs (in that case, it's far better to create your own myth), your interpretation of the meaning of a myth will always be filtered through your own context. As a new mother, I am moved by Demeter's power and strong love for Her daughter. This part of the myth never spoke to me before I had my own daughter.

Sixth, the meaning of a myth can change depending on the audience. The version you're reading might be one of several that existed for different groups of people. Imagine the same myth as told to a child; among a group of women; or by an elder to a community. The meaning can be interpreted very differently just by emphasizing different parts of the story. For a child, the myth of Persephone could be told as a lesson in being careful of strangers and sticking close to mom. For a woman, it might be a dark compelling love story. For a farmer, it's all about the cycle of the seasons.

Seventh, myths may require you to gain additional knowledge to deconstruct effectively. If you don't understand the context or have no basis of comparison for the symbols in the myth, you may miss important meanings. For example, to understand the myth of Persephone and Demeter, it's a good idea to know about the Eleusinian Mysteries, the role of agriculture and grain in Greece, the symbolism of the pomegranate, the descent of Inanna in Sumerian mythology, and so on.

Finally, it's important to trust your instincts and allow your creativity to flow. One good technique is to envision yourself as the various characters of the myth. How do you feel? What would you do in the same situation? What might motivate a mythological figure to do what they do? Examine possible ulterior motives. Replay the myth, assuming various levels of omniscience/precognition on the part of the characters. What if Persephone (who is a Goddess after all) knew exactly what was going to happen to Her? How does that change the tale?

When a myth calls to you, there's probably something there you need to know. It may be a lesson you have to learn or advice that you need. But it can take time and contemplation to discern what is it that's triggering your interest so strongly. By moving past a literal interpretation of the myth, you should be able to extract the essence or key symbol that speaks to you.

STUDY TIPS FOR READING
AND UNDERSTANDING

Reading a hard book is, well, hard. If you haven't had much practice at it, you might start out feeling pretty lost or frustrated. Reading a textbook isn't the same as reading a novel—reading a spiritual text is even more different. But there are some ways that you can make the process easier.

Before anything else, you must realize that when you attempt a complex book, you aren't simply reading, you're studying. Just like in school, you're attempting to assimilate and understand material that's unfamiliar to you and that requires an approach different from the one taken when reading fiction. You wouldn't expect to be able to read a chemistry text the same way you would a fantasy novel. A spiritual book is as different from those as they are from each other. When you read a book for spiritual purposes (whether it's an ostensibly spiritual book or not), you are attempting to extract information from the book that you can fit into your own framework. You can't just accept everything you're reading (as with a book on organic chemistry) and you can't put your brain in neutral and lose yourself in the story (as with a fantasy novel). You have to continually think about and question the text—and you have to understand it.

To comprehend what you're reading, you must understand the words, the sentences, and the ideas. With some books only one of these presents a challenge, with others it may be all of them. Start by making sure that the vocabulary in the book is familiar to you. This can be particularly difficult with older works where word usage may have greatly changed over the years. Read with a dictionary nearby if necessary. In addition, spiritual works will sometimes encode their text in euphemism. For example, many texts on alchemy are really about sex magic. All that heating and grinding and distilling of the essences takes on a very different meaning if you understand the context.

Next, make sure that you are following the germ of each sentence. One hallmark of difficult works is a more complex sentence structure filled with various clauses and subclauses. The trick here is to read slowly. Fortunately, we're not in school. There's no teacher to assign us too many chapters over a long weekend. Spiritual growth requires patience, and there's no hurry to finish a complex book. Take your time and make sure that each item the author is presenting makes sense to you.

Finally, you must understand the whole concepts that make up the book. This can be tricky. You may follow every word and sentence but still not grasp the idea they are describing. My experience with *The White Goddess* is an excellent example.[7] Graves's book is a notoriously difficult read, but one that is almost mandatory for an understanding of Witchcraft. Yet, in my work with this book, I constantly find myself thinking "Well, I get what he's saying . . . I just don't get what he's saying." That is, I understand the words and sentences but not the concepts. When I have this response to a book, my technique is to put the book aside for a time to allow the concepts to gestate within my brain. This serves two functions.

First, by allowing my brain to digest the information slowly, I avoid brain indigestion—the feeling that my brain is full and bloated. Difficult concepts are like spicy or rich food, best consumed slowly and in moderation. By giving my brain time to deal with a particular nugget of data, I can then return to the book with a fresh understanding. Second, by giving myself a break, I open the door to seemingly coincidental events that can help me. I can't tell you the number of times I've struggled with an idea, only to find the answer in a completely different book, movie, chance comment, or event.

Another great way of understanding a difficult concept is to discuss it with someone else. If you and several friends are each reading the same book, you can get together to talk about and help each other understand the work. Alternately, you can discuss a difficult idea with any sympathetic friend, whether or not they are reading the book. Finally, if you're really stuck, writing out your thoughts can cause a breakthrough. Think of this kind of writing as a journal entry, personal and free-form. Don't worry if the things you write won't make sense to anyone else.

Finally, I highly recommend that when you find a book that really stretches your brain, you buy it for yourself. One, you'll be able to proceed at your leisure. Two, you can make notes and come back to the book again and again. Three, the book will become a valuable part of your spiritual library. Great books are worth reading multiple times.

You'll gain new perspective every time you read them and will be able to chart your own growth through how your opinions change in relation to the text.

A few other study tips:

- **Jot down notes in the margins of your books** or under-line relevant passages. When you have an "ah hah!" moment, when you make a connection, when you disagree with some-thing—make a note of it. Not only will it help remind you of these things the next time you read the book, it will chart your own growth as your opinions change or those "ah hah!" mo-ments become simply another part of your spiritual practice. If you're an obsessive bibliophile like I am, make your notes in light pencil.

- **Point yourself to other books with similar ideas.** If an idea in a book reminds you of something in another book, go find and read that passage as well. Since all things are connected, this holistic approach can only improve your comprehension. Besides, in spiritual matters you don't want superficial knowl-edge based on rote memorization of ideas. You need a deep and richly connected *understanding* that you can rely on.

- **Look for multiple levels of meaning.** A text can seem to be about one thing but actually be about several different things. *The White Goddess* seems to be about poetry, but it's also about the practice of Witchcraft. The myth of Apollo's musical contest with Pan seems to be about King Midas's folly, but it's also about a cultural clash between the old Gods and the new. Always look to find the deeper or subtler interpretation.

- **Remember that this is not just theory.** Your spiritual reading shouldn't be for bland, academic purposes. You need to bring your knowledge from books back into the real world. How many Pagan books have you read that included lessons or exer-cises? It's a common practice in many modern texts (including this one). How many times have you actually done those lessons or exercises? Even if a book doesn't list suggested exercises outright, you should still endeavor to create your own and then do them. We practice a participatory, experiential religion. The "armchair Pagan" is an oxymoron—avoid being one.

HISTORICAL VERSUS INTUITIVE KNOWLEDGE

Fundamentally, spirituality can be described as the search for truth. This can be tricky, however, as we try to balance relativism with fact and historical accuracy. Unfortunately for the student of ancient mysteries, the personal biases of observers always color the research they do. This means that many works are hotly debated and both sides of the debate have their own agendas. For example, the work of Marija Gimbutas (*Goddesses and Gods of Old Europe*) has been revered and reviled for over four decades.[8] Currently out of favor with serious scholars, her descriptions of ancient Goddess-worshipping cultures still resonate with many Pagans. Yet, it's clear that the earliest archeologists from the 1800s had their own cultural biases and were also hampered by poor technology and underdeveloped excavation techniques.

So how can the curious Pagan find the truth? First, we have to be honest with ourselves. The works of Margaret Murry, Barbara Walker, James George Frazer, and Robert Graves (among others) have all come under critical scrutiny for their lapses in historical accuracy, ignorance of archeological fact, and author bias. But that doesn't mean we should toss out these works in their entirety. While the criticism is legitimate, the conclusions gained from it (that there never were pre-Gardener Witchcraft groups or ancient matriarchies or dying-king cults) are equally based in a certain biased worldview.

Since most of us won't have the opportunity to participate in archeological digs, interview indigenous peoples, or devote our lives to research, we have few options. First and foremost, we must *remember to take everything with a grain of salt*. The canon isn't the canon forever.

Things do change—sometimes embracing truth, sometimes ignoring it. We should always seek out alternate points of view, competing opinions, and rational debate. Just because something has always been considered true doesn't necessarily make it true. However, just because something is criticized by the established hierarchy doesn't make it automatically true either. There's a certain element of conservative, hidebound autocracy in every area of study. But that doesn't mean there's a huge secret conspiracy to keep us from discovering the truth. Sometimes the "old guard" criticizes a work because it's legitimately flawed and not simply because it questions their authority.

We must also try to embrace accuracy when we find it. Modern archeological digs are as meticulous as police investigations of homicide scenes. While we might question the accuracy of a researcher's conclusions, we cannot ignore the facts. Always try to find the original sources of information and question the biases of authors.

In addition, just because a book isn't accurate doesn't mean it's not useful. Things can resonate with you on a deep and personal level that goes beyond historical accuracy or literal truth. This is where intuitive knowledge comes into play. You must embrace these things whether or not they are backed by science because they obviously have power for you. But do not make the mistake of trying to proclaim their objective truth to the world. Despite the fact that many of the authors I've listed above have works that are considered historically flawed, I still recommend these books, because they are very valuable and useful on an intuitive level.

In addition, we have to remember that what people did thousands of years ago doesn't necessarily have anything to do with what we do today. It's useful to study past cultures, particularly if we are interested in Deities from that culture. But in the end, we are modern people and we are worshipping our Gods *now*, in this time. You would probably have a very difficult time sacrificing a black lamb or dog (or worse) to Hecate at the dark moon. But wouldn't you also be very surprised if She demanded it? We're different people with different needs.

Frankly, most of us will never have the life or death experiences that our ancestors did. Even during times of financial trouble, most of us are safe from the raging cold of winter, unlikely to run out of food, and not apt to be struck down by the plague.

The things the ancients did are certainly interesting and sometimes useful—but not always. There's excellent evidence that groups of the Celts (remember Celt refers to a racial designation, not a cultural one) were quite misogynistic and practiced human sacrifice. The Druids embraced early Christianity in the British Isles (whether from honest belief, self-interest, or self-preservation, we will never know). But there's no reason to get upset at these facts, because they have nothing to do with us now.

The "great global matriarchy" dispute has been going on a long time. Neither side of the argument is particularly objective or above selectively interpreting the facts. But the truth is that it doesn't matter whether a global matriarchy existed or no matriarchy *ever* existed (newer evidence shows both conclusions are probably false). We live and practice our religions right now, in this time and place. We have to accept that and follow our hearts and the dictates of our Deities.

Finally, we must make an effort to think for ourselves. One complaint about Gimbutas's work is that so many of her "goddess figures" were actually discovered in midden heaps (ancient trash pits). The criticism is that if these objects were routinely thrown out, they couldn't have been very valuable. However, I wonder whether it's not culturally biased to assume that these ancient cultures viewed trash in the same way we do. In a time before "nonbiodegradable" was invented, a time when these midden heaps were often very near human dwellings, perhaps people saw these places in a different way than we do. Or perhaps not. The point is that you cannot become an advancing student of the mysteries by meekly accepting whatever an author tells you. First read and then think, question, and do. That is the path toward real understanding.

FOOD FOR THOUGHT—WORDS
INTO THE WORLD

All your reading will be for nothing if you can't bring the knowledge you've gained back into the world. Sure, you'll have a head full of useful facts, but they won't be worth anything to your life or your spiritual path.

A number of years ago I became fascinated by beekeeping and read several books on the topic. But aside from a greater appreciation for the work bees do to produce honey and the environmental hurdles they face, I gained nothing from the experience. Why? Because I don't keep bees. I have no plans to keep bees. I live in a suburban neighborhood where I simply can't keep bees (and at the time, years ago, I lived in an apartment). In addition, my husband is seriously allergic to bee stings. The only way we will ever be able to have an apiary is if we have a large enough piece of land to keep the hives away from the house.

Maybe someday that will happen (and by then I will have forgotten everything I read anyway), but not now. Of course it wasn't a complete waste of time. I do have that greater appreciation and respect for those tiny creatures. But, while it assuaged my curiosity, the information I gathered wasn't particularly useful.

Information only becomes useful when it's *used*. This applies to any type of reading, but particularly reading for spiritual purposes. You can't be a Pagan or Witch just by reading about it. It has to be a part of what you do and a part of your life, a part of your thoughts and a part of who you are. That's why we say we "practice" Witchcraft—we don't "read" Witchcraft. We're lucky to live in a time and place where printing is easy, paper cheap, and information free and available. Most of us grew up in a literate society, and books are simply the easiest way for us to access and process information. But books are not everything.

That's why the rest of *this* book focuses not on reading but on thinking, doing, and experiencing. If you do nothing but read this book and shove it on your shelf, ignored, you will have missed the point. And no, you don't have to do every single exercise I've thought up. Think up your own. Incorporate the ideas into your life in your own way.

~~~~~~

CHAPTER 2 EXERCISES

The Hard Books

Find a book that challenges you and read it. It doesn't necessarily need to be spiritual, but it should be interesting and of some value to you. Work at understanding the words, sentences, and ideas. Attempt to create exercises to bring your knowledge into the real world.

Challenge yourself to learn something new. Because everything is connected, you'll often find nuggets of wisdom in the strangest places—astrophysics, for example. I can highly recommend books for the layperson such as Stephen Hawking's *A Brief History of Time*.[9] This is truly mind-bending stuff! Embark on a study of something you've never considered before. The cyberpunkish novel *Snow Crash* sent me to the library to read every available book on Sumerian mythology.[10]

Make sure it stays fun. Most of us probably remember a time when learning new things was enjoyable and exciting. But somewhere along the line we forget or lose the knack. If you're going to progress past the basics in any field, you're going to have to allow it to be fun again. And what could be more fun than studying to advance you on your spiritual path?

Know Thine Enemy

Find books that you don't agree with and read them. Reading only those things with a similar perspective is like reading only easy things—it's limiting. You don't necessarily need to agree with everything you read; finding a persuasive book that takes the "other side" of the debate will give you practice at critical thinking. In addition, it's important for you to know who your enemies are and how they think.

The books you choose are going to depend on your perspective. Being a Pagan or Witch, a book on conservative Christianity is probably a good start. Are you moved by ecological concerns? How about a volume describing how global warming is a falsehood? Wherever you stand on any divisive issue (abortion, gay rights, religious freedom, and so on), you will be able to find a book that takes the other side. The point is not to get angry. The point is to learn critical reading skills and find out how other people think.

Literary Criticism

One way of understanding the things you read is by studying literary criticism. This area of academia describes the ways in which you can view or understand a work of literature or poetry. Criticism in this context doesn't mean "complaining about" so much as critiquing—understanding, judging, or describing.

There are numerous schools of literary criticism and some are going to make more sense to you than others. For example, feminist criticism focuses on women in the text and how they are perceived, coupled with the perception of women in society when and where the work was created. Deconstruction, on the other hand, "assumes language refers only to itself rather than to an extratextual reality, that asserts multiple conflicting interpretations of a text, and that bases such interpretations on the philosophical, political, or social implications of the use of language in the text rather than on the author's intention."[11]

Scholars like to take literary criticism very seriously, debating the relative validity of the different schools, but I've always thought of criticism more as a fun tool for playing with comprehension. That is, I'm not convinced that any school of criticism is any better than any other, but they are all useful for teasing meaning from a work. That several meanings can always be discovered is just part of the fun. *A Handbook of Critical Approaches to Literature* is a good overview text.[12]

CONCLUSION

Far from suffering a dearth of good reading material, the Cusp Witch is literally inundated with information. All that's required is a shift in perspective and the acquisition of some tools to help with comprehension. Remember: read, question, think, and do. Take the challenge and work through a difficult or complex work. Ask yourself about the biases of authors, usefulness of information, and links to other things you already know. Learn to think for yourself—take everything with a grain of salt. Finally, bring what you have learned into reality by making it a part of your life and practice.

Once you begin collecting this advanced knowledge, you will have to form it into some cohesive whole. As a beginner, perhaps you simply took the system of your teacher or favorite Pagan author as delivered in its entirety. But discovering information for yourself means adapting to some new ways of thinking. Otherwise the results are chaos. These new modes of thinking are what the next chapter is all about.

CHAPTER 3

Changing Your Mind:
NEW WAYS OF THINKING

ONE OF THE MOST IMPORTANT THINGS YOU MUST DO TO PREPARE FOR your journeyman or -woman period is *change your mind*. If, like many Pagans, you came from a monotheistic religious background, you came to your new religion with a number of preconceptions and in-grained thought patterns. Even if you didn't, if you grew up in the United States or Europe you still suffer from cultural conditioning and societal memes that are largely based on a Judeo-Christian model.

You have no doubt already been working on adjusting some of your thinking. Many see the process of converting from Christian to Pagan as one of disposing of old, unhelpful memes like guilt, dogma, and materialism. This is a conscious process that the new Pagan is usually very aware of. You know what concepts were harmful to you that you wish to be rid of. However, with what do you replace those ideas? Without some structural base for thinking about the world, you may experience chaos instead. If you consciously shrug off your condi-tioned mental responses, you should pursue new ones equally con-sciously.

What follows are some concepts that I have found particularly use-ful in following my spiritual path. Some of this material might be familiar, but without training to bend our minds in these new direc-tions, the implementation of advanced material will be haphazard and chaotic.

C. G. JUNG

Carl Gustav Jung was an eminent nineteenth and twentieth-century researcher, a student of Freud, and the founder of analytic psychology. His importance to modern Paganism is undeniable—if somewhat ironic. Jung popularized the concept of synchronicity and developed the theories of the collective unconscious and archetypes (all of which we will be discussing in this chapter). Jung even experienced what we would call visions and prophetic/mystical dreams. Yet his life's work was dedicated to rationally explaining these strange occurrences.

Despite his assertions that there is nothing "nonrational" about these events, his theories outline a wonderfully complete logic of psychic power, dream messages, and magical theory. His work is especially valuable for the modern Pagan because it *is* so very rational, appealing to our scientific mindset. In addition, coming from a background of psychiatry, his focus is on helping people overcome mental illness, solve psychological troubles, and know themselves better. This is not useless academic theory!

Most people will never read much of Jung's work. *Man and His Symbols*, which he wrote with his associates for the lay reader, is a challenging read.[13] His work for his psychiatric peers is even more difficult. Jung's work is worth reading, however, even though it's tough. He has also inspired a number of other authors, many of whom are more ostensibly Pagan or mystical. In truth, most of this book owes a great debt to his work.

SYMBOLIC THINKING

Our modern society is based on rational thinking, but this is not necessarily a bad thing. Much of the technology we enjoy (like computers, medicine, and engineering) is based on this rational, scientific model. But however useful rational thought is for material advancement, it is not very useful for spiritual advancement. For example, modern society's poor environmental record comes directly from an inability to see the environment as having a spiritual component and therefore requiring more than rational thought to understand and appreciate it.

So what takes the place of rational thinking in spirituality? Some will have you believe that irrational thinking is the solution. According to them, you must either "take it on faith" (thereby applying no mode of logic at all) or, alternatively, you can "believe anything," however internally inconsistent. Neither of these options fosters spiritual growth, and in fact they may even be harmful. The first leads to spiritual stagnation and the second, to confusion or even insanity.

However, there is a third option. Instead of the rationality that can't acknowledge the existence of a spiritual path or the irrationality that doesn't give us a map to follow, we can endeavor to view the world symbolically. Symbolic thinking is about connections and correspondences. It is cyclical and multileveled. Yet it also requires an internal consistency and affords us the opportunity to apply a spiritual litmus test to new ideas.

Unlike rational thinking, symbolic thinking starts with the premise that *there is more to the world than can initially be seen or understood*. It presupposes an underlying conscious order manifest in all things and that, therefore, there is no such thing as coincidence or chance. Or, as Ray Grasse puts it in his excellent book *The Waking Dream*, "the symbolist standpoint considers life to be a living book of symbols, a sacred text that can be decoded. Through applying the proper key, the patterns of the world reveal hidden resonances and levels of information overlooked in our contemporary preoccupation with literal meanings and surface interpretations."[14]

Unlike irrational thinking, the symbolic worldview acknowledges that there is a patterned order to existence. We must be discerning in creating our symbol sets for ourselves, and our symbology must be internally consistent, archetypally resonant, and intuitively logical.

Symbolic thinking is based on our search for meaning, not simply the surface meaning, but a deeper significance.

You begin to cultivate symbolic thinking when you make an effort to connect disparate ideas through some sublevel (or superlevel) of commonality. *As above, so below.* This is where the "keys" that Grasse spoke of come into play. These keys include the Tarot, astrology, dream work, augury, mythology, meditation, chakras, and so on. Focus on the ones that resonate with you. Note, too, that while some of these keys can be used for divination, there is always a symbolic subtext that can be used, not to tell the future, but to divine larger truths about the meaning of the universe.

Is the color green associated with spiritual healing to you? And does it perhaps also connect with the Empress in the Tarot deck? The Empress is associated with the planet Venus, which is also linked to copper, emerald, and the color green. In my deck she is described as representing health, fertility, and nurturing—a Great Mother figure. Venus is also associated with the fourth chakra, the heart chakra, which governs our emotions and relationships with others.

From this small series of connections you can begin to think symbolically. If green is the color of nature and also of spiritual healing, what does it portend that our Great Mother Earth is now suffering ecological sickness? Can you outline a healing ritual (for yourself or another) using a series of healing connections? What does it mean when a patch of fuzzy green moss begins growing on your front door after you begin a new relationship? What even deeper insights might you gather about the nature of healing through meditation on the Empress card or the nature of heartache or a green meadow or your mother's emerald ring?

You can't force these kinds of connections. Either they inspire you or they do not. However, you may find that many of them do inspire you. This is because some of these connections are very old and have the cumulative energy of multitudes of believers. This is described below in the section on relativism. In addition, the symbolism of many objects, particularly in the natural world, is based on the very specific energies they give off.

The most important aspect of developing symbolic thinking is that it is *useful*. It furthers you on your spiritual path. As you broaden your web of connections, the world will begin to resonate with a deeper meaning: for example, my fascination with the moon as a child. I now understand not only the moon's material nature (a ball of rock hurtling around our own planet, reflecting the light of the sun) but also its hidden or occult nature. I understand it because I know the moon's connections that make up its symbolic language.

This is the source of understanding. The keys to the mysteries are all here. And while many of these revelations are incredibly subtle and personal, requiring much inner work on your part, others are immediate and quite noticeable. One of the ways in which symbolic thinking opens you to this hidden meaning is through the effects of synchronicity in your life.

SYNCHRONICITY

According to M.-L. von Franz, one of Jung's close associates and author of several of the essays that make up *Man and His Symbols*, "Dr. Jung put forward a new concept that he called *synchronicity*. This term means a 'meaningful coincidence' of outer and inner events that are not themselves causally connected. The emphasis lies on the word 'meaningful.'"[15]

Synchronicity is officially defined as "the coincidental occurrence of events and especially psychic events (as similar thoughts in widely separated persons or a mental image of an unexpected event before it happens) that seem related but are not explained by conventional mechanisms of causality."[16]

Jung observed that these coincidences were common among his patients. He believed that synchronicity accounted for psychic phenomena such as dreaming of the future, thinking of a friend just as he or she calls you, or knowing when some event has happened at a distance. He also tied these events to his concepts of archetypes and the collective unconscious (more on this below).

The key to understanding synchronicity is *meaning*. A clock stopping is not meaningful. A clock that stops at the exact moment of its owner's death is a meaningful event. If you open yourself to this concept, you will begin to see how meaningful coincidence moves throughout your own life. More important, you can *learn* from these occurrences as opposed to simply being subject to them. When I put aside a difficult book because I'm just not getting it, only to find the answer in another book, movie, chance comment, or other unrelated place, that's synchronicity.

Pagans and Witches commonly believe in psychic powers. They would not be at all surprised to be thinking of a friend just as the telephone rings. But synchronicity also moves more subtly, and these less obvious messages are often the more important ones. A bird appearing in the sky may not be synchronous at all, while a bird crashing into your window very well might be. However, to truly understand these messages of the universe, we have to look deeper. What kind of bird was it? Does that type of bird have a special significance in mythology or folk custom? Does the name of the bird have some meaning? What were you doing when the crash occurred? And how do you *use* the event to chart your course, make decisions, or learn something new about your spiritual path?

If a bird crashing into your window sounds like what's commonly known as an omen or portent, it might well be. After all, an omen can be easily defined as a meaningful coincidence (for more on omens, see the next chapter). However, synchronicity encompasses more than that. It is focused equally on relativism and the archetypes. Relativism insists that a "meaningful coincidence" must first have meaning *for you*—based on your own symbol set and perspective, while archetypes remind us that there are broad human meanings that go beyond the individual or even the cultural.

RELATIVISM

Jung postulated that there are two kinds of symbols: personal and archetypal. Both are important for understanding synchronicity and comprise our own, personal book of symbols. Most Pagans are now familiar with the concept of archetypes. However, there is somewhat less of a conscious understanding of the nature of relativism in Pagan spiritual practice.

Beginners are often focused on finding the "right" or "real" ways of exploring their spirituality. This is particularly true of converts from monotheistic religions. They feel that their old religion is totally wrong and that, therefore, there must be a religion that is totally right. This is the explanation for the period of backlash and rigid dogmatism that many new Witches and Pagans go through. There's a sense that the seeker has finally found the right way, so the old way is open to ridicule or even hatred. This is also the source of arguments regarding certain ideas in Wicca and Magic such as which elements correspond to which directions and whether the blade is associated with fire or air.

Most Pagans eventually graduate to the understanding that these issues are relative and personal. What's right for me may not be right for you. However, to truly understand the universe, we must take this a step further. It's not whether a symbol is right or not, it's that no symbol has any more rightness than any other and that anything might become a symbol. The colors that correspond to the four directions can be red, yellow, green, and blue; white, red, grey, and black; citrine, olive, russet, and black; or any other colors. While one option may appeal to you more than another, all the options (and *any* other combination you can think of) are valid and true. The only requirement is that, internally, they make sense to you and correspond with the energy you sense. In fact there need not be four elements at all. There may be six, or three, or none.

As I mentioned in the section on symbolic thinking above, some correspondences naturally resonate with us. This is because the cumulative belief and power of millions of people and thousands of years have created a connection far stronger than a single person could. Excellent examples of this phenomenon include the symbolism associated with the planets, Qabalistic sephiroth, Tarot, chakras, runes, and so on. Of course, these symbols still come from someplace. Natural objects all have their own energies that we can sense and our interpretation of the symbolism or specific power of these objects is based on the quality of that energy. However, the important thing for the advancing Witch or Pagan to remember is that these are all still options, possibilities for your own spiritual path, and not requirements. These symbol sets have power; however, adopt them consciously as relative symbols, and avoid labeling them as truth or dogma.

When you are just starting out, these symbols can give you the sense of order and structure that you may need. Of course you may choose to continue working with them throughout your more advanced studies. However, remember that any practice that becomes rigid also becomes limiting. Relativism teaches that what you believe is true for you . . . just make sure your truths are helping you grow and not holding you back.

ARCHETYPES AND THE COLLECTIVE UNCONSCIOUS

Unlike personal symbols, some other symbols seem to be a deeply embedded part of our subconscious. In fact Jung traced the appearance of these metasymbols throughout history and culture. Like instincts, they come from an unconscious source. However, Jung described the difference between the two.

What we properly call instincts are physiological urges, and are perceived by the senses. But at the same time, they also manifest themselves in fantasies and often reveal their presence only by

symbolic images. These manifestations are what I call the archetypes. They are without known origin; and they reproduce
themselves in any time or in any part of the world—even where
transmission by direct descent or "cross fertilization" through
migration must be ruled out.[17]

Many of the archetypes that Jung analyzed will be familiar to Pagans: the great mother, the dying god, the initiate, the hero. However,
it is important to realize the difference between the archetype of the
great mother and the Great Mother Goddess that you may have chosen to believe in. Archetypes are teaching tools. They are like meta-
symbol categories that you can use to help analyze your experiences.
They are not Deities to be worshipped. When you call on a God
and Goddess, you are not invoking psychological constructs but living
beings who are as autonomous and self-determining as you are.

Archetypes have great power. You can easily argue the meaning of
a relative or personal symbol. For example, many Native Americans
believed the owl to be a death omen. A European viewpoint would
more likely associate the owl with the Goddesses Athena or Bloduwedd—and therefore see it as a symbol of wisdom as opposed to
death. However, neither viewpoint is more correct or right than the
other. What you believe is going to be relative to your personal experience, cultural context, and so on. With archetypes, things aren't as
flexible. You can't simply disbelieve an archetype. In fact, if you repress an archetype, it simply reappears in a negative or shadow form.

In our culture, the "dark side" is commonly repressed. We don't
like to acknowledge that death, darkness, violence, and sex are as valid
as life, light, peace, and love. We label one set of ideas good and the
other evil. The truth is that these halves are part of a whole—a contin-
ual cycle or spiral—and both are necessary. But because we repress
the ideas that our culture considers evil, they reappear in forms more
destructive than before. This is the shadow. And it is applicable not

only to elements of human nature (like violence, life, and sex) but also to the archetypes.

The tendency to ignore the darker elements of existence is a feature of Neo-Paganism as much as Christianity. We can't view the Goddess only as loving mother . . . because She is, and has always been, a being of death and war as well as love. We can't tell ourselves that we will never feel anger or act violently. Those emotions are as much a part of our humanity as happiness and joy. If we do not acknowledge those parts of ourselves, we will never be able to control them. It is the uncontrolled, shadow aspects of these very archetypes that are the cause of so many of humanity's problems.

Where do these archetypes come from? Jung felt that there was a level of the unconscious mind that was shared among all humans. He called this the *collective unconscious* and felt that the archetypes were, in part, generated there. But he also came to believe that the archetypes created existence as much as existence created the archetypes. This particular idea could potentially spark a number of fascinating spiritual meditations. More on this in the chapter on altered states of consciousness.

In metaphysical or theosophical literature, the Akashic Record refers to a similar if not identical concept. Everything that occurs is recorded in an etheric substance known as akasha. In the right state of consciousness, individuals can access information from this record. From this perspective, past life regression, divination, and psychic power all rely on the Akashic Record or collective unconscious to operate.

~~~~~~

FOOD FOR THOUGHT—THE HERO'S JOURNEY

One of the more compelling of Jung's archetypes is that of the hero. Renowned comparative mythologist Joseph Campbell expanded this archetype into the hero's Journey. What Campbell noticed was that heroic stories from around the world all had similar steps or stages. He categorized these steps in his book *Hero with a Thousand Faces.*[18]

What makes the hero's journey so useful is that, while it describes fictional or mythological stories, those stories in turn describe actual reality. You can probably match the steps of the hero's journey to occurrences in your own life. A hero's journey is marked by a fundamental change in the hero through events in the tale. Any events in your own life that cause you to change mark your own hero's journey. Naturally, not every story contains every step, particularly in the real world, but the motifs recur enough to make its study a useful spiritual tool.

What follows is an overview of Campbell's hero's journey and its application to the movie *Star Wars*, episode IV (the first of the movies made).[19] This is not as bizarre as it seems. One hallmark of an archetype is that it transcends culture, time, and place. The hero's journey is as applicable and meaningful to us today as it was to people thousands of years ago. George Lucas read *Hero with a Thousand Faces* in college. When he set out to write the space opera, his interest in the hero's journey was rekindled. Lucas became a friend of Campbell's and a student of his theories. In fact, Campbell's interviews with Bill Moyers (compiled into the documentary *Joseph Campbell and The Power of Myth*) took place at Skywalker Ranch.[20]

Since the plot of the film follows the journey so faithfully and just about everyone has seen the film, it's helpful as an example in understanding the various stages and steps. Note that "hero" can, of course, refer to a person of either gender. I've mixed pronouns in the explanations below.

STAGE ONE: DEPARTURE

Every hero starts as a normal person in a normal world. To find adventure, change, and the knowledge of the self, she must leave this world behind and travel to the land of adventure.

Step 1—The Call to Adventure

The hero is called by his destiny to leave the familiar and journey into the unknown. The hero can be called by either danger or reward (or both). He can answer the call willingly or be forced into the journey by either malicious or friendly beings or events. Finally, the journey can start with an accident or mistake (being in the right place at the right time or the wrong place at the wrong time).

In *Star Wars*, our hero, Luke Skywalker, is called to adventure by his destiny as the son of Anakin—former Jedi Knight and adventurer in his own right. Luke wants to leave the farm and attend the academy, but he feels constrained by familial duty. Luke complains at the very start of the film that he's "never gonna get out of here." But we know that he *will* answer the call. As his aunt comments in the film, "Luke's just not a farmer, Owen. He has too much of his father in him."

In addition to his own adventurous spirit, Luke's call to adventure also comes in the form of Leia's message to Obi-Wan. When Luke discovers the message carried by R2-D2, he unwittingly facilitates the droid's escape. His comment to C3PO is amusingly prescient: "You know, that little droid is gonna cause me a lot of trouble!" This accident, and Luke's decision to follow the droid on his own, begins his hero's journey adventure.

Step 2—Refusal of the Call

Our budding hero decides against following the call to adventure. Whether from a sense of duty, fear, insecurity, or any number of reasons, our hero decides she would rather stay in familiar circumstances than stray into the unknown. This decision is usually based on a certain selfishness or narrow-mindedness. At this point, the story takes a negative turn. Either the hero becomes a victim in need of rescue, or she is literally forced into adventure by her situation.

In *Star Wars*, Luke initially refuses to get involved with Obi-Wan and Leia's message. Obi-Wan plainly insists that Luke "must learn the ways of the Force if you're to come with me to Aldaraan." But Luke's reaction is one of fear. "I've got to get home," he insists. "I can't get involved . . . I've got work to do . . . there's nothing I can do about it right now." And finally, quietly, "It's so far from here." Luke's initial refusal of the call is based not in his uncle's logic (needing him for the harvest) but in his own fear of the unknown. In reply, Obi-Wan only says, "You must do what you think is right, of course."

But Luke doesn't have a choice. After discovering his home and relatives destroyed, he must accept the call. "I want to come with you to Aldaraan. There's nothing here for me now," he says. "I want to learn the ways of the Force and become a Jedi like my father."

Most heroes will initially refuse the call, but if the hero refuses the call consistently, she will become an antihero. Even so, antiheroes usually end up back on the heroic path by the end of the story—no matter how much they fight it. In *Star Wars*, Han Solo is an excellent example of the antihero.

Step 3—Supernatural Aid

Once the hero accepts the call to adventure (either deliberately or unwillingly), a magical guide appears. Typically an old man or woman, this guide or helper represents the protective powers of the universe that are now available to the hero because of his decision. The guide commonly gives the hero an amulet to use in the coming battles or trials. There is also usually a point where the guide will step back and let the hero continue on his own. To win through to the end, the hero must begin to rely only on himself, having internalized the lessons of the guide and his adventures.

In *Star Wars*, Obi-Wan is Luke's supernatural guide. The movie refers to him as both a "strange old hermit" and a "wizard." The talisman is, of course, Anakin's light saber. Obi-Wan saves Luke from the storm troopers ("these aren't the droids you're looking for") and in the tavern in Mos Eisley. He teaches Luke about the Force and continues to play a role in Luke's journey, even after his own death. After being captured by the Death Star, Obi-Wan insists on disabling the tractor beam alone. When Luke protests, he only comments that "Your destiny lies along a different path than mine." This is his way of saying that Luke is on his own.

Step 4—Crossing the First Threshold

Before the adventure can really commence, our hero must take that first step into the unknown. The threshold acts as a significant gateway, well guarded, that leads from the hero's regular life to her new life of adventure. The guardians represent the limits of our hero's current experience. While many people are content to stay within the bounds of the known, the hero must battle the guardians to embrace her destiny and continue the journey. Once again, the hero doesn't have much choice. By answering the call to adventure, her old life is either symbolically or literally dead to her. Before she can go back, she must go forward toward change and self-actualization. It's no coincidence that so many heroes' journeys are partially or wholly coming of age stories. Coming of age is a time of learning about oneself and this is, at its core, what the hero's journey is about.

Luke's threshold is the tavern at Mos Eisley. This "wretched hive of scum and villainy" abounds with dangers that Luke believes he's ready to face. But though he makes it through the gate (and into the larger unknown of space), he begins to realize how much he has yet to learn. This is also where Luke meets Han Solo and Chewbacca, some of the companions who will play large roles in his future journey. The jump to light speed that allows them to escape is a literal first step into the unknown. Obi-Wan tells Luke after his first successful experience with the Force, "You've taken your first step into a larger world."

Step 5—The Belly of the Whale

After crossing the threshold, our hero comes to a moment of final separation. He already knows that he can't return to his prior, "normal" existence. After this moment, he will also be unable to turn aside. Named after the biblical story of Jonah and the Whale, this step is where his first, fundamental internal change comes about. The belly of the whale can be seen as the person's lowest point, but it's really a transition from one world to another and from one person to another. By entering this stage of the story, the hero demonstrates his commitment to metamorphosis.

The belly is generally represented by something dark, unknown, or frightening, but what it really symbolizes is the womb. Our hero must return to the womb in order to be reborn as someone new. Like the barrows of the British Isles, burying the dead is literally returning him to the Great Mother's womb. The hero will need to die to himself in order to be renewed and changed. Depending on the story, this step can be tightly coupled with the crossing of the threshold or part of the next stage of the journey as one of many trials to come.

For Luke, this is quite obviously symbolized by the Millennium Falcon being swallowed by the Death Star. Before this moment, Luke had been very much a victim of circumstance. He is saved by his companions; he doesn't do much to direct his own destiny. But as Luke emerges from the belly of the Falcon (itself within the belly of the Death Star), he knows he can no longer remain passive. He must begin to act. This stage culminates in the trash compactor. Another womb or belly, the water, with its mysterious creature, represents the unconscious.

STAGE TWO: INITIATION

The hero's departure is only the first step. As the old cliché states, "Out of the frying pan and into the fire." The thresholds passed are only the beginning. A long road still lies ahead.

Step 1—The Road of Trials

For our hero, the road ahead will be filled with tests or ordeals that she must undergo in order to transform herself. She may not pass all the tests, but experiencing them is vital to her successful navigation through the journey. These trials often appear in threes and can be of various common types:

- Dragon battle—a fight with a dragon, either literal or figurative.
- Brother battle—a fight between two brothers or between parts of the hero's psyche.
- Crucifixion—a literal or figurative hanging, with an element of sacrifice.

- Dismemberment—being torn asunder, physically, emotionally, or mentally.
- Abduction—being stolen away or stealing someone else away.
- Night / Sea journey—travels through mysterious realms (inner or outer).

Luke's trials in *Star Wars* include his rescue of Princess Leia culminating in the trash compactor with its strange monster (dragon battle), the gunfight and leap across the chasm, and the spaceship gunfight that facilitates their escape. Note, too, that Obi-Wan's lightsaber battle with Darth Vadar is very much a brother battle. Obi-Wan and Vader represent the two sides of the Force as well as being comrades and fellow Jedis who have taken different paths.

Step 2—Meeting the Goddess
This represents the step in which the hero experiences an unconditional love or connection very much like the love that a mother feels for her children. The experience can be external (literally discovering a partner or other half) or completely internal (experiencing great marriage or union of opposites within). It is usually a mixture of both.

The Goddess in this step does not necessarily have to be female. For a female hero, it can be the discovery of her own Goddess nature and also of the Divine consort, the male aspect of Her love and power (which lies within every man). For a male hero, it can be the experience of the Divine Feminine in the form of a human woman or a coming together of the male and female essences within himself. For a literal meeting of man and woman, it will be a deep and sacred connection—not necessarily culminating in physical love.

Leia very strongly represents the Goddess in *Star Wars*. She is not only young and attractive, she is also strong, intelligent, and knowledgeable. She is the keeper of the grail or boon—the plans to the Death Star that are required to defeat the Federation. Although she and Luke do not yet know it, they have a long history together as twins separated at birth. It is clearly their destiny to meet again. Luke's attraction to her is undeniable, and she acts as his prime moti-

vator throughout most of the film. Yet there is always a sense of a
higher sort of connection between them.

Step 3—Temptation

Campbell originally described this step as "Woman as Temptress."
But while women have been cast in this role, a broad look at hero's
journey stories shows that the temptation is as likely to come from a
male figure or from within. Our hero must face temptations that
threaten to distract or deter her from her journey. She may also face
the temptation of her former, earthly self in relation to the person
she is becoming. To continue with her journey, she must stay her
course and focus only on the result of her quest.

Though Luke learns early about the temptation of the dark side of
the Force, his temptation in the first movie is a small one—his moment of despair after Obi-Wan is killed. Luke's comment—"I just miss
him so much" is proof that he has not yet internalized the lessons he
was taught. But his willingness to shrug off his despair to continue
the battle shows that he is well on his way. If you are a fan of all
the *Star Wars* movies, you will begin to recognize these steps in the
other movies. For example, in the later films Luke is very much
tempted by the dark side of the Force.

Step 4—Atonement with the Father

As the Goddess symbolizes unconditional love and acceptance, so
the Father symbolizes ultimate power in the hero's life. Our hero must
come to terms with a literal or figurative father figure, the person or
entity that holds the power of life and death over him. This is the ful-
crum of the journey. All the trials and struggles so far have served to
bring the hero to this place. In many tales this is literally a male
character. The atonement (or at-one-ment) with this character is the
hero's ego-shattering initiation.

In the first *Star Wars* movie, the atonement with the father is
Luke's internalization of Obi-Wan's lessons about the Force. While
Obi-Wan is a literal father figure (his disembodied voice a symbol of
his becoming one with Luke after his death), the Force is a figurative

one. Luke has to become one with this powerful and dangerous energy to fulfill his role as hero. The culmination of Luke's self-actualization comes when he takes the risk of relying only on the Force to help him target the vent opening and blast the Death Star. This occurs while he is being pursued by his biological father, Darth Vader (with their own atonement still two movies away).

Step 5—Apotheosis

To apotheosize is to deify. After our hero dies (either literally or spiritually) she moves away from duality and to a state of perfect knowledge, happiness, and bliss. She becomes godlike, an avatar. In many tales this is a period of rest and peace before the hero must return to her life.

Luke's moment comes as he integrates the Force and realizes its true nature. As Obi-Wan tells him, "the Force will be with you." That he can feel and use the Force allows him almost godlike power. He can target and blast the Death Star (a chance Han describes as "one in a million") because his old self has died and he has become a new person.

Step 6—The Ultimate Boon

This is the goal of our hero's quest: the object or grail she was sent to find, or the task that she needed to fulfill. If the boon is an object, it is rarely just a material thing; instead it symbolizes something greater. The philosopher's stone, the elixir of eternal life, the holy grail, all are representations of an internal change. If a task, it is a task that transcends the hero herself and affects / benefits all people.

The boon in *Star Wars* is both an item and a task. The item, the plans to the Death Star, are what the characters struggle to deliver throughout most of the film. However, the plans then designate the task, to use the knowledge gleaned from them to destroy the space station—a task of monumental difficulty. To make matters worse, the task must be performed or the entire rebel base will be destroyed. The survival of the alliance depends on this task. Therefore, everything depends on Luke and his ability to use the Force.

STAGE THREE: RETURN

Everything the hero learns in his initiation must be brought back with him to the real world. Whether the hero experiences a literal return or only a symbolic one, he must re-enter the world of mortals with all his acquired skill and knowledge.

Step 1—Refusal of the Return

Like the refusal of the call, our hero may refuse to return to the "normal" world. She may not see the reason for bringing back the boon or knowledge to help her community. It may be simply a moment of doubt or a serious refusal, but it's common for heroes to doubt themselves and their wisdom and abilities.

In *Star Wars* the return is symbolized by the attack on the Death Star. Luke must take his knowledge of the Force and use it to help the alliance. This is specifically symbolized by his reunion with Biggs, his friend from his home planet. He's using his powers to help not only himself but all the people he left behind. Although Luke never experiences a refusal, in the movie, Han experiences it for him. Throughout the film Han Solo acts as counterpoint—antihero to Luke's hero. Luke asks Han to stay and help, but he refuses, putting his own self-interest ahead of the needs of his community.

Step 2—The Magic Flight

Our hero may need to escape with the boon. Alternately, he may need to use the boon to perform some dangerous task. Either way, our hero learns that coming back to the "normal" world—the return—can be just as dangerous as everything that went before. This is why so many heroes leave triumphant . . . but at a run.

For Luke, the magic flight is his assault and escape from the Death Star at the end of the film. He has to dodge danger to destroy it as well as to get away safely. Using his knowledge to save the rebellion almost kills him.

Step 3—Rescue from Without

Our hero needed help in setting out on her quest. This is the role of the supernatural guide. However, she might also need help in her return. Perhaps she has been injured or weakened. Or she could be in such a state of bliss that she doesn't wish to return. Or she may not understand that a return is possible.

In *Star Wars* Han rescues Luke during his assault on the Death Star. He returns to blast Luke's pursuers and clear the way for Luke to destroy it and complete his quest. Han's comment—"You're all clear, kid. Now let's blow this thing and go home"—clearly demonstrates that the goal is not simply to destroy the space station but to return home afterward.

Step 4—The Crossing of the Return Threshold

The crossing of the threshold thrusts our hero into danger and onto his quest. To return again, he must recross into the everyday world, bringing with him his boon or powers. This is usually a very difficult task.

For Luke, taking the theory of the Force and applying it to a real task (destroying the Death Star and returning alive), shows his success as a hero and his ability in crossing the return threshold.

Step 5—Master of the Two Worlds—and Step 6—Freedom to Live

The end of the hero's journey leaves our hero a new person. Her reward is that she is now the master of both the spiritual and material realms. She has achieved balance and can live in both places at once. In addition, she has the freedom to continue her life. No longer a pawn in a transformative experience, she can move forward, using the lessons she's learned. Having died to herself, she no longer fears death.

Star Wars only hints at Luke's experience after returning from destroying the Death Star. We know he's enfolded in the arms of his friends and considered a hero by his community. We suspect that he can go on with his life, experiencing the Force and making a difference. Of course having seen the next two movies, we also know that more adventures are before him and that he has a great deal more to learn before he will become a Jedi. However, we also know that, as Obi-Wan tells him, "The Force will be with you—always."

CHAPTER 3 EXERCISES

Finding Synchronicity

In order to integrate the lessons of synchronicity (including omens and portents) into your spiritual practice, you must first become aware of them. Even people who believe in these subtle hints don't always recognize them at the time. Have you ever looked back after a bad experience and realized that your instincts told you there would be a problem, but you ignored your gut feeling at the time? Or have you had an experience where everything around you seemed to be pointing you in a certain direction, but you only recognized it after the fact?

Well, there's nothing special or intuitive about 20/20 hindsight. If you want to take advantage of synchronicity in your life, you have to make a deliberate effort to recognize these signals in advance. One good way of doing this is to note any unusual occurrences at the time they happen. After some practice, you can simply make a mental note, but it's best to start by actually writing down what happened. Making note of these events is important because, as with many other spiritual phenomena (including dreams, revelations, and conversations with your Deities), there's a tendency for the conscious mind to forget the event later.

This doesn't require a special book or a lot of time. A little notebook in which you can scribble a few notes will do. You'll learn how much information you need to include through trial and error. Later, if you can't remember what your notes are about, add more detail. If your hand cramps up, add less. Here's an example:

Monday 12/10/01—Crow on porch. Screamed at me as I took out the trash. Cold gust of wind. Sense of foreboding.

Later, when something happens that seems to fit, you can append the note with the details:

Monday 12/10/01—Crow on porch. Screamed at me as I took out the trash. Cold gust of wind. Sense of foreboding. Sunday 12/16/01— J——'s dog hit by trash truck!

Another great way of noting these events is to share them with a trusted friend. This can be particularly useful if you can e-mail your friend regularly. You'll have both a written record of the event and a second perspective on its meaning. Do make sure, however, that you share a strong bond with the other person. Synchronous events can be very personal. You need someone whose discretion and objectivity you can count on.

By noting the things that happen and any later ramifications, you'll discover that there are plenty of events that don't lead to anything at all. These are just the occurrences of life and don't particularly apply to you. But sometimes there are deeper messages that you need to recognize. When you get the hang of it, you'll be able to *feel* the difference between a significant event and an insignificant one. Finally, please remember that this is an imperfect science. If we could know everything in advance, I'd have won the lottery by now.

Creating a Symbol Diary

To begin thinking symbolically, you have to connect things that at first seem to have no direct connection. These connections are known as correspondences. A list of similar correspondences is called a concordance. For example, a list of the colors, metals, stones, and meanings of the planets is a "planetary concordance." Books that include this type of information are quite common—Web sites even more common. In fact, it's a hallmark of a beginner's Pagan site that the author includes a concordance—usually containing information, often verbatim, which is already available from numerous published sources.

Concordances have their uses. As I mentioned above, many of these connections are backed by long and venerable histories. But they must also resonate with you personally. If you use a standard set of color correspondences for the planets, they will very likely work for you. If you change these correspondences, you must make sure that the new colors resonate as strongly. However, the most potent symbol connections are those that come to you personally. These won't be included in every book and site. In fact they may be unique to you. But it is because of their uniqueness that they can be so powerful.

If you are not yet familiar with a broad range of existing correspondence sets from various sources, you should make an effort to incorporate as many as possible into your worldview. That means you need to obtain a good book of this type of information and study it. *The Magician's Companion* is one decent source of this type of data.[21] Its strengths are that it includes an encyclopedia's worth of different symbol sets from around the world and presents the information simply. Its major weakness is that the information cannot be completely trusted. For example, the section on magic squares includes several egregious mathematical errors.

Once you have become an expert in multiple concordances (and you will need to be an expert to truly incorporate symbolic thinking into your life), you can begin to personalize those connections. This is where the fun starts. When a personal connection presents itself to you, you will want to make note of it. In addition, you'll want to incorporate it into your practices as soon as possible. For example, if a certain fruit or vegetable suddenly suggests itself as belonging to a particular Deity, make offerings of it to Him or Her. If a shape or design strongly implies protection or safety, draw it out, empower it, and place it in your home or car.

Most personal correspondences come under the heading of "trade secrets." This is mainly because the connection may be so personal that it won't even make sense to other people. Besides, if you discovered a powerful protection symbol, would you really want to advertise it? As you log more of these connections you will be creating a personal concordance—a truly powerful book of symbols. If you've ever wondered what to include in your Book of Shadows or Grimoire, well, this is it. Skip the pages and pages of correspondences that you can find in a hundred books and focus on those that are truly and completely yours.

A Novel Idea—The Hero's Journey in Fiction

When Joseph Campbell described the hero's journey as an archetype, he wasn't kidding. The story arc he describes appears again and again in both ancient and modern fiction and mythological stories. It's so ubiquitous that you will almost certainly be able to trace the various stages and steps in just about any book that you pull off your bookshelf. I originally tried this as part of a college class assignment. My choice was *The White Raven* by Diana L. Paxson.[22] This is a great book with a wonderful Pagan story in its own right, but when I began matching the tale to the hero's journey, I was absolutely stunned. However, it wasn't just me. The entire class had the same experience with their choices as well—books ranging from historical fiction to adventure to mystery to romance.

Pick a book—truly, just about any work of fiction will do—and as you read, try to recognize the hero's journey in its pages. You will not only get more out of the novel; you will also come to a greater understanding of the archetype. However, be warned. Once you begin to look for it, the hero's journey will appear in every story, tale, movie, and even TV series you encounter. It is everywhere.

Your Life as Hero's Journey

It's important to remember that the path of the advancing Pagan or Witch is never simply academic. Theory is nothing unless you can begin to apply that theory to your own life and path. An idea might be interesting, but unless it's also *useful*, it will not contribute to your spiritual growth. The hero's journey isn't just a fascinating way of critiquing fiction, it's also a way of viewing your own life. You *are* the hero in your own personal journey. Perhaps you will never be called to slay the ultimate evil and bring freedom to all humankind, but nonetheless, your own path will include challenges and trials that will ultimately change you.

Take a momentous event in your life. Pick a time when you underwent a change as a result of the event. Now starting thinking about all the events leading up to that change and all the events after it. Can you begin to see connections with the stages and steps of the hero's journey?

CONCLUSION

The road of the journeyman Witch or Pagan is focused not only on new ideas but also new ways of thinking. When you learn to think symbolically, you will notice greater comprehension of the workings of synchronicity in your life. Finding the connections between apparently unrelated systems or ideas is the key to unlocking spiritual mysteries. In addition, symbolic pattern recognition will allow you to discern between relative symbols and powerful archetypes. Archetypal tools like the hero's journey can help you find and walk your spiritual path.

This chapter touched briefly on omens as they relate to synchronicity. The symbolic connections that describe the holistic nature of the universe drive your ability to "see" future trends—what's known as divination. However, to divine the future with any sort of accuracy, you need to have a clear understanding of how the future manifests itself in the present. This is discussed in detail in the next chapter.

CHAPTER 4

Interconnectivity:
OMENS, PORTENTS, AND DIVINATION

A LARGE CHUNK OF MODERN PAGANISM SEEMS TO BE FOCUSED ON DIS-covering the future. During your initiation into the beginning stage of your path, you were probably introduced to some form of divination such as runes, Tarot cards, or astrology. There is long historical prece-dent for this focus. One of the primary tasks of the Witch, shaman, magician, or Druid is to determine the future course of events. In classical Greece, people traveled many miles to consult oracles who could help them make decisions about their lives by exposing (how-ever cryptically) their future.

But how does divination work, and why? And how do we integrate ideas about knowing the future with the exercise of free will? The fact that divination works is obvious to anyone who has been "blown away" by a particularly accurate reading. But why doesn't it work all the time? The answers are both more complex and simpler than you might expect.

DESTINY, FATE, FREE WILL, AND THE NATURE OF TIME

On the surface, destiny and free will seem like mutually exclusive con-cepts. Either you are controlled by a particular destiny or you have free will—but not both. The truth is that we are controlled by destiny, but we also have free will. How can this be? Like many seemingly inconsistent ideas, the reality hinges on perception and the nature of the universe.

Everything in the universe is connected. While many Pagans would eagerly attest to this fact, very few have the tiniest inkling of what this really means. This is because, as humans, we are hindered by limited perspective. To the average person, the world is imprisoned by the march of time, the reality of cause and effect is immutable, and much of human behavior (including her own) is chaotic and unpredictable.

In fact, the primary difference between that average person and a Witch is that the Witch has the perspective to begin testing the bounds of time and "logic." I use the term *Witch* here to describe all who test or even notice these limitations—no matter what they call themselves. Throughout history, there have been numerous people (from shamans to Sufis to metaphysicians) who—to make ironic use of a corporate metaphor—see the box and can think and operate outside of it.

However, as humans, we all have to contend with our physical limits. Transcending them is difficult—and for good reason. It is through those very limitations that we learn. Human beings learn through experience. It should be obvious from the most cursory review of human behavior that you can't *tell* people anything important. Inevitably they must discover for themselves what is important. Our limited perspective is designed to facilitate our growth. To put it bluntly, we would be a lot less likely to learn anything if we knew the details of our lessons in advance.

This is why, in general, people are completely controlled by their destiny and fate. The perception of free will is an illusion. From a much wider perspective, every purportedly free decision is simply the culmination of everything in the decision maker's experience to that point. If you knew everything about a person, you would have an unfailing ability to predict their behavior. Of course, with our limitations, it's impossible to know everything about another person. For most of us, it's difficult to know even the most basic information about ourselves and our own motivations.

At the same time, we do have free will. Illusion or not, from our point of view (and an inordinate amount of truth and reality is simply a matter of point of view) we *do* have free will . . . and therefore must exercise it. In fact, as we come to realize our limitations and work at transcending them, we can begin to understand our own fate and destiny. It is through that understanding that we discover our True Will: free will—freed of perspective. This is why your first and foremost task is to know yourself.

But what does all this have to do with divination and knowing the future? As humans, one of our most persistent limitations is time. This is particularly true of those of us in the modern Western world. In the past, time was a much more relative concept. Yes, humans have understood the passage of time for many thousands of years (as "celestial clocks" such as Stonehenge demonstrate). However, on a day-to-day basis, time was a much more malleable concept. With the invention of more and more accurate timepieces, we have allowed ourselves to be trapped and limited by time.

Practically speaking, knowing what time it is and being "on time" are reasonable ways of making the world work. However, as with many of the ideas we hold to be truth, the passage of time is a useful metaphor, not rigid dogma. As a side note, this is why you should never wear a watch in ritual. You need to divorce yourself from many of the rules or constraints of the "real world"—and time is one of the most persistent and difficult of these—when you enter ritual space.

Please understand that I am not advocating what has become known as "Pagan Standard Time" in groups and covens around the country; in fact I advocate just the opposite. Being chronically late is not only rude and inconsiderate, it actually demonstrates an *inability* to transcend the limitations of time. People who understand the passage of time enough to know its relativism are, as a consequence, rarely late unless they choose to be.

But if the straight passage of time is simply an illusion (albeit a useful one for getting to work in the morning), what then is the actual nature of time? Interestingly enough, modern scientific thought is beginning to come into agreement with mystical ideas on the topic. Special relativity, for example, has long postulated that time is relative to your position and movement. Scientists studying quantum mechanics have recently postulated that all moments in time are actually occurring at once and that humans simply move through the moments. From this perspective, everything has already occurred and individual decisions are simply branches to new realities—yes, plural realities. This model of the universe includes alternate realities, multiple dimensions, and time travel. While still scientifically controversial, these theories are very useful indeed for spiritual purposes.

For example, a spell has you going back in time to contact your younger self at a particularly important or vulnerable moment. By giving your younger self the information or support he or she needs at that time, you can effectively change your own history and become a new person in the here and now. Many people, including magicians, might say that this spell has a primarily psychological component; however, there's no reason not to view the spell as time travel on the astral plane (or even on the literal one).

A much more ancient and mystical view of time is that of the spiral. The spiral appears in enough places and enough times in history to be considered an archetype. In fact the labyrinth (with a single path—as differentiated from the maze, which has many possible directions but only one "right" way or solution) may be considered a sophisticated spiral. But what does the spiral or maze signify? Many people have described it as a symbol of our journey through life. But it also symbolizes our journey through time. From our perspective within the maze or spiral, there is a single current; only one direction is possible. But from a broader perspective, we have only to step off the path and we can move to any other location just as easily.

Stepping into another time (to help your younger self, for example) is a sophisticated and advanced working. But we all have the ability to see the other loops and swirls of maze—if we know how to look. Not only because the future has, in effect, already occurred, but because events in the future have specific repercussions here in the present. Even if you don't have the ability to literally see into the future (what's known as precognition), you can still learn about it by taking a close look at what's happening in the here and now.

This is how divination works and why you can, if you choose, use divinatory tools to see not only the future but also the past and the present. You can also use divination to learn more about yourself. As you advance, you may find yourself preferring this kind of knowledge over the standard prediction results. Using divinatory tools to perform self-analysis and examine your own motivations you can gain some of the most useful benefits of divination.

Divination and Augury

The terms divination and augury are synonyms; in practice, however, their usage differs slightly. Divination is attempting to acquire knowledge (particularly of the future) by deliberately creating conditions that allow interconnectivity to operate. That is, you actively divine the future through the use of cards, coins, chicken entrails (ick!), and so on. Augury is attempting to acquire knowledge (particularly of the future) through interpretation of existing omens or portents. That is, you simply make yourself aware of the synchronous events that already regularly occur.

So by this definition, reading Tarot cards is divination, while interpreting the activities of a bird outside your window is augury. Apart from the linguistic difference however, the two are very similar. They both work for the same reasons and have the same pitfalls. In addition, they can impart the same types of information. The primary difference is that, because you deliberately arrange it, divination can give you more detailed information as well as the higher probability of tampering—either conscious or unconscious.

Divination and augury work because of the age-old magical maxim: As Above, So Below. This saying is specifically associated with astrology (that is, the planets above are connected to our lives below); however, since each thing is connected to every other thing, it actually describes a much broader realm of influence. More specifically, you might say that the larger structure (the planets in the universe) contains the same data as the smaller (the human life), or the reverse—that the smaller structure (the Tarot deck) contains information relevant to the larger. If the theory behind this idea interests you, you may want to explore chaos mathematics, fractals, and self-similar systems.

But practically speaking, what it means is that you can gain additional information about the world (past, present, and future) through the practice of divination or augury.

The Pitfalls of Prediction

There are several pitfalls or problems with prediction or foretelling of any type. The first is a matter of objectivity. This problem particularly applies to divination but also affects the accuracy of augury. Simply stated, it can be very difficult for the average person to be objective enough about himself or his close friends and family to be accurate in predictive interpretation. The information you already have (or think you have) about yourself or the querent can color the outcome and your analysis of it.

The more subjective you are, the less random the reading will end up being. Of course, prediction is never really random. If it were, it wouldn't work. But from our point of view it must operate that way if it is to accurately tap into the interconnectivity or synchronicity inherent in all things. For example, if you laid out a Tarot reading for yourself by deliberately selecting those cards you felt matched what you wanted to know and placing them in the correct positions, you would not be practicing divination at all. Or imagine that you place a bird feeder on your porch and then count every avian visitor as an omen. Or perhaps you find yourself shuffling your Tarot deck to bury a particularly unpleasant card at the bottom.

These are particularly obvious examples, but what about more subtle things? For example, if you do a reading, not to discover something you don't know, but to verify what you do know, you may get your wish. That is, the divination will reflect your own opinions about the situation as opposed to the truth. For example, you find yourself in love and want to know whether your feelings are returned. Or you plan a spell that you're sure will work and want to verify a good outcome. By not being open to alternate results or possibilities, you may affect the result so that it tells you only what you want to hear.

One of the best ways to avoid this problem is not to perform divination for yourself. If you have a friend who's regularly accurate (even if their predictions aren't always happy ones), that's the person you should approach for a serious reading. Also, avoid doing serious readings for others with whom you know you cannot be objective. Note that you can still use divinatory techniques as tools for self-knowledge or symbolic thinking. Meditating on a selected Tarot card works well for this purpose.

Another way to avoid the objectivity trap when you feel obliged to read for yourself (and it will inevitably happen) is to choose divination techniques that allow as little interpretation as possible. For this purpose, Tarot and *I Ching* are better than runes or tea leaves. The more structured the divination system, the more it forces you to be honest in your interpretation. Scrying, in particular, is very nebulous and has little structure or guidance. Force yourself to be scrupulously honest about what you learn and see. Write down your results to avoid selective memory after the fact.

I can't overstress the importance of writing down the literal results of your divinations (for yourself or others). Don't bother with the interpretative stuff, simply write down the relevant objective details (card or rune titles and locations, astrological charts, relevant *I Ching* hexagrams or geomantic symbols, and so on). Later, go back and take another look at the information. Does it still seem to be saying the same thing as in the original heat of the moment? Does hindsight give it a new perspective? Did you blatantly ignore the obvious or add information that simply wasn't there? Remember that honesty is as important in divination as in life.

Of course there are people who don't seem so affected by the objectivity trap. They can read for friends or family or even themselves without much trouble. They simply have great skill at being completely honest with themselves and others. Ironically, these same people are often pretty unpopular. Our society doesn't reward this kind of hard-core honesty and labels it tactlessness, rudeness, or cruelty. However, if you want to cultivate this skill for yourself (bearing in mind the potential consequences), you can begin by practicing complete honesty, particularly about your own motivations.

The second potential pitfall of prediction is that of overuse. This problem applies to both divination and augury; however, it's easier to avoid in divination. Basically, you can't govern your entire life by the stars, cards, omens, or what have you. In divination, there's a kind of rule of diminishing returns. The more you read for yourself or for the same questions, the less interesting and accurate your readings become. If you do a divination and the results seem to be saying "mind your own business," "how the heck should I know," or "outcome unclear"—give it a break. If you don't like the reading you got, the least helpful thing you can do is to try again in order to get the result you want. Instead, try analyzing what current situation or decision leads to the undesired outcome and change it. In fact, the most important thing you can do *before* performing divination is to examine your motivations for doing it.

The overuse pitfall operates in a different way for augury. If you don't want to overuse divination, you simply stop divining as much. However, in augury the situation is more one where you have to accept that not everything is an omen. Remember that synchronicity is defined as *meaningful* coincidence. And synchronicity is, in one respect, the perception and acknowledgment of omens in your life. So, while you need to be aware of omens when they occur, you can't go around looking for them. While everything may be symbolic—part of a huge interconnected whole—that doesn't mean everything is specifically related to you and your life every moment. Or, as Freud said, "Sometimes a cigar is just a cigar."

Real omens have a certain quality about them. Not only will they have special meaning for you, they also have a certain flavor—a tingle or chill, a sharp contrast from the rest of the day, or a later haziness of memory or recollection. You can't force an omen. If you are being deliberate about finding something out, that's divination (with its own pitfalls and problems). But you can't simply say "If the wind blows through the trees, it means I should do this"—particularly when a hurricane's coming.

ACCURACY IN DIVINATION: YOU HAVE TO WANT IT!

It's often after a terrifying or deeply confusing or emotional time that Pagans turn to divination to try to get some helpful information. However, it's often at these very times that people don't get the information they are looking for. That's because to be accurate, you have to accept the news that accuracy might bring. If you are afraid of what you might find out, if you are not really ready deep down for the information, you will not discover it through divination.

After the terrorist attacks on September 11, 2001, many Witches and Pagans of my acquaintance did various divinations to discover what was going to happen next. There was quite a sense of desperation and of wanting all the information we could get. However, few got many specific details. That's because although we all said we wanted the data, deep down we really didn't.

That's also why you didn't hear stories of Pagans predicting these disasters in advance. Few people do a divination looking for that kind of future. And what was to happen if you did predict it? Unless you knew someone on the scene whom you could warn away, it wouldn't really have helped. If you announced the specific details of a catastrophe in advance, all you'd get for your trouble would be a visit from men in shiny black shoes and dark glasses, convinced that you had a hand in it. After all, the world at large doesn't believe in the validity of divination. Or what if you discovered the details about an upcoming disaster and didn't tell anyone? That would be even worse. We are not equipped as a society or as individuals to handle that kind of information, so for the most part it's not available to us. And perhaps we should be grateful.

On a more personal level, however, this same mechanism operates for things that we might think we want to know about even though we already have the outcome firmly in mind. For example, if you are very excited about a new business venture you might simply refuse to believe it when the cards or coins tells you that it's bound to fail. You will probably get a vague reading as your unconscious mind impacts the energies involved. Ironically, in this situation, you'd be better off not doing a reading at all. Instead, allow your positive attitude to act as projective magic to keep things on track, and do everything you can in the real world to achieve success.

Dream Work

A unique area of potential prediction that lies outside the realm of divination or augury is dream work. Your dreams can contain a wealth of interesting information about yourself as well as the past, present, and future. Dreams are highly symbolic because they tap into the deepest recesses of the unconscious mind. Much of Jung's work is based on the messages that appeared to his patients in dreams. Yet dreams are more slippery than the waking world, hard to control or analyze.

Many books on the subject will attempt to divide dreams into categories or types. This is a valid idea, as not all dreams are the same. However, the categories can be deceptive. Each person will have a different labeling system and structure. What you want to avoid is allowing other people's ideas about the nature of dreams to affect your own experience of them. All dreams are highly personal, and you will need to create a personal way of understanding them. What I have detailed below is my understanding of types of dreams, based not on arbitrary labels, but on how useful these dreams are to me and my spiritual path.

Dreams that are not useful: Many dreams don't seem to help me at all. Of course, this is deceptive. Even the act of dreaming is useful and researchers know that the ability to dream is important for mental and physical health. However, most people, including myself, have a number of dreams that simply seem to involve some kind of dumping mechanism. The sleeping brain creates collages out of stored information that appear as dreams.

Another kind of dream that isn't useful is one whose purpose or message I do not understand. I believe these dreams are actually quite common among people. There may be information that I am missing or details that I misread. I might consider a dream to be simply mental detritus as described above, and only later discover that it had some importance and relevance.

Finally, dreams I don't remember upon waking aren't particularly useful. If the message of the dream comes from my unconscious mind, then it didn't complete the journey to my consciousness. Of course, dreams that come from elsewhere will have still embedded themselves in my unconscious mind and therefore be one step closer to being consciously realized.

Dreams that are useful: Of course dreams can deliver all sorts of information about the unconscious mind. In dreams, the presentation is symbolic and needs to be interpreted to make sense. But this kind of dream information can be useful in discovering underlying concerns, issues, or anything I've repressed psychologically. Often, nightmares operate quite well in informing me about unconscious or semiconscious fears. Like hints and tips about the psyche, these types of dreams lack coherence and simply bubble up out of my brain. They may appear in the midst of less useful dreams that are simply rehashing the day's events.

For example, a dream of going shopping isn't particularly useful. If the dream includes some recurring imagery, however, such as buying weights or exercise equipment, it could be a message that my unconscious mind is focusing on issues of strength or health. If the dream includes a stressful component (say, I'm hunting for the sporting goods store and can't find it) it could mean that I'm subliminally concerned about my health. Maybe my unconscious mind knows that I need to get in better shape—even though I'm not ready to admit it. Alternately, I could be coming down with a cold or will soon be in a situation where I will need my strength. This second interpretation is what I call a mundane clairvoyant dream.

A mundane clairvoyant dream is a dream about the future that later comes true. However, in this type of clairvoyant dream, the subject matter is usually boring or involved with trivial matters. It's certainly interesting when I dream that a friend arrives with a pizza and then it happens, but not too useful. Of course in the example above, I can learn from the shopping dream to take really good care of my health or conserve my strength for a few days. Still, while knowing you're going to get sick in advance can come in handy, it's not exactly earth-shattering.

Dreams that are very useful: More rarely, I'll have very important and useful dreams. These are imprinted with a great significance on both my waking and sleeping minds. I'm often compelled to write them down immediately and in great detail. Later analysis will show multiple layers of symbolism and the appearance of archetypes. These dreams generally incorporate a very strong emotional component. Whatever emotion the dream elicits (joy, terror, awe, peace) will stay with me for up to several days.

These dreams are what might be called spiritual epiphanies and I don't think they always come from the unconscious mind. Sometimes, dreams give the impression of traveling, to the degree that I wonder whether I've been wandering the astral plane in my sleep. Other times I've received a message from my Deities and not from my own mind at all (except inasmuch as we're all connected). It's also possible to tap into the collective unconscious while sleeping. The texture of these types of dreams can be hard to describe. Suffice it to say that when you've had one, you'll know it.

Other very useful dreams are those of serious clairvoyance. Again very rare (for me at least), dreams which give useful and specific information about the future do happen. Dreams can also "foretell" the past, as anyone who's had a very powerful dream about a prior life can tell you. We've all heard stories about people who dream that their plane is going to crash and therefore postpone their journey, saving their lives. While I don't have such a dramatic tale to tell, I have had dreams that foretold the future enough to help me make decisions. I've also had general, nondream "bad feelings" about something in the future that later came to pass.

~~~~~~~~~~~~~~~~~~~~~~~~~~~

FOOD FOR THOUGHT—A COUPLE OF PERSONAL ANECDOTES

Reading about divination or augury isn't any fun without a couple of campfire tales. Here are a couple of episodes from my own life that can underscore how prediction can work . . . and not work.

THE TAROT READING

Once, some years back, I was considering starting a business with a friend. We'd discussed it a lot and were very excited about the prospect. At one point, I asked her to do a reading for the outcome of our business. Far from a glowing report, however, her reading said that while we might someday work together, we wouldn't be starting this business at this time. The reading spoke of traveling and hardships and difficulties that we were going to have to focus on.

While I'd like to say that we both wisely decided against going forward, that wasn't the case. I remember that I simply refused to believe the interpretation even though it was strongly backed by the cards and not wishful thinking. I simply couldn't be objective about the idea and wanted to turn the cards around to make them say what I wanted them to say. Naturally, the business did not come to fruition. My friend did move away and we both had our share of the hardships and troubles that her reading predicted.

THE BIRD

Once, while I was standing in my boss's office, a bird fluttered down dead outside the office window. When I went out to check on it, I discovered that it was still warm, with no sign of injury. Wondering whether this might indicate some environmental problem, I called the local fish and wildlife department. They said that small birds do sometimes fall dead from starvation or cold. When I described the bird, they surmised that it was a king finch.

The fact that I happened to look out the window just as the bird fell, coupled with a general sense of foreboding, made me think that this was an omen. The type of bird and the fact that I was standing in the company president's office led me to believe that the company was not going to go well because of the actions of the president (the king is dead). My suspicions soon proved correct and I ended up finding another position as the company began struggling because of the president's actions.

JUST A BAD FEELING

The future doesn't always come to us in specific omens or deliberate divination. Sometimes our instinct or gut just tells us something. For example, my husband and I were planning on driving home for the holiday season to be with our families. We live about an eight-hour drive away and typically made a visit home every year. But this year we both began to feel very uncomfortable about the idea of driving home. The feelings didn't seem to be coming from anywhere specific, but they were very strong and caused us a lot of stress.

It was only after we told our families that we would have to postpone our trip by a week that we felt better. Naturally, they were confused by our change in plans and disappointed that we would be missing typical family holiday events. However, we were insistent. When a huge snowstorm blew in and caused havoc on the roads during the very time we would have been driving, we knew we'd made the right decision in listening to our instincts.

CHAPTER 4 EXERCISES

Beyond Runes and Cards

Because of the interconnectivity of all things, we can divine using literally anything that has meaning for us. Of course, it can be less trouble to stick with an existing system as opposed to inventing your own. However, the process of creating a divination tool for your own use can be quite educational. In addition, the results can be very good.

The easiest types of divination to create are those in the category of symbol chits. You might not be up for creating and illustrating a whole new deck of Tarot cards, but there are many interesting possibilities here. They may take some thought but shouldn't take too much time.

For example, if you are interested in stones and crystals, you may have a box of them at home. Why not create a set of personal runes from them? Give each rock a meaning based on its composition, shape, or personal association. Then grab a handful and toss them out. What do their positions suggest to you? Are there specific meanings that come from having two items touching? To make the system even more detailed, paint a cloth with various personal symbols and toss your runes onto it.

During a slow week at work, I once developed a system of divination based on a handful of colored pens. First, I gave each pen a planetary association based on color. The meanings of the pens were based on the planet (red for Mars, for aggression, green for Venus, for love, and so on). I also had a pen that I used as the base, symbolizing the querent or question. To use this system, I would ask a question and toss the pens onto the floor. Ones that fell parallel were working in concert. Ones that crossed were opposing each other. The reading was based on location and position of the base pen.

Despite sounding silly, this system worked amazingly well for me. The readings were always quite useful and accurate and the only problem was that my coworkers wondered why I kept knocking my penholder over.

Try creating your own system of divination. It doesn't have to be something you want to use forever (my pens ran out of ink, alas, and work got busy again), but it should be something that includes enough symbolism to be useful for you.

Folklore

One interesting way of becoming more comfortable with augury is to make a study of your local folklore. Often, these ancient nuggets of wisdom are simply omens disguised as natural phenomena (or natural phenomena disguised as omens—take your pick). For example, people used to predict the coming winter by the actions of birds or the fuzziness of caterpillars. Imagine scientists' surprise when these "old wives tales" were proved true.

Most of these tidbits are going to be specific to your particular geography and climate. By researching old folklore, you can learn more about the natural environment where you live. In the U.S., American Indian folklore can be a rich addition to observances made by the earliest settlers. In much of Europe, the folklore goes straight back through to mythology and the Old Ways.

In prior generations, people spent a lot more time observing nature. They relied on being able to predict the weather and the movement of animals for their very survival. By watching what plants and animals did to prepare for the coming winter, they could prepare their own families. From this detailed focus came folk and weather lore such as "red sky at night, sailors' delight; red sky at morning, sailors take warning," or that the halo around the moon meant coming snow. Their knowledge might seem like magic to us, but to them it was simply part of living. By learning more about this old wisdom, we can sharpen our own perception and improve our own abilities to augur the future.

CONCLUSION

Divination and augury are powerful tools for learning more about the past, present, and future as well as the nature of your own soul. Hidden behind the outward simplicity of consulting the cards or a crystal ball are keys to understanding your limitations as a human and how to transcend those limitations to discover your True Will and become master or mistress of your own Fate and Destiny. Yet, to become adept at prediction is a matter of the most mundane skills: objectivity, honesty, and desire.

Consulting an oracle (whether a stranger, friend, or yourself) is serious business, not to be taken lightly. At the same time, too much of an emotional attachment will be a detriment to your accuracy and ability to interpret honestly. Finally, it's important to remember that you must make decisions and live out your life, no matter what the runes foretell. Omens are all around you, hinting and directing your actions, and yet not every bird or breeze is significant to you specifically.

Like the other areas discussed so far, prediction is a tool that's only useful when it's used. This doesn't mean that you read the *I Ching* whenever the phone rings (Caller ID is a lot easier to use). It means that you have to get out there, into the realms where the action is, to find and walk your path. The next chapter describes where to find the temple of wisdom, the archway to adventure, and the entrance to other worlds.

CHAPTER 5

The Nature of Things:

YOUR TOUGHEST PAGAN TEACHER

THERE'S NO GETTING AROUND IT—PAGAN PATHS ARE NATURE RELI-
gions. The lessons, the holidays, the very source of these traditions are
nature based. Whether you live in the city and consider yourself an
urbanite is irrelevant; if you're a Pagan, you're going to need to look
to nature. Lessons are everywhere in this world, but for the Witch,
Mother Nature incorporates some of the most important mysteries.

This doesn't mean you need to become a hippie and live in a commune to be Pagan. It doesn't mean if you live in the city and enjoy its
comforts and excitement that you aren't a real Witch. What it means
is that you cannot pretend to be one with nature and know Her lessons
if you never worship outside of the house.

There's nothing like a Pagan fireside chat to stimulate great discussion and ideas—a few good friends, a libation, and a fire to ward off
the chill (or a cool basement nook in summer). Pagan "Witch and
Bitch" sessions are wonderful and can teach us a great deal. Getting
confirmation, sharing stories, gaining perspective—all are good lessons
that make for great memories. But there are some things that we can't
learn at our hearth. Some lessons—powerful ones—we have to seek
out for ourselves. Some lessons can only be discovered in the wild
places.

GAIA

It's always amusing when science *finally* catches up to spirituality. For
example, the Gaia Theory: "the theory that our planet and its creatures

constitute a single self-regulating system that is in fact a great living being."[23] Not a very surprising idea to Pagans. Yet, many Pagans are divorced from the power of the planet. Be assured, there are great and powerful lessons to be learned from this Greatest of all Great Mothers.

The Earth goes beyond simply Goddess. She is the face behind the face—the nurturer and destroyer of us all. She is both literal (the spinning rock we cling to) and symbolic. She is our Mother Nature, and if you want to know Her, you will need to seek Her in the natural places of the world.

Humans have a symbiotic (and, too often, parasitic) relationship with Her. She can be found in an old growth forest as well as your vegetable garden, in a wild hedgerow and a formal Japanese garden. She is the mistress of the wild things that kill us (from predators and diseases to earthquakes and floods) as well as the nurturing tools of agriculture and animal husbandry.

Enter a cave and you are in the womb of Gaia. The rivers and springs are Her blood; the forests and oceans, Her lungs. Spires of rock are Her bones, while rolling hills are Her fleshy curves. Your square little houses can't compete. You must leave them behind and seek out growing and living things—and bring Her growth and life inside with you to transform your home into Her domain as well.

You don't have to live in a rural area to enjoy nature. Even in cities and suburban neighborhoods you can find an abundance of plants and wild creatures. Look around you, pay attention, walk instead of driving. Our tiny apartment in the middle of urban Denver didn't seem like a good place for communing with the natural world, but nearby we discovered the creek and river with their winding bike paths and lush greenery. Coursing below the level of the city streets, it was sometimes like a quiet peaceful realm—and at other times like a big outdoor party.

I worked in a huge downtown skyscraper, yet a few blocks away there were ethnic neighborhoods where wild gardens of flowers and vegetables hid behind rundown apartments. It doesn't matter how urban or modest your own home may be, you can find room for a few potted plants and a birdfeeder. I never was a city girl; urban life is too fast-paced and crowded for me. But we all have to live in the real world, where practical considerations and spiritual ones intermingle.

It can seem like a challenge to be a "tree hugging" Pagan when the only nearby trees are stunted from pollution. Yet with an eye to the wonders of nature, you can find green places that soothe your soul wherever you may live. We discovered areas both in the city (like the creek and its paths) and outside of it (like the green valley where we flew kites). Even in a manicured city park, you can find a quiet spot to simply commune with the unpaved ground.

But no matter how you fit nature into your life, you should definitely make an effort to do so. I am no Luddite. I work in a technical industry, live in the suburbs, and enjoy having food delivered and visiting amenities like bookstores and chocolate shops. I like gourmet coffee and DVDs. But I am still awed by the wonders of nature, both raw and cultivated. I find a wild stream as moving as a lush fertile farm.

If where you live suffers from a dearth of wild places, you will simply have to make a greater effort and go a farther distance. Even a few days camping away from people can feed your soul and teach you great lessons. It doesn't have to be as rigorous as an Outward Bound excursion. If you're new to camping, team up with some friends who know the ropes and go car camping. Drive to an accessible site, pitch a tent, and spend the night. If the very idea of camping is distasteful, consider renting a remote cabin for a few days or even staying in a hotel or B&B in a small village that enjoys close natural beauty. You may not be able to afford accommodations in a resort town, but there are many small towns that don't see regular tourist traffic. Do a little research into the locations of wilderness trails, lakes and rivers, hot springs, or national parks and forests.

Finally, if getting out of town takes more time and money than you can spare right now, take a closer look at the parks and gardens where you live. Are you fortunate enough to have a botanical garden or arboretum? Or perhaps your city boasts a high quality zoo (the kind where you don't feel bad for the animals). Many urban areas have wildlife rescue groups for which you can volunteer. If no other option immediately presents itself, I can recommend a visit to your local garden store or greenhouse. Enclosed greenhouses in particular are moist, soothing havens where you can browse to your heart's content and learn a great deal about plant life (in fairness to those that provide this sanctuary, you may want to adopt a small plant of your own and take it home with you).

The more you get out there and enjoy nature, the more sensitive to it you will become. Take every opportunity to feel the energy in forests and glens, under old trees and in fields. Practice near streams, rivers, ponds, seas, and the ocean. Climb mountain paths and explore caves. Each spot will have a different feel and, with practice, you will begin to learn to distinguish and work with the varied energy of the planet.

SACRED GEOMETRY

When we cast a circle, we create a sacred space—a place where the veil between the worlds thins. The natural world includes places like this too. Marked by both natural phenomena (such as springs, groves, and spires of rock) and man-made ones (holy wells, stone circles, even churches), the other world seems closer here than at home.

Lines of power circle the globe and can be sensed and measured by the discerning psyche. Where these lines cross, swirl, or eddy, places of power emerge. Again, these places were marked by earlier cultures. Dolmens, menhirs, and stone circles are common markers of these energy crossroads in Europe and the British Isles. Ancient streets often followed the paths of power. In the U.S., Native American sacred sites mark the same types of locations.

On a local scale, the tributaries of these rivers of energy shift and move. You may find your own power spot in a neglected corner of a park, wilderness area, or your own yard. With practice, you can even shift one or create a little circle spot of your own. But you will be hard pressed to even notice these subtle currents from inside your home. As you begin regularly exploring wild places, you may come upon a place that seems to resonate with power for you. These natural temples are perfect for outdoor worship.

Many Pagans are nervous worshipping outdoors. They feel exposed on property that they do not own or worried about being discovered. If you require flowing robes, flaming candles, and exotic tools and trappings to do your work, who can blame you for such nervousness? However, you don't really need all those things. The beauty of the land and the natural energy can be enough to put you in the proper frame of mind. Go in your regular hiking or walking clothes. Wear proper shoes and take a staff to help you along the way. You can pack an offering in your backpack. With the right frame of mind, you can commune with nature, do a ritual, even work major magic—and no one will be the wiser.

Witches of the past didn't need exotic tools or strange props. Their walking staff, knife, and kitchen broom all served another, hidden purpose. You can do as much or more with even fewer outward props. Through visualization and practice, you can create whole, detailed workings in your mind while your body sits in meditation (more on this in the chapter on altered states). Even if you choose to physically work your ritual, the energy you raise should protect you from prying eyes. Go at odd hours, choose a secluded location, shield your working, and send out your energy with a "nothing to see here" message.

If you find an outdoor spot to work at regularly, it will become something of a permanent temple for you. Marking the site is not necessary. Your energy and attention will make the place sacred and increase the power flow and energy there. The veil between the worlds will thin and you can use the spot as a launching pad for other-world journeys and religious and magical workings. With enough effort on your part, the site will become a part of you—you will create an intimate connection between the location and your own spirit. To encourage this process, there are several things you can do:

- **Treat the land with respect.** On your visits, collect litter and dispose of it properly. It doesn't matter who dropped it, make it your responsibility to clean it up. Obviously, you must also clean up after yourself and any pets you bring. Don't damage the site by digging or removing ground cover.
- **Follow all human laws pertaining to the area.** While it can be frustrating, most of these guidelines are logical and based on the well-being of the site. Coming from the desert Southwest, I know well that a ban on fire in dry or drought-stricken areas is a serious and necessary safety precaution. Rules regarding access, tree cutting, deadfall collection, and water use are the price we pay to enjoy the beauty of natural flora and fauna on public land. With more and more human visitors to wildlife areas, the most beautiful sites are often put under great pressure and ecological strain by our very love and interest as thousands of tourists visit them and leave traces of their presence.
- **Bring nothing that's not biodegradable.** Leaving an offering is always a great idea. Food, herbs, and water or liquor will be absorbed by the soil or eaten by the Earth's wild creatures. But don't deposit anything there that can harm the site or that doesn't belong there. This includes salt or salt water that damages plant life, seeds or pinecones that are not indigenous, and crystals or rocks that are not native to the site.
- **Take nothing with you when you go.** Admittedly, I'm just as guilty of collecting the odd rock or feather as anyone. But please use logic when taking parts of the natural world home with you. Don't dig items out of the ground. Don't remove whole plants or seeds. If you take a pinecone, make sure it's open and has already dropped its payload. Don't disturb wildlife or the things wild creatures need to survive (nests, logs, or burrows).

AGRICULTURE AND THE WHEEL OF THE YEAR

A close friend once told me about attending a public Imbolc ritual in Oklahoma. She had a difficult time keeping from laughing out loud at the high priestess's explanation of the holiday. The HP described the snows lying thick on the ground and the birth of the spring lambs and starving peasants celebrating the coming of new life—yet it was a sunny 70 degrees outside, at the end of a typically short, balmy winter.

Pre-Christian holidays have usually been focused on the seasonal turning of the year. But what we have to remember is that their timing varied from place to place. Being astronomical phenomena, the solstices and equinoxes are the same all over the globe (although at reverse times of the year in opposite hemispheres). Still, their interpretation would certainly vary depending on where you lived. Mediterranean Pagans would have had a very different cycle than those in Northern Europe. Other holidays with an agricultural theme might vary from year to year as well. The celebration of the first harvest or the migration of birds or animals would vary depending on a number of different conditions.

The interpretations that modern Pagans apply to the eight standard holidays are from a Northern European perspective. However, evidence suggests that the earliest British Isles Pagans celebrated either the quarter days or the cross-quarter days—but not both. Also, it seems that the cross-quarter days (commonly referred to as Imbolc, Beltane, Lughnasadh, and Samhain) were the older holidays, with Beltane and Samhain being the oldest of all. The timing of these holidays was based not on our calendar (which, of course, had not yet been invented) but on solar or lunar astrology and the turning of the actual seasons.

In addition, many Pagans celebrated other holidays based on particular Deities or festivals. Some of these holidays were agriculturally oriented and some weren't. In Northern Europe, the solstices and equinoxes are tightly linked to an agricultural mythos based on the change of seasons (the Goddess and her Consort or the Goddess and the Twin Gods). The cross-quarter days, however, are typically more focused on sex, death, and inspiration.

But whatever holidays you choose to celebrate, the agricultural cycle of the British Isles is simply not going to match that of most of the United States. Maine might be the exception and the seasons in Minnesota are pretty close, but most of the U.S. is much warmer and, in many areas, drier than England, Ireland, or Wales.

Perhaps you're wondering whether it really matters what the weather is like outside. Tradition is tradition, right? Well, maybe not. If you want to base your festivals on the turning of the year wheel, then the least you can do is to match them to the way the wheel turns in your part of the world . . . especially if you want to practice outdoors. In fact, if you are working alone, you can adjust your rituals to match the agricultural cycle—marking the first flower of spring, the opening weekend of the local farmers' market, or the start of the fair. Every summer, we enjoy visiting our local Renaissance Festival. Pagan types abound and it's definitely a time of celebration. Visiting favorite vendors (and spending money), watching the jousting, enjoying the shows and music—it's a party upholding the tradition of festivals and fairs that marked the year's turning and were often combined with more esoteric or spiritual pursuits.

When you tie your celebrations to the land you live in, you make a close connection to that land. But that doesn't mean you have to throw out all tradition. I celebrate Imbolc as the feast of Bride and Lughnasadh as the feast of her male counterpart, Lugh. Both are tightly tied to inspiration. To me Beltane is all about sex, while Samhain celebrates death—two sides of the same coin. It doesn't matter what the weather's doing.

I also enjoy celebrating the solstices and equinoxes, especially Yule. I've talked to Pagans who have a difficult time with the Christmas holiday season. I've never really understood this. In my mind, the winter solstice has always been the perfect time for integrating traditions. Fortunately, my extended family isn't overtly Christian, so

Christmas has primarily been a time for getting together as a family, putting aside our differences, and sharing gifts and good food. The crass commercialism is disgusting, but most of the other aspects of the holiday are already pretty darned Pagan! All it takes is just a little tweak of the mindset and the whole U.S. will be celebrating Yule and the birth of the Sun along with you.

I wouldn't feel comfortable at some midnight mass or participating in Bible readings, but I've always been comfortable with Christmas. The excess of candles, indoor foliage, quasi-pagan mythological figures, and "love and joy come to you" energy (which I need a dose of after Samhain) has always tickled my fancy!

After all, Jesus is just one in a long history of dying gods like Osirus, John Barleycorn, Odin, and the Oak King/Holly King. Sure, he had better spin doctors and a more aggressive marketing campaign, but he's just another seasonal male deity—dying and being reborn each year. And Santa Claus is a very Pagan figure indeed. Think of him less as a jolly bringer of gifts and clogged arteries, and more as a dark bringer of wisdom—a shaman high on death cap mushrooms, slipping into the house of your consciousness late at night—a dark fairy of the Northern woods, renowned in earlier times for bringing punishment to the wicked as well as treats for the good.

When you tie the festivals to tradition as well as to the land you live in, you will have created a very powerful combination. As you move beyond the standard (and often locally inappropriate) agricultural meanings of the holidays, you will be making a close connection to the place where you live. It is this connection that allows us to begin creating a relationship with those creatures of the land—beings, far from human, that are only to be found in the wild places.

LAND SPIRITS AND GUARDIANS

Natural wonders are often watched over by various land spirits or guardians. These creatures are tied to the land and can be sensed, if not seen. Watching over the land and its denizens, guardians are responsible for the wilderness terror or nervousness that occasionally overcomes people when they spend time in a remote area. While people new to camping or trekking are particularly prone to this kind of thing, even visitors more used to the outdoors can be overcome by a strong sense of discomfort. When you consider what humankind has done to the Earth, it's not really surprising.

The way to deal with this situation is with caution and respect. The fear can be banished by loud music and chatter, but I wouldn't recommend it. Instead, face your feelings head-on to determine whether you're simply overreacting to the energy of nature. In serious cases, you may need to leave the area. Land spirits can be mistrustful of human presence and are not shy about letting you know it.

If you are a regular visitor to a guarded site, you can eventually enter a guardian-type relationship with the land itself. This is not something to be taken on lightly. Having respect for a natural location is very different from swearing to protect it. Be especially careful of this with land that you do not own. The land will draw on your energy and attention to keep itself safe and protected . . . but what happens when the area is slated for construction?

If you want to help protect an area that's under this kind of threat, the best options are to rally a group with public support and to protest, both within the system (petitions, letter writing campaigns) and outside of it (sit-ins, protests, chaining yourself to trees). Not everyone is cut out for this kind of activism. But the price for failure, while sad, is not as serious as breaching your oath to a land guardian. The Earth and its natural creatures and spirit beings do not understand or appreciate land ownership, and indeed they are correct. You cannot ever really own the land. But a philosophical truth won't help you when you're in a court of law trying to stop the draining of a swamp or the felling of trees.

Usually, a land spirit acts as a silent sentinel—a quiet presence that watches over the area. These beings can be associated with a particular location like a tree, stream, or rock. They are a part of the land and primarily focused on it. Other beings that prefer wild places are more autonomous—and potentially more dangerous.

Fairies

Fairies and fairy lore fascinate many Pagans. There are even Pagan paths, like certain branches of Wicca, that are specifically focused on these beings. Folklore is very clear on the location or habitat of fairies. Apart from the "house sprite" or "brownie" (who might be poking through your cupboards at night), fairies live outdoors. They can be found in forests, glens, rivers, and ancient trees. They dance in clearings or stone circles. In Britain, they wander the moors and fens. Here in the U.S., you can feel their touch in many wild places. They even exist in the wild corner of your garden and in fields and farms. But you will rarely find them haunting your living room.

After Christianity came to the British Isles, cautionary tales about the danger of fairies were common. God-fearing folk were expected to stay near the safety of home after dark. To venture out unprotected was to be abducted by the fairy folk. To avoid your prayers was to invite strange nightly visitors. When the tides of nature shifted and that strange wind blew, the wild hunt would ride forth into the night. At these times, good Christians would be in church praying; they'd avert their eyes from the sound of hounds baying in the sky. Being neither God-fearing nor Christian, you can take these tales as instruction manuals for fairy encounters.

As folklore tells us, there are many kinds of fairies: from shy little forest dwellers to the Horned Lord Himself—often called the King of the Fairies. The Lady of Witches is also frequently known as the Fairy Queen. Whether you want to catch a glimpse of a sprite or meet these Deities face to face, you need to seek them outside the walls of your home.

Even if you choose to deal only with those who linger at your hearth or in your attic (potentially a smarter choice), you must carry the core of the land inside. You have to learn to see with wild eyes and hear with wild ears. You have to bring the spark within you and within your home. The dusty cupboard, neglected corner, and over-grown plot of land are your invitations to the Fey. The lessons for finding them are out under the sun and moon and stars.

Whenever you deal with the spirit realm/fairy realm/choose your set of noncorporeal beings, what you bring to the experience *shapes* the experience to a high degree. This is true of all of life, but especially so with fairies. That's why, traditionally, the Fair Folk weren't all good or all bad. In the old folktales they were basically amoral and could engender great fortune as well as great suffering. The point is that, while these spirits exist outside you, your expectations have a lot to do with your interaction. If you think you can communicate with them, you probably will be able to at some point. If you know you can't, then you won't be able to. If you believe in certain "classes" of these beings, those are the ones you'll run across. Or, to quote Tom Wolfe: "Not 'Seeing is Believing' . . . but 'Believing is Seeing.' "[24] But just because you must believe in fairies to see them does not mean that you create them. They do exist, and they serve their own needs and lives and not ours. They are not *safe*. They are not *predictable*. But if, nonetheless, you choose to try to find them, you cannot be safe and predictable either. Have courage and confidence and the will to get out of your protected sphere and into the wild places. Perhaps you will meet them. And if they don't level you with terror or trick and embarrass you, you might make a friend or two.

FOOD FOR THOUGHT—THAT WOLF JUST ATE MY FLUFFY BUNNY!

Throughout history, humans have had certain preconceived notions about the natural world. Often, these are based more in philosophy than reality. For example, in the eighteenth century, scholars of the

Enlightenment described the concept of the "noble savage."[25] According to this worldview, humanity in its natural state was innocent and pure, noble and incapable of deliberate harm. It was only with the advent of civilization that human cruelty was invented—the natural state was the pure state. This concept tied neatly into the British and American Romanticism of the eighteenth and mid-nineteenth centuries.

Romanticism was marked by a departure from older, more formal structures in art and literature. Because the process was so gradual, it's difficult to pin down, but hallmarks of Romantic thought include "primitivism; love of nature; sympathetic interest in the past, especially the medieval; mysticism; individualism."[26] The Romantic view of nature was, well, romantic. It used nostalgia as well as pastoral and bucolic imagery to describe the natural world as a place of peace, balance, and beauty.

In the late nineteenth century however, Darwin's theories of evolution and survival of the fittest led to the view that nature was a harsh and brutal place. "Nature Red in Tooth and Claw" became the prevailing view.[27] In addition, the discovery of species extinction shocked the religious and nonreligious alike.

Of course, all these views are human views. People put their perspective onto the planet without considering the planet itself. A more realistic point of view draws from each of these extremes. Nature is beautiful and peaceful as much as it is brutal and violent. Getting "back to nature" can be a liberating and soul-mending experience. Still, living in the days before modern medicine, electricity, and factory farming would very likely have been "nasty, brutish, and short."[28]

Modern Paganism seems to take its primary view of nature from the Romantics. Mother Nature is wonderful, gentle, nurturing, and beautiful. She loves us unconditionally and exists for our pleasure and enjoyment. Of course, this shows a real lack of awareness about the cruelty that is inherent in the natural world, and indeed *required* for it to function. Living in industrialized nations, few of us have been in a situation where bad weather might spell the death of our entire family. We typically don't have to grow all our own food and raise and butcher our own meat. With office jobs and light housework, our lives are so much easier than even our great grandparents' were. It's easy, under these conditions, to romanticize the great outdoors.

Pagans tend to have an inherent love of nature. However, we can't let that love blind us to either practical necessities such as wilderness survival and preparedness or the balance in all things. Life and death, birth and decay, beauty and ugliness are equally required for the world to function. There is enough hate and cruelty out there for us to want to embrace love and kindness, but that doesn't mean that the darker side of things is wrong or evil. It's simply necessary.

When you approach nature with a one-sided view (that nature is all good or all loving) you greatly limit your experience and may even put yourself in danger. You can love nature with all your heart, but that won't keep you from getting killed by a sudden snowstorm, flash flood, cold, or heat. Always be prepared when you venture out (get a good book on the topic if you are unfamiliar with the basics).

Alternately, if you approach nature as being annoying or inconvenient, you limit yourself in another way. Exploring the great outdoors can be dirty, buggy, and sweaty. The wind and weather are unpredictable. If you are used to working or meditating in your house, the lack of structure can be maddening. The sun is too bright. The breeze tickles. The ants have invaded your circle. You have to come to terms with this capriciousness—it's all a part of the experience.

In addition to these practicalities, you must also accept and remember nature's less beautiful side because it's a part of the cycle and of the lesson. Death and birth are at the core of Pagan practice. You must come to understand both to truly understand the mysteries.

CHAPTER 5 EXERCISES

Exercise . . . Literally

If you want to get out into nature, you will need to be in shape. There's only one way to accomplish that . . . get up, turn off the TV,

and get out there. No matter who you are or what your personal
physical limitations, you can probably be in better shape than you are.
Handicaps don't have to keep you on the sidelines. Blind people climb
mountains. Women recovering from breast cancer run marathons.
People with missing limbs enter adventure races and go whitewater
rafting.

You don't have to go nearly this far. Being obsessive about it isn't
appropriate either. But when you take a walk, each step increases your
physical fitness and your connection with nature. If you can't walk,
you can still roll or even ride to places of natural beauty. Either way, if
you can't manage to go more than a few feet without being out of
breath, that's still a few feet more than before.

I'm not one of those intrinsically fit people. I'm clumsy, have no
gift for athletics, and never got very much exercise growing up. I'm
no poster child for extreme sports or heavy exercise. But I love hiking
in the mountains, or biking down a wooded path, or blading in the
city. It makes me feel good, happier, more in control and balanced.
Had I known what a little moderate exercise could do for me, I'd have
started years ago. Yeah, it's hard sometimes. I get sore muscles, aches,
and pains. I sweat and don't smell very good. There are times when
I'm too lazy or busy (or both) to exercise. But it's always worth it
when I do. My most mystical experiences outside of my dreams have
all been out of doors. I wouldn't have had those experiences without
the willingness to get out there, and a body that could support me.

If you're a very sedentary person, you will want to see a doctor
before starting any major exercise regime. Heavy people are particularly prone to injury and need to approach things more cautiously. In
addition, disease, handicap, or pregnancy places special restrictions on
what you can do. If, on the other hand, you get regular exercise in a
gym, now is the time to get outside and take a look around you.
Walking a trail or hiking a hill might be less efficient than a Stairmaster,
but so what? The experience will be well worth it.

One Tree, One Year

A good way to get more in touch with the natural world is to see how it changes from season to season. Observing a deciduous tree is a great way of accomplishing this. Pick a tree near where you live that drops its leaves in the winter. Now observe the tree for a whole year. How does the tree change in each season? Are there buds in spring, or does a late frost kill most of them off? How does it deal with the summer months? Is it wet where you live? If so, the tree might collect moss or lichen.

As the months pass, make it a regular habit to check out your tree up close. Are there any animals or insects around the tree? Do birds nest in its branches? You can even climb the tree. Tree climbing is wasted on young people. There's nothing quite like sitting in a cathedral of leaves. Most people won't even notice you there. How does the trunk of your tree grow? What's the bark like?

Keeping an eye on a tree for a whole year may sound boring. But that's the pace at which most of nature moves. Sure, rain showers, floods, and earthquakes are sudden events, but the majority of the Earth moves very slowly indeed. If you want to understand nature better, you have to slow down a little bit too. You could watch any natural object for a year (although you'd have to be very observant to see the changes in a rock), but trees are particularly useful. They are large enough to see from a distance and to afford shade and a place to rest beneath. They change with the seasons. They have a great soothing energy. Your tree may become something of a friend to you over the course of the year.

All Your Tools for Free

There's a certain tendency to occasionally want to shop your way to Witch-hood, a feeling that a visit to the occult or new age shop to buy cool stuff will further you on your path. I know I've succumbed at times to "cool toy-ism". But the power of the tools we use comes from the symbolism they hold, coupled with the energy we put into them. That's why making your own tools is supposed to make them more real or powerful. But that isn't because they are inherently better if homemade; it's because by the time they are complete, you've already put a great deal of thought and energy into them.

Nature is a wonderful source of magical working tools. Because so much of Pagan symbolism comes from the natural world, natural objects will reflect that symbolism quite well. In addition, objects that have been created by the Earth have the Earth's energy within them. Of course, the Earth originally created everything, so from that point of view, everything is natural, even plastic. But objects that are more closely linked to the planet can manifest the appropriate energy quite clearly.

Try collecting a set or group of working tools directly from nature. Use them in ritual and see how they feel. If a particular tool feels right, make it your standard working item for a while. If you need to modify the item in any way (like cutting a wand to length), you will simply be adding your own energy to that already within the object.

If you had to collect every tool from the natural world, which would be the hardest to find? Spend some time thinking about it. There are some real insights to be had about the nature of the tools we use and what they symbolize. To quote a Pagan parent, "Athames don't grow on trees, you know!" Instead, they are forged in the smith's fire . . . the fire of consciousness and inspiration. What if you needed to represent the element of fire using only natural objects? There is a lot of power inherent in these kinds of thought exercises. You will become more in tune with the subtle differences in energies stored in different kinds of objects.

Grow Something

Another great way to really participate in the spirit of nature is to grow something from seed. It can be an extensive garden or a pot of parsley on your windowsill. You can tend a high-maintenance bonsai tree or an easy-to-care-for cactus. But closely watching over a living thing can be highly educational.

Of course, you can take this idea even further. Caring for an animal is also growing something. There's a reason that humans have shared their lives with animals for thousands of years. Whether it's a bowl of fish or a pack of dogs or an exotic reptile or bird, taking the responsibility to care for another being is a serious and powerful commitment.

Of course, to really benefit from the relationship, you must make sure that your animal companions are getting the very best care possible. Please keep this in mind before acquiring a pet. Different animals have different needs, and some of them are extensive. This is particularly true of the exotics—reptiles, amphibians, birds, and salt water fish.

While we're on the topic of animals, please be cautious in calling your pets your familiars. The traditional Witch's familiar is a semiautonomous creature with magical powers that can be directed by the Witch to perform various magical tasks. And I'm not talking about "sit" or "fetch" here. A real familiar is a creature that doesn't even necessarily exist on the physical plane. In one school of thought, the familiar is a gift to the Witch from his Deities. Another school of thought has the Witch creating her own familiar as an astral entity.

Either way, it's unfair to adopt just any animal and label it as a familiar—unfair to the animal. One of the great things about animal companions is that they love us for who we are. We should give them the same unconditional love. Our pets can become very special friends: loyal, protective, and intelligent. Certainly they have emotions, care about their human families, and carry certain magic about them. But that's not necessarily the same as being a familiar. If you tell your dog or cat to leave the house in spirit form tonight, find the ring you lost while hiking, and return it to your house by morning, what will your pet do?

CONCLUSION

The natural world is your occult schoolhouse, sensual playground, healing temple, and initiatory trial. It is the literal and metaphorical body of Mother Earth, who looms behind the veil of experience. As the keeper of keys, she holds the mysteries in every cell and atom.

The Earth is home to all creatures, from physical denizens like ants, cows, and humans to nonphysical beings like spirits and fairies. The special wisdom of the plants exists here too. The planet itself pulses with power. The devoted seeker can access ley lines, dragon tracks, and power spots. These special places can act as doors to other worlds, including the fairy realm—the hollow hills of lore. As a Cusp Witch, there is so much you can learn and discover in the natural world. You simply have to get out there and begin the adventure.

Above all, being a Witch is about *living*. You can read about it, you can even think about it. But until you get out there and *do* it, it will not be real. When nature becomes more than a picture in a book or on TV, then you will be a real student of that wild power. When the tools and skills that you learned as a beginner become part of your everyday existence, then you are truly on your journey as an advancing Pagan.

The next chapter is about that most common of witchy topics, magic. However, far from a simple list of spells or elaborate rituals, the focus there is on incorporating magic into your day-to-day routine. The goal is to integrate your practice as a Pagan and your everyday life as a human into a seamless whole. As you do, your power to chart and direct your own life will grow and you will be taking your first step toward mastery of the magical arts.

CHAPTER 6

Magic in the Everyday

"DOUBLE, DOUBLE TOIL AND TROUBLE; FIRE BURN AND CAULDRON bubble."[29] When you imagine Witches casting spells, what do you picture? Dark robes? A huge cast-iron cauldron? Or maybe a workroom filled with magically prepared herbs, cleansed stones, and handmade candles in different colors? While these images can certainly be true, also true are the following:

- The Witch at work in her cubicle, performing a quick spell with a paper clip to help her focus on a deadline.
- A magic vegetable garden, where charms for health and prosperity are buried among the tomatoes and zucchini.
- The witchy condominium, with crystals on the windowsills, chimes at the doors, and dream pillows under the mattresses.
- A Pagan on the road, making magic for a safe journey and good gas mileage.

MAGIC WORKS!

We know magic works because it's a natural force, like gravity. Yet, there's still a tendency to see magic as something exotic, something requiring a massive amount of effort, elaborate ritual, and the blessings of the Deities. Many beginning Witches and Pagans are even taught to fear magic, to see it as something unpredictable and dangerous—or for which you have to give something else up. Others have a holier-

than-thou attitude, as if a charm for health or money is somehow
wrong and an affront to the God or Goddess.

The truth is that magic is simply a tool that, with skill, we can apply
to improve our lives, help our friends and families, and yes, even harm
people. Magic is neither unpredictable nor inherently dangerous. It's
governed by a basic set of rules or laws and works as a combination of
art and science. Done correctly, it works correctly. Magic need not
necessarily be coupled with religion. Getting to know your Deities is
a wonderful experience, but there's no reason to bother a powerful,
noncorporeal being every time you work a charm to remember your
dreams or keep your family healthy.

For the beginning Pagan or Witch, the casting of spells is sur-
rounded by more mystery and confusion than any other part of our
practice. Requests for spells are met with ethical lectures as well as "go
make your own" stoicism. Books of spells are out there, but the new
Witch can be frustrated by their lack of effect. Covens often focus
primarily on religious aspects (and that's as it should be), leaving a
Pagan to wonder just why her magic isn't working.

Part of the problem is that when magic works, it really does feel
mystical and wonderful. A good spell gives you a sense of having
touched another world, making order from chaos and manifesting a
power that seems to come directly from the Deities. In fact, that's
exactly what has happened. However, the reasoning behind the reality
is as simple as cooking. You add the right ingredients, you cook it up
correctly, and something delicious will result.

THE DIFFERENCE BETWEEN MAGIC AND RITUAL

To my way of thinking, magic and ritual are not the same thing. Magic
is, very roughly, making something happen or "causing change to
occur in conformity with Will."[30] Ritual, on the other hand, is an
event or practice designed to worship your Deities and celebrate your
connection with them. Of course they can be combined; however,

they don't necessarily have to be. When you work a ritual, you are creating a sacred space and asking various entities (your Deities, helpful spirits, or ancestors) to be there with you. Yes, you might work a spell while in your sacred space; you might even ask that your working be blessed. However, the presence of a God or spirit isn't necessary for magic.

In fact, combining magic and ritual might even be an imposition. Do you really think the God and Goddess want to sit around watching you cast a spell for a new lover? Do they need to literally be there while you create a bunch of household charms? Or maybe they expect that, because you are human and have the spark of the Divine within you, you can do some of this basic stuff on your own.

If you ask your Deities for help, that's prayer. If you use the spark within to make it happen yourself, that's magic. Yes, there's a gray area where the two overlap. But without an understanding of the difference, magic starts to seem like an overly complex and specific practice. In truth, you can cast a spell without a formal circle, without tools, without privacy. You can cast standing on a busy street corner.

So why involve religion at all? Well, first of all, with religion comes a moral code. Your Deities are going to expect certain behavior from you, and you ignore Their expectations at your spiritual peril. In addition, the Deities can be of particular benefit in certain kinds of spells. Healing spells are a good example. If I were going to try to improve someone's health, I would definitely combine my spell work with a full-on ritual. I'd ask that my particular God and Goddess help the person in question as well as working whatever spell I'd devised. But I figure that getting a better job is a personal matter, too trivial to bother my Deities with. As they say, "The Gods help those who help themselves."

THE LOGIC OF THE CIRCLE

When you cast a circle, you are accomplishing two important things. First, you are creating a barrier. Circles have edges and those edges can be used to keep certain energies in and others out. Second, you are creating a crossroads between the worlds. Inside the circle, other planes are much closer. This can make talking to your Deities easier (hence the common use of a circle in ritual as sacred space in both Pagan and non-Pagan religious systems).

While you can cast a spell anywhere with little or no preparation beyond your own visualization and will, there are good reasons to use a circle in magic as well as ritual. Standing between the worlds, as you are when you're in a circle, can make reaching the astral plane much easier. And as we'll be discussing below, magic occurs primarily on the astral.

Another example is in "baneful" magic. Now, many people say that negative or repellent magic is never a good idea, but I've always felt it's best to consider the intent. For example, a healing circle can be just as much about harming or banishing illness as it is about attracting health. Ridding yourself of a bad habit could be thought of as destroying it. And exorcising a personal demon such as a painful childhood memory is as challenging and powerful as exorcising a real demon (and a lot more frequently necessary). In any case, magic along these lines requires a certain amount of protection—both of yourself and any "innocent bystanders." A circle is an excellent way to accomplish this.

HOW MAGIC WORKS

So if magic isn't getting your Deities to do something for you, what is it? What are spells and why don't they always seem to work? Basically, all those different tools, charms, chants, and other magical trappings are window dressing (albeit sometimes necessary window dressing) for the real process—the stuff going on behind the scenes.

Magic is the act of projecting power to accomplish something. The power travels from your conscious mind to your subconscious, from there to the astral plane, and then back again to the physical world. The thing you want to control is the shape that your power will take.

Spells can generally be divided into attractive (drawing toward) and repulsive (pushing away) spells. The spell stretches either between you and the object of the spell or between two different objects. So, getting rid of an old friendship stretches between you and the other person and is a repulsive spell. Sending healing energy to your mother is an attractive spell between her and good health.

The Four Powers

You've probably read about the four powers of the mage or the Witches' pyramid: To Know, To Dare, To Will, and To Keep Silent. You may also know that these powers correspond to the four classical elements and are supposed to be keys for working magic. But how does this help us make spells that work? The following is my own theory on the nature of the four powers and their reflection onto the practice of spell casting. While no more true than any other metaphor, this particular framework has improved my magic a great deal.

For a successful spell, the four powers must manifest in both inner and outer forms. For example, you have to know what you want to accomplish and you must know yourself. The first is the outward aspect of the power of knowledge, the second is the inward manifestation. This is true of each of the four powers. That means that there are potentially eight steps or parts to successful spell casting. For example:

Power	Element	Outward Aspect	Inward Aspect
To Know	Air	Know your objective	Know yourself
To Dare	Fire	Create the symbol set	Raise and target energy
To Will	Water	Link to the physical	Send the energy
To Keep Silent	Earth	Don't talk about it	Clear your mind

The order in which these parts are accomplished has to do with the natural "direction" of spell casting. A spell begins with a conscious (outward) decision. Then, the process of casting the spell is one of going inward to the subconscious and astral. Finally, the manifestation of the spells is a movement back out to the physical world. So we start with the outer powers, move to the inner, and finish with the outer again.

Power	Outward Aspect	Inward Aspect	Power
To Know	Know your objective		
To Dare	Create the symbol set		
		Raise and target energy	To Dare
		Know yourself	To Know
		Clear your mind	To Keep Silent
		Send the energy	To Will
To Will	Link to the physical		
To Keep Silent	Don't talk about it		

How does all this work? Let's go over it step by step:

Know your objective (outward knowledge). Really *think* about the parameters you want to involve in your spell. A good spell will have a combination of vague and specific clauses or parameters. For example, let's say you need a better job. Well, you don't just want to ask for a different job. That's too vague. You might just end up with a similar job, one that's much worse, or one that is better in all the wrong ways. Instead, analyze the things your new job should have (better money, safer environment, more challenge) and make a list.

However, you also probably don't want to do a spell for a specific job ("I want my friend Bob's job"). It's too limiting and it doesn't allow the optimal solution to come to you. It's important to specify what you want, but not always exactly how you will get it. That allows the energy to accomplish its task in the easiest way. It also keeps you from worrying whether you're the reason that Bob just got fired. Note: if you don't know enough about the job you want to create a detailed symbol set, you can always do a spell simply for prosperity and happiness. Presumably, you know what being happy feels like. If you can also envision prosperity, then you can create a spell to allow those things to come to you in whatever way makes sense.

Create the symbol set (outward daring). The place where magic comes from within you (the subconscious) and the place where its primary effect occurs (the astral) are both symbolic. They function not in words but in symbols and patterns. This is where all that symbolic thinking comes in handy. You have to take the thing you want, with all its parameters, and transform it into a symbol. That's what all those trappings are for: the magic words, special herbs, planetary alignments, lunar aspect, and so on. Those are just ways of "saying" what you want without words.

Creating your symbol set takes a certain amount of daring. Remember that the power of daring is associated with the element of fire. You'll need to touch that inspirational fire within you to find a symbol set that works just right. This is also the moment when you take your knowledge and make it concrete. It's really a kind of art form and requires not only that you know your symbols intimately but that you know how the symbols "vibrate" or feel to you.

When you pick a spell from a book, the symbolism might not work for you. Perhaps you are unfamiliar with some of the ingredients, or maybe the associations simply don't click. Maybe the symbolism *kind of* works (being based on type of energy) but you have a much stronger connection or preference to something else. In any case, if the symbols don't work, the spell won't work. That's why it's always best to create your own spells. Why is Friday the best day for love magic? Because of ancient connections that set up systems of vibration or resonance here and now. The right symbols make harmony, the wrong ones, discord. Or, for the less musically inclined, think about the "smell" of the thing you want. How does the odor of a time of day, a herb, a crystal work to make a pleasing perfume that brings the results of the spell to mind? If you are a tactile person, think in terms of feeling and texture. What does Mars feel like? What's the magical texture of basil oil?

The more complex the spell, the more important symbol creation becomes. However, it's always possible to simply use the symbol mentally. If you do a spell frequently (protection for example), you will eventually just know what protection energy feels like and won't have to work out a symbol every time. This is how the skilled Witch can cast a spell standing on a street corner. He or she already knows the sound, smell, taste, or texture of the desired result. See the exercise at the end of this chapter for more details on creating symbol sets.

Raise and target your energy (inward daring). Use whatever technique works best for you to generate the energy you will put into your spell. Then take that energy and imprint it with the thing you want. That is, use your symbol set to get a sense of what the result of the spell *feels* like, astrally speaking. This is why creating a symbol is important. A string of words means little to our unconscious. The symbol for the string of words is what we need to use.

This is the moment where daring really comes into play. You have to imprint the energy strongly, firmly—without doubt or uncertainty. If you are hesitant, the energy won't clearly shout your need to the astral and the effects of the spell will be equally muddled.

By the way, if you need to go through a whole song and dance to raise energy, you may want to break that habit. Elaborate techniques for raising energy work great for groups but aren't always necessary for the individual. You can draw energy up from the Earth after centering and grounding, or from above you through the top of your head (the crown chakra). This allows you to cast anytime, anywhere.

Know yourself (inward knowledge). It's very important for you to really know yourself to work magic. If your conscious mind believes that you need more money, but your subconscious feels guilty or fearful of success or resentful of successful people, all the money spells in the world won't help you. Since the subconscious mind is your connection to the astral, you'd better have a good idea of what this part of yourself is feeling and doing before you send that energy out.

Clear your mind (inward silence). This is of primary importance. To send out the energy you have targeted, you need to connect to the astral plane. This is accomplished in an altered state of consciousness. It's the place within you where your conscious mind is still and your subconscious can operate freely. The point of the symbol you created for your need is to help you take the energy you've generated and connect it to the astral plane. The way to do that is by moving through your subconscious. This is why casting a circle can be useful for spellcraft even though it's not necessary. The circle itself is a doorway, and standing in it you are halfway there.

The more complex the spell, the deeper you will need to go. This also improves with practice. If you need to cast a spell while driving and you are familiar with the spell you want to cast, you can simply calm yourself for a moment and send the energy out. You don't always need to enter a full trance—although you can choose to do so (although, please, not while driving).

The power "to be silent" is often interpreted as meaning that you should not talk about your spells once they are cast. While that's true, the inward power of silence is much more important for successful spell casting. This is what many spells found in books never seem to mention. Without the ability to silence your conscious mind, the power will move no further than your own thoughts.

Send the energy (inward will). You can either send the energy directly out into the astral or program an object to give off the energy over time. The method depends on the type of spell. For a new job, I would just send the energy out in a wave. However, for a charm to remember my dreams, I would send the energy into my symbol to be slowly released during the night. Candle magic is an example of empowering an object (the candle) with your energy. When you burn the candle, the energy is released. You can also empower charm bags, stones, crystals, incense, and so on.

This type of spell casting can be used to strengthen the overall effect over time. For example, you can imprint your need for friendship on a candle that you plan on burning each Friday night for the next seven weeks. Since Friday and the number seven are classically associated with Venus, the planet of love and friendship, each time you burn the candle you are strengthening and adding to the initial energy through your symbolic associations. Just remember that the associations must make sense to *you*.

Another example of spell casting with an object is imprinting a clay figure with something you want to be rid of (an illness, bad habit, or negative trait). Place the figure in a running stream, and as the clay is washed away, you or your environment will also be washed clean.

Link to the physical (outward will). You need to create a way for the energy of the spell to operate using everyday means. Spells work on the astral plane because the rules there operate very differently. On the astral, time and distance are irrelevant and energy and symbols work like machines do here. But the new job you want will still have to come from the physical world.

This means that you will have to put some energy into creating opportunities for the magic to help you here on this plain. For a job spell, you need to get out there and start looking for work. But even if there's nothing you can do physically, you can still create links mentally and emotionally by having the right attitude.

Don't talk about it (outward silence). You have to be ready for the results of your spell to work. This is why it's traditional not to talk about your spells after they are complete. In fact you shouldn't dwell on them at all. Why? One reason is that many Witches cast a spell and then spend as much or more energy worrying about whether it will work than they spent on the original spell. That doesn't create an environment that's at all conducive to a successful spell. Instead, spend your energy helping to make things happen here and now. This is not to say that you can't revisit the spell to add additional energy. In the example above, where you burn a candle for seven Fridays, you aren't dwelling in a negative way on the outcome; you're adding additional *positive* energy over time.

Another reason not to talk about your magic is that some people will not understand. People who don't believe in magic or who, for some reason, aren't supportive of you can cast a pall over your work. Research into psychic powers seems to point to the fact that a skeptical observer can affect psychic ability. Therefore it's a good policy to just keep the details of your workings to yourself until the effect is realized.

Taking Steps

As you become more familiar with a particular spell, you won't have to walk through a specific bunch of steps. This is why a skilled Witch should be able to cast a spell wherever he is and whenever he needs to. In addition, remember that this framework is simply one way of viewing spell casting. You may decide that a different method or structure works better for you. However, the basics (deciding what you want, symbolizing it, sending it out, and making a link for its return) are going to remain the same.

Understanding the mechanism behind the outward trappings allows you to create spells for any need or purpose. You don't have to limit yourself to preexisting spells from old books. In fact it's smarter to create spells for yourself than use someone else's. You can tailor a spell to your exact requirements and use your most powerful symbols. You can also mix and match from existing spells to create the perfect new spell. This allows you to take from whatever sources make sense, including old magic books and new. Innovation is the key.

ADVANCED MAGICAL ETHICS

Since ethics is considered primarily a matter of religion, this section might seem to belong to the next chapter. However, the ethics specifically associated with magic are important enough to warrant their own discussion. Many beginning Pagans go by simple ethical rules or guides without ever looking deeper into the nature of right and wrong and their own standards of ethical behavior. Ethics is a complex subject, however, and Pagans do themselves a disservice by simply parroting an ethical rede or rule without knowing their own minds and hearts.

What is ethics? Ethics encompasses your own set of rules for behavior. These rules are influenced by a number of factors including the society in which you live and the religion you practice. Your standard of ethics comes from your upbringing as well as your true nature or character. If this definition sounds very relative, well, it is. Just like so many of the symbols we take for granted, the concepts of right and wrong are influenced by relative forces to a much greater degree than we would like to think.

For example, during the industrial revolution, child labor was considered ethical by societal standards. In many places and times, what we would consider child marriage was very common. Even obvious examples are requirements of society as opposed to any natural law. In our society it is wrong to steal. That's because we are capitalistic and driven by the concept of ownership and private property. In societies that have no ownership or property rights (like some tribal societies), the taboo against stealing is unnecessary.

Religion is also a primary source for rules of ethical behavior. For example, there's a long history of murder in the name of a God: Thou Shalt Not Kill—unless it's a heretic or nonbeliever. In the past, Gods and Goddesses have demanded sacrifices that, to our modern eyes, seem unethical. Spiritual self-mutilation (from flagellation to tattooing and scarification) might also be considered unethical. It just depends on whom you ask.

So are there any absolute standards of ethics? Things that are always right or always wrong? This is the question that scholars of religion and philosophy have been pondering for millennia. A better question for us as individuals is "What is my own standard of ethics and where does it come from?" What you consider ethical or unethical behavior depends in large part on your society, time, culture, and family. In addition, as Pagans of various types, your Deities will have ethical rules that you must follow. For example, Wiccans follow the Wiccan Rede. The shortened version "An it harm none, do as you will" is just the beginning of a long poem, extant in several versions, that describes the ethical behavior that Wiccans should emulate.[31]

But rules and guidelines are going to be, at times, unequal to creating a standard for a complex world. For example, you can't really go through life harming nothing and no one. It's simply impossible. A million microbes die every time you breathe or move. Even if you are a strict vegan, you have to admit that you are harming plants by eating them.

Even the most obvious rule can be modified depending on the situation. For example, I'm certainly glad that our society generally supports people not killing one another. I would never choose to kill someone, and most people would agree that killing another human is wrong. However, what about self-defense? What if the choice is between killing someone else or being killed? Then the issue is very different, isn't it? Or what about killing someone who wants to be killed (euthanasia), or killing yourself (suicide)?

Another ethical issue is how the threat of getting caught affects your choices. You have to ask yourself whether your standards are based on your own internal motivation or whether the threat of punishment plays a part in your ethical decisions. Getting to the real answer to this question can take a lot of introspection. Would you steal if no one would ever know? What if your ATM accidentally gave you an extra twenty dollars? This works in both directions. Are there any laws you disagree with based on your set of ethics? Does the fear of legal repercussions keep you from breaking those laws? If you're honest, you might surprise yourself with some of your answers.

So what does this have to do with magic? Ostensibly, magic allows us to do things that we can't do in any other way, and *allows us to do them without getting caught by mundane means*. This throws many people into an ethical tailspin. Sure, a few will take advantage of their abilities, but many more go in the opposite direction, limiting themselves with extreme interpretations of what's permitted. For example, you might simply refuse to do magic for personal gain for fear of unethically taking prosperity away from someone else. However, if you view magic as something normal and natural, most personal ethical dilemmas will fade.

If you are considering a magical act, begin by imagining that you could reach the same result through purely normal means. If you could find your dream job by simply looking in the want ads, you wouldn't turn it down because you might be "taking" that work away from someone else, would you? No, you'd polish your resume, put on your best clothes, and sell yourself to them with everything you had. If there was a real threat to you or your family, you wouldn't stand back and do nothing. You'd get an alarm system or a large dog and maybe learn some self-defense or martial arts. If you were being stalked or harassed, you'd contact the appropriate authorities, and if that didn't work, you'd do whatever else you could to stay safe.

Of course the reverse is also true. If you wouldn't steal someone's property through normal means, you shouldn't do it magically. If beating someone up for simply looking at you is overreacting, you wouldn't curse him or her for something equally minor. If chewing someone out in a righteous, holier-than-thou "snit fit" is repugnant to you, then you shouldn't do it—either physically or magically.

In addition, knowing how your inner sense of ethics relates to your fear of the law can help you make ethical choices as well. If a wonderful natural spot were going to be developed, you might fear actually sabotaging the bulldozers physically because of the possibility of getting caught. But using magic, you very likely wouldn't get caught. Does that mean that magical sabotage is ethical?

In magic you have only your inner sense of right and wrong to guide you. Sure, if you step on enough toes, someone bigger might come along and "magic" you a sharp lesson in "do unto others." But at least the cops won't be knocking on your door with a warrant to search for eye of newt. Of course, this is no excuse for rampant ego gratification. Whatever your standards are, however much they rely on your religion, society, or personality, they should not be changeable. Your core ideas of right and wrong should stay with you and guide your actions—magical and mundane—no matter what the circumstances.

The two primary objections I hear against doing certain kinds of spells are that (1) with greater power comes greater responsibility and (2) when you get something you have to give something else up. There is truth to the first objection. The more you can do, the more you need to check your motivations and take full responsibility for your results . . . because your results will be more impressive. This is why knowing yourself is so very important, particularly as you advance. I don't think, however, this means that you must be cowed or terrified into doing nothing. Not doing magic because your spells work too well and scare you is really a cowardly reaction. Take responsibility for yourself and your needs and do what you need to do.

But while the first issue does have merit, the second objection is just silly. The idea that you have to suffer for your spirituality comes from religions like Puritanist Christianity. Sure, when you gain something you *may* have to give something up, but not necessarily in a negative way. It's simply the balance of the universe operating. One thing leaves and makes room for something new. Something arrives and therefore pushes another thing out. For example, magic for abundance can mean making some kind of exchange required by the desired results. For a prosperity spell, you might have to give up time (in order to work more) or friends (who are jealous of your success) or peace and quiet (because your lucrative new job is in the city). But it's not bad or good, just necessary balance.

Also, don't go around thinking that your increase in fortune is causing someone else to starve. That's not how it works. There really *is* enough to go around. World politics, war, and corporate greed are the reasons that some have more and some less—not your little magic spell. Feel blessed with what you have and share your blessings as you can. But don't let guilt tie your hands and make you miss opportunities.

Magic is simply another skill or ability that you can use to know and help yourself. If a person was very smart you wouldn't want her to "play dumb" because others aren't as smart, would you? A friend who has a particular talent (music, writing, sports) shouldn't ignore it because someone else can't play a note, string three words together, or even walk and chew gum at the same time. We have to use the abilities we have to make our lives better, follow our path, and help others whenever possible.

Of course we should also never squander our abilities on meaningless power plays or silly games. Just as we may feel contempt for the smart person who uses her intelligence to make others feel stupid or the talented artist who mocks those with different or lesser talents, we should also feel contempt for the person who works magic simply to meddle, make trouble, or show off.

A Note on Love Spells

Rare is the book on magic that doesn't cover the topic of love spells—either by offering a list to try or by warning you away for ethical reasons. Obviously, there are a lot of lonely and unsatisfied people out there who are longing for love. In addition, love spells come from a rich magical background. The history of magic is full of spells to win or attract love, make oneself irresistible, or keep a lover faithful. Some of the oldest spells are concerned with these very issues.

What are the ethics surrounding these types of spells? Well, applying the rationale I set out above for getting a job to the issue of finding love, you might think that there was nothing ethically wrong with working magic for love. After all, if you were going to see your perfect someone at a party, you wouldn't avoid them for fear of some sort of repercussion. You'd dress to look your best, put on a winning smile, and try to appear witty without tripping over your shoes.

However, there are some additional ethical considerations to love magic that you have to consider. The first is the necessity of honesty for a good relationship. You certainly might try to look your best to impress a special someone, but if he's a "miniskirt and spiked heels" kind of guy and you're more of a "jeans and hiking boots girl," for example, you've got bigger problems than simply how you look. It won't do you any good to buy a pair of four-inch stilettos for the party because you're not being honest. Even if you don't stumble and twist your ankle, eventually he'll realize that you'd rather be hiking than shopping, and strife will ensue. Or for a reverse example, if she's interested in a steady career guy and you're working part time and playing in a local band, it doesn't help to tell her you're a doctor, lawyer, or CPA. Eventually the truth will come out.

So what's my point? The wrong type of love spell is just as deceptive as pretending to be something you're not. Whether it's a spell to make yourself irresistible or to make someone else fall in love with you, it's still based on deception. Eventually, the spell will run its course and you'll be forced to base the rest of your relationship on who you both *really* are. Depending on the circumstances, that could come as a terribly unpleasant shock.

And in fact this ethical issue isn't so different from a job spell, after all. If you work magic to find that perfect job (one that you're qualified for or that gives you an opportunity to learn a new skill) you are basing your spell on honesty and it should work well. However, if you create a spell to get a job through magic that you simply cannot do, eventually your boss will discover that you are completely unqualified and you'll either get fired or promoted to middle management.

What kind of spells might you work to find love? Well, first of all, you could work on being worthy of love. Everyone deserves love in his or her life, however many people simply refuse to believe it. And since our beliefs work magic to create our reality, we will certainly not find love if, deep down, we think we don't deserve it. If this sounds a bit too easy or fluffy, it's not. Our beliefs about ourselves are deep-seated in our subconscious and usually come from childhood. Digging around in the "bottom" of your brain can be a terrifying and emotionally difficult process, particularly if you have painful past experiences.

You might also do magic to call the right person to you. Like any type of spell, it helps to keep a balance between specific and general parameters. You may want someone who is as bright as you, has a good sense of humor, or is exciting and adventurous (or alternately, stable and steady). You don't want to get too specific (36-24-36 with blond hair and blue eyes) or too general (oh, just anyone will do). Or you might simply ask that you find your "soul mate" or perfect match. People are notoriously biased when it comes to being in love. It would be far too easy to create a "nonspecific" spell with one eye on the guy or gal you're currently infatuated with. In the process, you might miss out on some great opportunities.

Finally, it's important to note that power itself is attractive. As you move past the beginner stage, you will be gaining a lot of personal power. Just as people who are supremely self-confident attract a lot of attention, so, too, do people who take responsibility for their actions, know themselves well, work hard to improve themselves, and walk their own path without apology or excuse (in fact that sounds like a good definition of self-confidence). Doing so creates a kind of aura that can affect other people. Some will feel uncomfortable or even fear you. But many more will find it very compelling. The opportunities for rampant ego gratification become quite numerous, and adding a love spell to the mix can cause a lot of problems. There's a fine line between feeling confident and getting a swelled head, and walking that line is one of the greater challenges of the advancing Pagan.

SPREADING IT OUT—CHARMS AND BLESSINGS

The majority of magic you read about in older books comes under the heading of folk or kitchen magic: spells that require only a few basic ingredients and have a simple purpose such as protection, health, or harmony. These little charms are easy, but they have a cumulative effect, particularly in your home. As simple as these can be to invent and implement, I'm surprised that Pagans and Witches don't use more of them. I think the reason has less to do with ability than with perspective.

Magic is very cool. But this doesn't mean that it's always earth-shattering, life-changing, or intensely difficult. As I've said, magic can be done anywhere, with any tools or none, using whatever makes sense to you. When you are first starting out, magic can seem mysterious and secretive. However, one of your goals as an advancing Pagan is to integrate your life. When you have little boxes in your life that say "magic" or "religion" or "boring, mundane crap," you end up scattered. You can't do a spell because you have to clean the house. You can't deal with bills because you're working money magic. When you create these types of arbitrary rules, you only limit yourself.

I have a close friend, a Witch who's always impressed me with her ability to get things done. She has multiple projects and interests, a full spiritual and social life, a busy job and home business, and great relationships. How does she fit it all in? From keen observation, I've discovered that it's because she doesn't limit herself. She makes room for everything in her life by integrating it. Sure, she still has to focus (just like the rest of us) to do her work or magic. But she doesn't let arbitrary distinctions sidetrack her. If she needs to accomplish something, she does it when it fits into her schedule. If she tires of a hobby she puts it aside for a time—without guilt. She knows how to say no and how to say yes. She makes good use of her time, including time to do nothing but relax. While she occasionally gets overwhelmed (just like the rest of us), she also accomplishes a lot of things that feed her soul and make her happy.

When you begin to mix everything together in your life, you may find that more magic begins to creep in. It's the antithesis of the "Sunday Christian." These are the people who spend all day in church on Sunday, but who ignore their faith the rest of the week. When you live your path all the time, you end up with both more path and more time. You don't have to wait until you can perform a full-on magical spell casting extravaganza . . . it might never happen. Tuck your magic into your day. When you remember the basics it will work just as well.

And if a project or chore seems intensely normal or boring, make it magical or spiritual—all it takes is a shift in mindset.

THE DISHES OF LIFE

Years ago, my friend and I came up with a theory that we jokingly called "the dishes of life." The premise is that, no matter who you are or what you do, you still have to live in the physical world. Whether you're just beginning or are the ultimate spiritual guru, the dishes still have to get done. Even monks and nuns in retreat from the world do these basic chores. But far from being a necessary evil or the price you pay for living, these chores are part of the path and the spiritual journey.

When you can see the magic or spirit in washing your dishes, you can begin seeing it everywhere. This is how we integrate our lives. Plants are magic. Clouds are magic. People are magic. Even mundane people are magic, just by being alive. In fact life is magic (particularly if you consider the Gaia Theory). Truly seeing this and living it can be the work of multiple lifetimes. I know that when confronted with a sink full of grimy pots at the end of a long day, I'm not exactly feeling spiritually moved. But washing them is still magic. The truth is that ignoring these simple magics is a great loss. The dance of life includes many different steps. To truly live, you must not only learn as many as you can, you have to get down and really boogie.

When beginners discover Paganism and magic, it can be like seeing a bright light for the first time (being illuminated). The trouble is that, after seeing that brilliance, the rest of your world can seem very gray in comparison. This can cause real world avoidance that creates an imbalance in a beginner's life. Alternately, a person can spend so much time staring at the light that he sees nothing but afterimages wherever he looks. This is the cause of what my friend Elizabeth calls "D&D Syndrome"—the illusion that you're living in a live-action role-playing game.

You have to allow the light to *clear* your vision so that you can see things in their entirety. This means that you view your religion and magic with objectivity, but you also see the physical world as the beautiful and magical place that it really is. A spider spinning its web in the garden is just as cool as fairies dancing under a full moon. Your pet cat hunting a cricket is as magnificent as the jaguar in the forest. Magic is already everywhere; you don't have to put it there with flights of fancy.

Yes, there are deeper mysteries, powerful spiritual beings, and life-changing lessons. But life, with its ups and downs and endless sinks full of dishes, is the greatest and most beautiful mystery of them all.

TRUTH, HONESTY, AND KEEPING SECRETS

I've always believed that the greatest secret is that there are no secrets. There's simply knowledge I'm ready for and knowledge I'm not. If I'm not ready to absorb a bit of information, it doesn't matter how clearly someone tells it to me; I just won't get it. But once I'm ready for it, nothing can keep me from knowing what I need to know. When a teacher poses a riddle or makes a student dig for an answer, it shouldn't be simply a game to frustrate the student or a ploy to make the teacher seem powerful. It can actually be a way of helping the student get ready to absorb the idea.

The irony is that most of these "hidden pearls of wisdom" sound pretty basic and even silly if someone just tells them to you. For example, "people are not all good or all evil." It sounds so obvious! Yet, when I first really understood this idea with my heart as well as my head, it changed my life. Understanding this simple phrase was my comprehension of the fallacy of duality. People have everything within them, and you can't divide them with labels (good/evil, saved/sinner, man/woman).

But in my example above, there's no real secret. That little tidbit is there for everyone to access, no matter what path they're on. In fact, that's true of all knowledge. The part of you that's connected to the divine always knows everything. It's just a matter of seeking the information and opening your mind. So what's the point of even having secrets? There are some good reasons to keep things secret, just as there are some bad ones.

When you are presented with information that's supposed to be kept secret, your job is to analyze whether there's really a good reason for the secrecy. Of course, for the protection of the members, you might take an oath not to divulge the identities of people in your group. Not everyone is openly Pagan, and unfortunately discrimination still exists. In addition, there may be parts of your practice that might offend some people, like ritual nudity. There's certainly no reason for every person you come across to know every minute detail about what you do. In addition, when I work magic for another or give someone spiritual counseling, I consider myself bound by "doctor/patient" confidentiality—just like a therapist or clergyman or -woman. Finally, there are some spiritual experiences that are too personal and special to divulge. Sharing them would make them less, diffuse them somehow. And occasionally, you may get information directly from your Deities that They ask you not to share.

These are all good reasons for keeping information secret; however, I've never really needed to take an oath to another person regarding any of these situations. My own sense of propriety usually keeps me from blabbing about my path to those who wouldn't understand or don't care. In addition, my relationship with my Deities demands certain conduct, including keeping the confidences of people I work with. It's not a matter of promising this or swearing that, it's just a part of my personality.

Sometimes people have reasons for keeping things secret that aren't really valid. It might be to create a barrier between members and non-members, or to seem cool, or to impress others. It might be out of a sense of mistrust or an urge to control the person to whom the secrets are told. In these cases, it's a good idea to remember that enlightenment has never been limited to one group or path. The answers are available to anyone who asks and who is ready for them. If you don't know whom to ask, ask your Deities. They should be able to point you in the right direction.

BUILDING THE BOOK OF SYMBOLS

Because I'm a writer, you'd think I'd have a comprehensive and complete Book of Shadows, neatly cross-indexed and containing all my knowledge to date. However, that's simply not the case. Having never been part of a traditional coven that mandated the copying of the group's Book, I found my fledgling attempts at creating a personal manual boring and useless. I realize now that my beginner's mistake was copying things from whatever book I was reading at the time.

Did I really need to copy the same old correspondences and basic material? I knew these things already and could look them up if I ever forgot. In addition, not being a member of a strictly interpreted tradition, my ideas and ways of working change over time. The correspondences I labored to copy neatly (I have notoriously inconstant handwriting) might not even reflect my actual practices a year from now. Finally, when I read beginners' books I certainly enjoyed them and learned from them, but they didn't have the sense of mystery I associated with a hand copied and illuminated Book of Shadows. Why then would I fill my Book of Shadows with the same type of material?

So what do I consider important to capture in writing? Over the years, I've learned what records to keep by what I later regretted not writing down—important dreams, for example. Any dream heavy with symbolism needs to be recorded. Dreams are slippery and the imagery will fade over time. In addition, it is very useful to review the dream later and see if you still interpret it the same way. I've never gone back to read my first scrawls about the waxing moon being better for attractive spells . . . but I regularly review my most potent dreams and still learn from them.

It's also a good idea to record the results of any divination or realization of omens. This type of information takes on the character of a diary more than a Book of Shadows, and you might want to keep the information separate. However, I always regret it when I don't jot down at least the basic results. Later, I'll want to refresh my memory or see how accurate I was, and won't be able to.

In addition, it's important to record any spell that works well. I once whipped up a dream sachet using whatever relevant herbs I found in my kitchen cupboard. I charged it up with a useful incantation, invented on the spot, then placed it under my pillow. For weeks I woke unrested after long nights of constant dreaming. First the satchel went from the pillow to the nightstand, then to the desk across the room, then out of the room entirely. It was finally completely dismantled and the ingredients discharged and burned. I had some truly life-changing dreams during that time, but finally needed more peaceful sleep. I only wish now that I had jotted down the herbs and incantation! Any personal symbols that you have discovered or realized should also be recorded. These personal symbols are great for creating future spells.

Finally, rituals and results should be recorded for later review and use. Not only can you use the information to refine your ritual practice, it can also become something of a profile of the various Deities that you've worked with. Any information you obtain either directly from Them or through meditation should be included no matter how odd or everyday it sounds. The work you do to find these keys is the real reason for being a Witch or Pagan.

FOOD FOR THOUGHT—BALANCING YOUR CHECKBOOK AS A MAGICAL ACT

Many Pagans I know have a love/hate relationship with the material world. They enjoy the benefits of modern technology, at the same time feeling that technological advances are bad. They aren't about to move to a commune or homestead in Alaska, but they dream of "getting back to the land." They have contempt for material success and successful people, feeling that they've sold out. And when they enjoy any success themselves, they feel unworthy or guilty. At the same time, they can't pay their bills or keep their finances in order and they spend a great deal of time worrying about money; they may even work money magic for themselves.

If you recognize yourself in this description, remember that these attitudes keep you from being successful. After all, the things we believe about ourselves become true for us. If you believe that having a comfortable lifestyle means selling your soul, then you will never have success without facing a moral quandary. If you live with a burden of guilt about having been born American, middle-class, and so on, you will never be able to take command of your life.

It would be nice if we lived in a place where we didn't have to worry about money, but we don't. For most people in the world, money is required and work is the primary way to get it. In fact capitalist societies such as most of us live in value money above all else. And while you don't have to fall into that trap yourself, you *do* have to live in this economy. Even if you feel that being a capitalist is wrong, there's nothing wrong with surviving and providing for your family

Capitalism in fact has a very unhealthy view of money and material wealth. Yet, feeling guilty for being successful or resentful of others' success is equally unhealthy. A healthier perspective on materialism and wealth can be found in Taoist philosophy embodied by the *I Ching* as well as practices such as feng shui. This philosophy has no problem with luck and prosperity, and practitioners make a concerted effort to draw these things into their lives. The healthy acquisition of wealth is considered a sign of a person who lives in harmony. And harmony here is the key. Instead of focusing on your spiritual life to the detriment of your material one, you have to find a point of balance.

Yes, rampant materialism, capitalism, and globalized exploitation have caused many problems. Among other things, the environment is being destroyed and millions live in poverty. However, just because we've gone to extremes or in the wrong direction doesn't mean that technology or material success is totally bad. Our ancestors would have jumped at the chance to enjoy a regular, year-round supply of food. They would have celebrated the medications and medical procedures that save lives. Our technological advances have given millions of people independence, democracy, widespread literacy, and more freedom of thought and speech than the world has ever seen—not to mention indoor plumbing and sanitary living conditions. That this wealth and luxury aren't spread evenly is a flaw of ideology and distribution, not materialism itself.

When we live in balance, then all things have their place in our lives: giving and receiving, leading and following, working and resting. In addition, balance means that we focus on both material growth and spiritual growth. Taoist philosophy doesn't tell us to feel bad if we have or want money. Instead it teaches that the wise person will nurture prosperity and work to be successful, while realizing that money isn't everything.

The optimal situation is to do what you love and earn enough money to be safe and comfortable. It's not an impossible goal. You may have to tweak your definitions a bit (I love to write, but know I won't make a living off my poetry), and it may take time to get there. But first you will have to work at ridding yourself of all those negative thoughts and self-defeating habits that keep you from being prosperous.

CHAPTER 6 EXERCISES

Symbol Creation

Despite this being one of the most "hands-on" chapters in the book, I'm only including one exercise. Having spent the preceding pages telling you to invent your own magic and create your own spells, it would be illogical of me to then fill the examples with suggestions for things to try. However, I have included one example of symbol creation for a spell, just to give you a sense of how the process might work for you.

Let's say that you need a new job. You've given some thought to the matter and have determined that your perfect job would include a better pay scale, easier work, and more convenient hours. So how do you create a symbol for "New job, better money, not manual labor, no night shifts"? There are many options, and they can be combined in any way that makes sense to you.

For example, you can pick a group of things that symbolize the different parts of the equation. A new coin for money, a daylily or morning glory for the day shift, a set of false fingernails for "desk job," sage for employment, patchouli for wealth—whatever clicks and feels right. While false fingernails may not seem very magical, as long as the symbol speaks to you, it will work. I once created a spell for a friend's legal troubles using the "Get out of jail free" card from my Monopoly game.

You can probably also think of some destructive symbols (like burning your uniform). One tip, though, if you are doing an "attractive" spell (that is, you are calling something to you—a new job in this case): avoid the use of "repellent" symbols. If you are doing a "repellent" spell (one to rid yourself of something—like banishing a bad habit) avoid the use of "attractive" symbols. Focusing on one thing at a time is easier for your subconscious to process. Notice in the list above that the daylily symbolizes "day shift," *not* "no night shift." This is an attractive spell and all the components and symbols should reflect that.

Another technique is the use of magic words. The goal here is to take the words for the thing you want and strip them down or combine them in a way that creates a symbol that still contains the essence of the original words. There are dozens of ways to do this including the use of sacred or magical alphabets, numerology and magic squares, text manipulation, and so on. A peek in any of the older books on magic (not necessarily Paganism) will give you a good start.

Once you have your symbol set, you can improve the "logic" of the spell by timing it correctly (that is, symbolically). Examine moon phase, time of day, day of the week, or planetary aspect. For our spell, the moon could be full or near full. The optimal time of day might be high noon. The planet that governs money and prosperity is Jupiter, and that would mean casting on a Wednesday. You could also do the spell just after the new moon, for new beginnings, and start at 8 A.M., the start of your desired "day shift." This flexibility is particularly useful for something like finding a new job, where you may not want to wait a couple of weeks for the right astrological influences.

In addition, the use of various herbs, crystals, scents, and so on can help empower the spell. I tend to take a very nondogmatic and flexible view of spell casting. However, as a friend recently reminded me, plants, stones, colors, and other spell components have their own energies that lend themselves to certain kinds of magic. A good reference book can point you to lists of components that might be useful. However, it's still important to remember that the things you use must click for you and put you in the right state of mind. If anise oil reminds you of when you had the flu and threw up your grandmother's spice cookies, you will want to avoid using it no matter how much it makes sense to the logic of the spell. It's also important to remember that some items have more nebulous definitions than others. Colors, for example, are particularly prone to multiple interpretations depending on the culture and philosophy. Don't worry too much about the "right" set of interpretations. Let your intuition guide you and keep tabs on how effective your spells are depending on what you've used.

Once you have the symbol, you'll want to decide how to imprint and deliver the energy. Perhaps you want to simply use your symbolic items and send the energy out in a wave. You can also store the energy in a battery like a candle or crystal. You might decide to destroy the symbol in the process of sending the energy, say, burning a piece of paper with your magic word and releasing the ashes into the wind or smudging with the appropriate herbs and letting the smoke carry your wishes outward.

Finally, you need to figure out some creative ways to help draw the energy back into the physical world. For a new job, the primary thing you need to do is get out there and look for work: read newspaper classifieds, send out your resume, apply for positions. But there are also less direct ways to create the channels you need. You can try getting up early to watch the sun come up, buy some office clothes to wear at your new desk job, or create a new budget to take into account your future income.

CONCLUSION

When you truly live as a Witch or Pagan, many of the barriers that divide sections of your life begin to fall away. As you comprehend that everything is magic and that even the most routine tasks are part of the mystery, your practice will become more integrated. This takes you beyond being a "Sabbat Pagan" to a place where all parts of your life work together as a whole and nothing is dismissed as *just* mundane.

In addition, by learning the behind-the-scenes operation of the magical process and coming to know the symbols and techniques that work for you, your spellcraft will be much improved as well. From basic household charms to complex spells, your magic will resonate with you and your environment—it will *work*. Another important task for your intermediate period is to examine your own sense of ethics and moral structure. Explore these issues with honesty and introspection and you can allow your inner sense of right and wrong to guide you in making the correct choices without feeling powerless or fearful.

Of course, whether your magic is for a new lover or the health of the whole planet, it's still peripheral to the primary goal of the advancing Pagan. Above all, we practice a religion, and getting to know and learn from our Deities is our principal objective. This is discussed in the next chapter.

CHAPTER 7

Advanced Ritual

IMAGINE A GROUP OF PAGANS MEETING ON A WINDSWEPT HILL UNDER a full moon. They build a fire, dance and sing, cast a circle, and call on the Lunar Goddess. They have created a temple, a space as sacred and holy as any cathedral, in order to touch the higher presence of the Divine. The time of night is perfect, the fire correctly laid, the altar perfectly dressed. They come with one mind, one intent, one purpose. And the Goddess responds, filling them with Her light and energy. She teaches and guides, answers prayers and requests. She tasks the Pagans based on their needs and expects to be venerated and loved. She will not leave the circle disappointed.

The primary purpose of doing any ritual is to meet and connect with the Deities. In this, Pagans are lucky because our religions tend to be nonhierarchical. You don't need a priest or pastor to intervene for you; you can work with your Gods and Goddesses directly. This is both good and bad. It's good in that we can build a personalized connection that resonates with our souls. It's bad in that it can be hard to grasp that relationship without help.

Coven members have an advantage because they are part of a group of people who are all working to connect to Divinity in a very similar way. Of course, the negative side of group work is that your connection with Deity will still be very personal and there may be times when there's a difference of opinion within the group. In any case, the core reason for ritual stays the same: to connect with and learn from Gods and Goddesses so that we can become more like Them. To my mind, this should be the primary purpose of any religion.

THE PANTHEON GAME

One of most obvious characteristics separating modern Neo-Paganism from other religions is the idea that you can choose your Deities. Most Pagans are familiar with the mythology and cosmology of multiple ancient cultures and may have been involved with several different pantheons. In and of itself, this is not a problem. In fact the lessons and symbolic connections that we can gain from a working knowledge of world religion and mythology are well worth the effort in study and reading. However, this extensive knowledge has caused a number of fascinating debates within the Pagan community.

One of the most controversial is the issue of mixing pantheons. There are many Pagans who frequently call on Gods and Goddesses from different times and cultures and see no problem with it. There are also many people who feel that this is completely inappropriate. In a related issue, some Pagans are concerned about the tendency to switch Deities at the drop of a hat. They feel that the lack of devotion to a particular Deity or pantheon is irreverent. Others feel that the freedom to explore is one of Neo-Paganism's better features.

Finally, there's the issue of the Wiccan Lord and Lady. Many traditional Wiccans call on a God and Goddess with no specific history before They were defined and named by Gerald Gardener. Other Wiccans have historical names for these Deities, or they may switch names, rolling all Goddesses up into the Lady and all Gods into the Lord. In fact "All Goddesses are one Goddess, all Gods are one God, and there is one Initiator"[32] is a commonly accepted point of view among Wiccans. Other Pagans feel this smacks of monotheism and is inherently disrespectful of individual Gods or Goddesses.

I think that most of these issues come from differing definitions and inherent contradictions about the nature of Divinity. The whole point of worshipping Gods and Goddesses is that They are larger / more aware / bigger than ourselves. If They weren't, why would we bother to devote ourselves to Them? Deities aren't just interesting symbol sets, archetypes, or psychological constructs; They are extant beings with Their own personalities, likes, and dislikes. From this point of view, the idea of "summoning" a Deity or "dismissing" one might seem disrespectful. Instead, we ask one or more Deities to join us in ritual or watch over us, and we hope that They do so.

In fact, one school of thought is that we don't choose a God or Goddess at all. Instead, They choose us. From this perspective, once you find the Deity or pantheon you belong to, you then dedicate yourself to that individual Deity or group. Of course, many Pagans haven't settled on a particular tradition yet, so they don't know to Whom they belong. Even so, focusing in one direction can often make for a better, more meaningful relationship with the Divine.

However, there's also nothing inherently wrong with exploring different pantheons or even mixing within the same ritual . . . as long as the Goddesses and Gods approve. Remember that each Deity has His or Her own perspective and personality and may not mesh with all other Deities. A little forethought here can serve you well. Even within the same pantheon, Deities are often very different and may not "get along" well in the circle. The Greek and Roman pantheons are good examples of this phenomenon. Many of the major Goddesses were often in direct competition. And Zeus and Hera never had a very good relationship, despite being married.

If you do call on Deities that don't mix, you'll often find that one Deity may simply not show up; either that or the combined energies will make for chaos instead of harmony within your circle. Still, since most Pagan Deities come from pantheistic cultures, They tend to be less "jealous" than monotheistic Gods who, by definition, want Their worshippers to focus only on Them. I've never felt uncomfortable as a guest at a Pagan circle that called on Deities that I was unfamiliar with. At the same time, I have Gods and Goddesses that I work with and am very devoted to. I wouldn't abandon Them at a moment's notice to go devote myself to someone else. In particular, if you call on a Deity for help and He or She answers your call, you then owe that being a debt of gratitude. A ritual or offering of thanks is not only polite but usually expected by the Deity. And as I said in the section on ethics in the prior chapter, when you work with the Deities, you ignore Their expectations at your peril.

But what about the idea that all Gods and Goddesses are really one? And if They are, then why do They have different names and personalities? It does seem illogical to say that a Goddess of love such as Aphrodite is the same as a Goddess of war and death such as the Morrigan. Yet, there's a certain logic and internal harmony to the idea that all Deities are really the same. I believe that one of the more challenging paradoxes of Deity is that this is both true and untrue.

At a very high level, we are *all* One. Every rock and tree, human and animal, God and Goddess are the same, holistically connected and part of the same energy. Yet, as limited incarnate beings, we don't often operate at this level, even though we may be aware of it. When we work with a particular God or Goddess, it's like working with a single facet of an infinitely huge, magnificent diamond. We can't see or even comprehend the whole in any useful way. So we focus instead on the aspect or aspects that call to us. This is why, although at one level all Gods and Goddesses really are One, on a more personal level They are all very different, with different preferences and areas of interest.

THE SEARCH FOR "GOD"

Many Pagans are still in the realm of searching for the right Deities. Perhaps they started with a certain pantheon and are now exploring to see if something else suits them better. Or, they could simply be in that experimental stage, trying different things to see what works. Sometimes the choice of Deity is a matter of expedience. For example, you find and join a great coven who worships a particular pantheon. As long as you feel the connection, there's absolutely nothing wrong with this. Alternately, you might have a strong interest in several Deities from different pantheons and call on Them for different purposes. Or you might even mix Deities, calling on several Great Mother Goddesses from various cultures and times in the same ritual.

There's another school of thought, however, that says each person has a patron God or Goddess. This is related to the concept of being chosen by a particular Deity. Of course this may not preclude your working with other Gods or Goddesses as well. However, if you find that there is a particular being that you are strongly linked to, there can be a great benefit to concentrating on that one Deity. While the Pagan faiths often hold that we are all clergy, to honestly declare that you are a Priest or Priestess of a particular Deity requires work, dedication, and a great deal of focus on that God or Goddess.

There are several ways you might be linked to a patron Deity. First, there's the issue of heritage. You may have strong ancestral ties to a particular geographical location or ethnic group that gives you a certain insight into the Pagan Deities of that culture. Second, you can consider physical location. This explains why some Americans of European heritage find themselves connecting with American Indian religions. Those Deities are "local" and tied to the land; that can have a strong effect on the people who live there. Third, we can't discount the effect of reincarnation. While not all Pagans believe that we experience multiple lives, for those who do, some may have connections to Deity that predate their current existence. Finally, some people are just picked by a particular God or Goddess for no obvious reason whatsoever. This type of call is as legitimate as any other. We don't have to justify our religion or choice of Deity to anyone.

Imagine for a moment a huge banquet of the Gods. All the Deities of every culture, past and present, are there eating, drinking, and having a great time. This can make an interesting guided meditation or thought exercise, by the way. Just visualizing the seating chart would be fascinating. Over there in the corner is Jehovah, grumpy because He's not the only guest. The Hindu Gods and Goddesses, peacefully munching their vegetarian entrees, sit far from the raucous Valhalla-style feasting of the Norse Pantheon. No one really wants to look too closely at what Kali chose off the menu, but Bride is enjoying milk and honey and Bacchus is already drunk as a lord. If you walked through this banquet, where would you sit? Which Gods would welcome you to Their table and where would you feel most comfortable?

If you are interested in discovering your patron God or Goddess, there are several things you can try:

- **Examine your dreams** for manifestations. Gods or Goddesses can appear to you with advice or information. If a particular Deity appears several times, or the appearance of a Deity corresponds with other omens in your life, that might be a good Deity to be working with right now. For example, you are given a book on German folklore, see a significant formation of geese in the sky, and then dream about a woman who is not only wild but also reminds you of Mother Goose. You probably want to learn more about Frau Holda with her wild Witch rides and nocturnal hunts.

- **Do a divination** specifically asking which Deity you should be working with right now. A typical divination might not give you an exact name, but it may point you in the correct direction. For example, the Magus card in the Tarot might indicate a Deity of magic, such as Thoth or Tezcatlipoca. The rune Kenaz (Torch) could point to a Deity of inspiration such as Bride. As with dream analysis, keep an eye out for related omens.

- **Work magic** to help you discover the right God or Goddess. Create a spell to draw your awareness to the right Deity or to open the channels of communication between you. Use general symbols that represent Deity to you (perhaps a white candle) so that you don't "bias" the spell toward a particular Divine being. And remember to create a sacred space or circle for this kind of work.

- **Pray**. Send out a general call asking that you be able to communicate with your patron Deity. Ask that the God or Goddess you need to work with appear to you through dreams or omens as described above.

Remember, too, that you may be called to a being who is not specifically a Deity but more of a spirit or avatar. Prometheus would be a good example of a human mythological figure whose imagery may speak to you. Various natural beings such as Nyads and Dryads weren't traditionally considered Deities either, yet you can create a powerful relationship with and learn a great deal from them. In the British Isles, many a stream, grove, or standing stone was tied to a minor God or Goddess.

If you experience a manifestation of a particular Deity, then your first goal should be to learn as much about that particular God or Goddess as possible. This has two fundamental purposes. First, it can help you identify the Deity you have experienced. For example, since dreams are symbolic, you may experience a Deity through His or Her aspect as opposed to getting introduced directly. Second, even when you know which Deity has contacted you, learning more about Him or Her can help you connect more strongly.

I recommend a two-pronged approach including both intellectual and inspirational aspects. Begin by studying the mythology of your Deity. For some Gods and Goddess this will be relatively easy. For example, the Greek and Roman Deities are well documented in a relatively unbiased manner. For others this may prove more challenging. In the British Isles, for example, many Deities overlap, and much of the information has been codified not in structured mythologies but in folklore. In addition, over the years the Pagan folklore has been overlaid with a veneer of Christianity. It may take some interpretation and digging to understand the real characteristics of the Deity.

In addition, while each God or Goddess has a unique personality, there are clear examples of multiple Deities who really are effectively the same despite different names. For example, Venus and Aphrodite

or (more arguably) Inanna and Astarte. It's also important to understand the relationships between local "minor" Deities such as the spirits associated with certain trees or holy springs. In Britain, there's a
long tradition of tying ribbons or lengths of cloth to a tree near a
sacred well or spring. Each offering is a wish or prayer for healing,
fertility, safety, and so on. This practice was widespread (and still occurs) no matter which Deity was associated with the site. These patterns can help you codify appropriate forms of worship for your
particular God or Goddess.

As you begin researching the knowledge that ancient people had
about your Deity, you should look for the following types of information:

- **Names and titles**. Many Deities have multiple titles that
  describe Their aspects or powers. For example, Loki is often
  called the "Sly One, the Trickster, the Shape Changer, and the
  Sky Traveler."[33] When you understand those titles, you will gain
  a better understanding of the Deity being described.

- **Plants and animals**. Many Gods and Goddesses are closely
  tied to particular plants and animals. These correspondences can
  create powerful links to call on the Deity in ritual. Demeter is
  associated with corn, barley, and other grains as well as the snake
  and the pig.

- **Holidays**. Ancient people gathered throughout the year at
  specific times to call on the Deities. Some Gods and Goddess are
  associated with holidays that will be familiar to modern Pagans.
  For example, Bride is closely tied to Imbolc. However, some
  Deities have special dates that are specific to Them and not at all
  associated with the Wiccan wheel of the year. November 16 is
  Hecate's night and the festival of Bacchus was celebrated in ancient Rome on March 16 and 17.[34]

- **Regalia and appearance**. What particular Deities wore
  and how they typically appeared to mortals are important hints

about Their natures and the lessons They can teach. For example, Mary is often shown mantled in blue with stars and standing on a crescent moon. Her more Pagan role as Queen of Heaven ties in neatly with her appearance and dress.

- **Behavior and worship.** What ancient Deities did and how They were worshipped can be a great starting point for modern ritual and practice. You may have to make adjustments for modern sensibilities and ethics (you probably won't be performing animal sacrifices, for example), but the basics are still helpful. In addition, you should pay close attention to the behavior of both the Deity and His or Her worshippers. Did devotees of a particular Goddess give up certain foods or behavior? Did a particular God act with wild abandon or intellectual reserve?

After you have explored whatever mythology or folklore you can find, complete your research by examining the work of modern Pagan authors. There are many good books that describe aspects and correspondences for various Deities. They may include all the information above as well as modern additions. While these books can be very helpful, I always recommend going to the earliest sources first. Researching in this way allows you to start with a firm grounding in the *original* practices (or at least the earliest ones recorded). You can then review modern compilations and works with a more critical eye. You will be able to see where a modern author has employed poetic or spiritual license in adding to the original material. These expansions may be perfectly valid, although it will be difficult to judge their veracity without a basis for comparison.

After you have gathered some basic details regarding your chosen God or Goddess, you can use that information to make a direct contact with the Deity. Building this kind of ritual is as personal as (and in some ways very similar to) creating your own spell. You use the symbol set your research has uncovered to help tune yourself to the frequency of your target God or Goddess. For example, a Deity's many titles can be incorporated into the invocation you write. You might decorate your altar with the plants or foods associated with the Deity. You could dress in clothing that's the appropriate style and color, reflecting the original Pagan worshippers. Incense, decoration, timing—correspondences of all types can be incorporated into your ritual.

Don't worry if your research uncovered only minimal facts. Even a little information can be used to create a ritual to help you get in touch with your Deity. You can then use that contact as a basis for learning more about Him or Her. This is where the inspirational information-gathering begins. Nothing you read in a book will be as powerful to you as the details you get directly from a Divine presence. A Goddess's message to you might be as simple as the name you should use to call on Her. Or your patron God might respond with detailed instructions for invoking Him. Write this information down and use it the next time you call on your God or Goddess.

DEALING WITH YOUR DEITIES—REWARDS AND RESPONSIBILITIES

Whether or not you are called to a particular Deity or work with many, there will still be certain responsibilities you must take in order to gain the wisdom, insight, and other rewards that They can bestow on you. This relationship is the core of Pagan practice and can be highly challenging as well as life-changing and beneficial.

Remember, once you've made contact with particular Deities, you can pray to Them for help or advice. However, They may make requests of you as well. For example, They might give you a task or test, ask you to change your behavior, or request certain ritual acts be performed. A lunar Goddess might expect you to leave an offering to Her at every full moon. A God of agriculture might impress you with a strong desire to grow a garden yourself.

Deities don't just ask these things as quid pro quo for their help to you. While any God or Goddess can answer a prayer or give assistance, the Deities' most impressive power is Their ability to impart wisdom. Their requests to you are often more about you and your growth than about Their own needs. This is why, often, the requests They make of us as modern humans are different from ones They may have put to our ancestors. In times when most people lived in agricultural communities, asking for an animal sacrifice would have been perfectly logical and acceptable. After all, on small farms, animals are slaughtered in order to feed the family, even today. To perform that necessary task in honor of a Deity would sanctify the act, not sully it. The point is that it is done mindfully and that a part of the bounty is shared with or given back to the Deity. Yet, today, it would be highly difficult, not to mention illegal, for the modern urban or suburban Pagan to perform such a sacrifice.

What might your Deities ask of you? They might give you a specific task. This could include performing a ritual on a regular basis or at a particular location. They might request a lifestyle change, that you stop a bad habit or adopt a good one. Or they could place a geas on you—some action that you are to perform or, alternately, avoid. Finally, they might not make a direct request so much as affect your unconscious mind. For example, after working with a Deity, you might begin considering life changes or suddenly take an interest in a new area of study, hobby, or activity. These kinds of changes can seem either subtle or shattering. They could affect you in ways that you aren't even aware of until much later, or shake your entire life at once. The details and specifics will depend on your path and relationship with the Divine. The challenges may seem difficult, but the rewards are worth it.

My only possible concrete advice is to take these requests seriously. If you ignore the guidance that a Goddess gives you, you can't then expect Her to provide other guidance when you ask for it. The point of having a relationship with the Divine is that it helps you grow as a person. It's a relationship with a higher being that allows you to connect with the Divinity within as well as outwardly in the world. It demeans the Deities and Their willingness to help us when we treat Them as toys, to be played with when we feel like it and then put back on the shelf and ignored when we don't. But the Deities are also forgiving. If your Goddess presents you with a difficult challenge that you cannot accomplish, that doesn't mean you no longer have a relationship with Her. You may try your hardest but still not achieve success. It could be the challenge itself that's the point and not the outcome.

Alternately, you really could fail at a task. Perhaps you felt called to leave an offering at a certain natural location, but then neglected to do so. Or you offered to do a thank you ritual on a certain date, and then forgot. This is much like breaking a promise to or letting down a friend. Handle it in the same way. Apologize sincerely and do what you can to make it right.

MOTHER GODDESS, BROTHER GOD

It's appropriate that we describe our interaction with our Deities as a relationship. The Deities are very much like the people we have relationships with in our normal lives: friends, acquaintances, and family members. Thinking of Gods and Goddesses in the same way can be very useful for getting the most out of our Pagan religious practice. The way you view particular Deities affects how you approach Them in ritual and prayer, the things you can request of Them, and the treatment you can expect.

Your relationship with a Deity depends on the Deity's character as well as your individual needs as one dedicated to Him or Her. For example, some Deities have reputations for being distant (like Jehovah) or motherly (like Quan Yin) or friendly and protective (like Bride). Some are serious-minded and scholarly (like Horus), while others are energetic and physical (like Thor). Isis is queenly and commands respect, while Pan is friendlier, inviting you to revelry. Some Deities have very well defined roles and qualities, while others are more complex, representing a variety of things at the same time. He-cate is the Goddess of witchcraft, but She's also Queen of Heaven and Earth, a much broader role.

These aspects are part of every Deity's character, inherent to who they are. Like the individual people in our lives, individual Deities have preferences, moods, pet peeves, and personalities. When you call on a particular Deity, you should always begin by taking a close look at the way He or She seems to prefer to relate to mortals. The Greek Pantheon's dislike of hubris and Norse Deities' concern with bravery are two obvious examples. Some Deities are sticklers for form and ritual (Zeus, for example), while others respond better to raw emotion (like Dionysus). This goes beyond simply choosing incense or dressing your altar in the right color. You have to see your Deities as *individuals*—albeit extremely wise and powerful individuals from whom you have something to learn.

Being aware of the types of "personalities" your Deities are isn't just important for crafting ritual. The Deities you choose to invoke can depend in large part on the type of person you are and the type of role models you need. How you see your Deities is as important as how They see you. Some Pagans think of their relationship with their Deities as that of a child to a loving mother and father. Others have more of a student–mentor relationship with their chosen God or God-dess, seeing themselves as apprentices or aspirants to the realm of wisdom. Some see the Gods as siblings or friends whom they admire and want to learn from. These Pagans might look on a God as an admired big brother.

The things we need from our Deities are as individual as the things They need from us. And because of this, some Deities are going to be more appropriate for you to call on than others. For example, if you are struggling with the death of a family member, you may need to seek refuge in the loving arms of one of history's great ancient Mother Goddesses. If you strive to perfect your knowledge in some course of study, find a Deity who appreciates the application of intelligence and approach Him or Her as student to teacher. If you have a problem with authority, however, perhaps you'd be better served by learning your lessons in a setting where you feel more like a friend and less like a worshipper.

One of the primary goals of the majority of Deities seems to be helping us mortals learn the lessons we need to in order to grow spiritually. Different Deities teach in different ways. No doubt you learn best in a particular way as well. Matching your learning style with a Deity's teaching style is hugely helpful in moving forward. For example, some Pagans thrive on structure and logic while others learn better through the application of intuition. The important thing is to remember to play your part in the relationship. For example, if you call on the Lord and Lady as divine parents, you need to respond to their authority as if you were Their child: If They ask you to do some spiritual chore (taking out your astral garbage, for example), it's in your best interest to do so. Reacting like a teenager will only cause stress (as any parent of a teenager can tell you). If, on the other hand, you approach your Deity in more of a sibling role, your actions should be very different: Your big brother or sister Deity might expect you to try to deal with your own problems first. They might even tease you to get you to learn the lessons that you need to learn. After suffering a spiritual "noogie" or two, you will be well motivated to make a change.

As a student to a Deity, you need to stay on your toes. You need to think, analyze, and ask intelligent questions. You should be ready for riddles and puzzles that contain the answers to your questions. If instead, you've squired yourself to a warrior Deity, be ready for quests and challenges of bravery.

This all assumes that having looked at your own needs and learning style, you have the luxury of approaching a Deity who interests you and getting a response. Sometimes, however, things work in reverse. The universe always gives us what we need, not what we think we need. In some cases, Pagans are approached by a Deity instead of the other way around. The Pagan in question probably has some lessons that they can only learn in a particular way or from a particular God or Goddess. Perhaps they don't know their own needs well enough yet to realize the kind of lessons they need to learn.

Viewing Deities in this way might seem rather cold and analytical compared to the warm and very emotional relationships we actually have with Them. However, remembering that we have relationships with our Deities based on both our needs and Theirs can help us deal with some of the questions that we as Pagans might face. For example, if you are dedicated to a particular Deity, would it be a bad idea to call on a different Deity? If you need a cathartic release, whom should you turn to? If you are calling on a Deity and getting no response, what are you doing wrong? Are your needs and learning style in direct conflict with the Deities you've been working with?

In the everyday world, we need to work at making all our relationships as good as possible. It's the same when dealing with the Shining Ones—only even more important because our own growth and progress hinge on the result.

PERSONAL RESPONSIBILITY

One of the core tenets of Pagan religions is the concept of *personal responsibility*. It's such a universal idea that it might even be considered one of modern Paganism's only "commandments": THOU SHALT PRACTICE PERSONAL RESPONSIBILITY. But what does personal responsibility mean? Without a thorough understanding of this commandment and the ways it applies to our lives, it becomes little more than meaningless dogma.

First, personal responsibility means being responsible for our own actions. When we do something, bad or good, we need to face up to the consequences. Note that I said "bad *or* good." It's as important to take credit for doing the right thing as is it to take blame for doing the wrong thing. Pagans who practice personal responsibility don't have time for false modesty. When they've acted rightly, with integrity and according to their own code of ethics, they aren't afraid to accept their rewards. When they've acted foolishly, without regard for others, or put their own ideas of right and wrong onto the people they deal with, they take the blame, apologize, and make whatever efforts are necessary to rectify the situation.

Second, personal responsibility means being responsible for our own lives. Not only do we take responsibility for our actions toward others but we don't ask others to take responsibility for us. While there's nothing wrong with asking for help when you need it, it's important to remember that your life is your own. It is an empowering but also sometimes frightening fact that Pagans should always remember: No one else can deal with their issues, problems, or duties. Indeed, when you give up responsibility for your own life, you give up your ability to exercise the True Will and magical power necessary to further spiritual growth.

Third, we need to make sure we are taking care of those who *are* our personal responsibility. We may consciously choose to take responsibility for family, friends, children, and pets. In some cases this exchange is reciprocal. For example, spouses typically take some responsibility for one another. In others, it's part of our role to take responsibility for those who can't (like our children, both two- and four-footed). When you make this kind of commitment to someone else, it's important to honor that commitment. Sometimes, we are moved to try to take on responsibility for someone else—for example by giving well-meaning advice—but even if your intentions are good, it won't always work as well as you might like. Sometimes you can't, and indeed shouldn't, take responsibility for other people, even though they seem to need it or have a problem taking responsibility for themselves.

Finally, part of taking personal responsibility is being responsible for our own emotions and reactions. In our day-to-day interactions, we don't have control over the things that other people say, do, or believe.

But we do have control over our own responses. This doesn't mean we never get angry or upset. Indeed, taking responsibility for our own emotions often means allowing ourselves to get legitimately angry when the situation warrants. However, it also means not letting our emotions get out of control without good reason. Responsible Pagans don't go home mad and kick the cat.

It can be difficult to practice personal responsibility in a society where it's not often valued or praised. However it's only through following this "commandment" that we can really take control of our lives and create meaningful change. In additional, it's through the responsibility we take for the people we care about that we learn what perfect love and trust really mean.

CREATING RITUALS

As with spellcraft, there's a misconception among some Pagans that ritual work has to be complex, lengthy, or difficult. And, of course, there may be times when it's all three. But it doesn't necessarily have to be. It can be simple, unplanned, even spontaneous, and still be powerful. It all depends on the purpose of your ritual. Yes, rituals are always about connecting with Deity (at least according to my definition), but there are a number of ways you can accomplish this depending on your intended results. You can leave an offering, converse through prayer, extend an invitation, or manifest the Deity through your body.

Note that in much Pagan and Magical writing, there's some common confusion with the terms "evoking" and "invoking" and different people define those terms in different ways. Both words come from the Latin *vocare,* "to call," and have similar meanings. Both include the definition "to call forth," with the focus on being "by incantation." *Evoke* includes the additional definitions "to bring to mind" or "to recreate imaginatively."[35] Some authors use *evoke* to mean "inviting into the circle" and *invoke* to mean "inviting into your body."

Others use *invoke* to mean both kinds of interaction, with no clear delimiter between the two.

To avoid confusion, I use the terms *invite* and *invoke*. Inviting a Deity means that you ask Him or Her to be with you in the circle, much like inviting a friend to dinner. Deities invited to ritual will usually appear in noncorporeal or energy form. Invoking a Deity means that you call the Deity into the body of a ritual participant. This is typically a much more difficult process—particularly for the person whose consciousness will be sublimated to that of the God or Goddess. Keep in mind that, when many printed rituals ask you to invoke the God and Goddess, they really mean that you are to ritually invite Them to join you, not call Them into your body.

No way of connecting with a Deity is better than any other. Each method has its uses and appropriate times. A standard Wiccan ritual would likely involve casting a circle, calling the quarters, invoking (or inviting) the Lord and Lady, etc. However, lighting a candle, saying a prayer, and leaving an offering in a sacred spot are as useful and powerful in their place. It all depends on the purpose of your ritual. So what are some common reasons to have a ritual, and what might be involved?

Holiday rituals are commonly performed with others and involve acknowledging the role of Deity for a particular day. The ritual may involve asking for some guidance or boon over the coming months, but energy is often raised simply to experience and share in the celebratory feeling. Many times, these rituals are more of a party that you invite the Deities to rather than a solemn or serious event. Feasting is a common activity at this kind of ritual.

While some traditions attempt to invoke their Deities at every ritual, this is not always necessary. However, to invite your Deities to manifest Themselves into the body of a ritual participant is a powerful way to connect with and benefit from Their energy and wisdom. The purpose of this ritual might be as simple as facilitating that connection, or might be partnered with any other ritual purpose (like prophecy).

When done correctly, this kind of ritual tends to require a lot of energy and effort. Yet it can also be uplifting, life-changing, and very intense. You are hosting Higher Beings and it behooves you to be a good host. When you ask the Queen to dinner, it's wise to consider what you will do when she arrives. While this is true anytime you invite the Deities, it is particularly true when you wish to invoke a God or Goddess into yourself. Not everyone has a talent for this kind of work.

Spellcraft doesn't necessarily require the presence of the Deities, but there may be times when you want Their input or help. A powerful healing ritual is one obvious example. Another is when you wish to raise a lot of energy to use for some larger purpose (the environment, peace on earth, etc.). Inviting the Deities to work with you can give your magic a powerful boost. Remember, however, that it may not be appropriate to invite them to every love or job spell that you do.

Unlike divination or augury, prophecy comes directly from the Deities. Traditionally, this involved invoking the God or Goddess into the body of the prophet or prophetess. The person would then speak as the Deity, his or her own consciousness sublimated. This isn't more common because of the difficulty, not only in invoking, but in sublimating the conscious mind enough to allow the voice of the Deity to come through unhindered. Another method of incorporating prophecy into a ritual is to invite your God or Goddess to influence the outcome of divination performed during the ritual. Certain holidays (like Samhain or All Hallows Eve) are traditional times for divination.

One of the simplest forms of ritual, making offerings to your Deities can be a very powerful way to strengthen your connection to Them. While rituals often revolve around asking Deities for information or help, making an offering is your chance to give back and acknowledge Their contribution to your spiritual growth. Offerings can be made part of any type of ritual, but all that's really needed is a grateful spirit and a few moments' time. While some types of ritual require a certain amount of effort to connect with the Deities, an offering (being a one-way connection) is much simpler. Dedicate your gift to the right party and He or She *will* get the message.

Many Pagans seem to think that Christianity has given prayer a bad rap. However, there's nothing wrong with having a little chat with your chosen God or Goddess. This is also a very simple way of acknowledging Their help as well as asking for it. While you may not get a direct response, if you are sincere you will get an answer. It can come through omens, dreams, or simply instinctual knowledge.

Of course, there are as many reasons to perform a ritual as there are Pagans to perform them. But the prior list should give you an idea about the breadth of what can be considered ritual practice. From toasting your Goddess at dinner to invoking your God in an all-night ecstatic ceremony, any act you do with the Deities in mind is a ritual. Yet for more complex rites, there are some common components and parts.

THE PARTS OF RITUAL

If you read published rituals, you begin to notice a pattern of repeating motifs common to most of the more complex rituals. While leaving an offering or saying a prayer of thanks requires nothing more than your Will and attention, there are good reasons for the practices that have become traditional parts of ritual:

- **Cleansing.** A typical first step in ritual is to clean the ritual area and participants. This has a dual purpose: first, to make the space as comfortable as possible, neat and free from clutter and distractions, and second, to facilitate the change in consciousness necessary for a successful ritual. A ritual bath or shower will rinse unwanted energy from your body. Sweeping the ritual space does the same for the location. It's a way of putting on a certain mindset, like you might put on special ritual garb. Much of the lore surrounding what you can and cannot use for ritual (only handmade objects, natural fibers, certain colors) is simply to help the participants reach the correct mindset.

- **Casting.** As mentioned in the chapter on spellcraft, a circle acts as both an energy barrier and a gateway between the worlds—both key for working with the energy of the Deities. It's important to have a sacred space in which to perform your ritual. This is true of any sacred place, from a consecrated temple or grove to the circle you draw on your living room floor. Much of the first part of published rituals involves casting the circle, but all you really need to create a sacred space is awareness and Will. The gateway allows your interaction with the Divine to flow much more smoothly, while giving you a sense of security and keeping your energy contained.

- **Calling.** Inviting or invoking your Deities and other helpful spirits is the primary focus of ritual. This is where knowledge of your Deities' preferences and symbols comes into play. This symbol usage is much the same as in creating a spell. If your Goddess is associated with roses, copper, swans, and honey, you use these things in the ritual circle to help attune the vibration to a particular frequency. The symbols help you focus on the vibration of your Deities and make Them feel comfortable in joining you. This part of the process often involves a change of consciousness or an altered state, particularly if the purpose is to invoke rather than invite. In either case, you will want to do everything you can to make and strengthen a link to Them.

- **Charging.** A common part of many group rituals is the raising of a cone of power. Energy may be raised to facilitate the purpose of the ritual (like a request for help or a healing spell); however, it also serves a second purpose. By raising a great deal of energy within the close space of the circle, you effectively raise the vibrational rate of the ritual's participants. Since the astral plane, the Deities, and noncorporeal beings in general vibrate at a higher rate, the raising of energy helps connect you to those higher states. Sometimes energy is raised before calling on the Deities, sometimes after, and sometimes both. This depends on the flavor and purpose of your ritual.

- **Breaking.** After the ritual has been completed, there's usually a reverse of the prior steps. Excess energy is grounded, the Deities and other beings are thanked, and the circle is uncast. Sometimes these steps get short shrift in rituals, but it's vitally important that they be performed thoroughly. One reason is that any beings you call must be thanked and then politely asked to leave. While we're always in connection to all things, including our Deities, there's only so much direct contact we can handle on a day-to-day basis. I've experienced what it's like to have a Deity linger past the end of a ritual. It can be both strange and difficult to deal with. A second reason for making sure you break cleanly and completely is that you need to take yourself and any other participants back to normal vibrational levels. Normal for you, that is. Everyone typically vibrates at a different level, and while higher is generally better, there's only so high you can go and still sustain yourself in the material world. That's why eating at the end of a ritual is so important. It's a normal and grounding experience that also celebrates a ritual well done.

These steps aren't mandatory. Nor do they have to be done in a particular order or way. When you create rituals for yourself, you have the ability to tailor them to your specifications. However, it's important to remember the reasons for these various steps so that you can understand the structure you are building. For example, when I leave an offering I take a moment to cleanse my mind of negative thoughts and push out a cleansed space around me, making a quickie circle. I call on my Deity before leaving the offering and then thank Him or Her and collect my energy around me again, effectively wrapping up a mini ritual.

Little Rituals

Unlike the more elaborate circle-casting brand, some rituals are the religious equivalent of folk or kitchen magic. They require few tools, little time, and no fancy structure. We might call them devotions rather than rituals. They include things like asking a quick blessing before meals, speaking with your God or Goddess at night before bed, or keeping a shrine to which you regularly give attention. These actions can be just as powerful as a major ritual and invocation because they form part of your everyday life.

Fitness experts say that it's better to exercise for twenty minutes three times a week than once a week for an hour. It's the same with ritual. The more often you can incorporate devotions to or conversations with your Deities, the closer you will become. And, ironically, it's actually easier to perform many small devotions than a large ritual because they fit more easily into a busy schedule. There are occasions, of course, when you will want to make the time for something more elaborate, but on a day-to-day basis it's easier to give up just a few minutes here and there than to devote an hour every evening to the task.

Morning and evening are often good times to do a small devotion because people typically already have a waking and bedtime routine that they follow. I know that I have to follow a pretty regular pattern in the morning, particularly during the week. Any change or deviation tends to throw off my whole schedule. Under these conditions, it can be hard making changes. But once made, you'll find your little ritual as much a part of your waking up schedule as having coffee or brushing your teeth.

Routine and Spontaneity—Finding Your Balance

The amount of elaboration and theater you go through for a ritual will depend on whether the particular ritual is done as a group effort or performed solitary; your own preferences also come into play, of course. Some rituals are very structured, while others simply seem to happen without a lot of planning. From attending various rituals in the past, I've observed that people typically have an aptitude and preference for a particular level of structure. And the nature of the ritual may also demand a certain amount of organization. As part of your quest to know yourself, you will want to give some thought to the kind of ritual work that best suits you. Following your instincts will make the rituals you do that much more effective.

In a group situation, people will typically need the cues that a routine provides. Participants will benefit from a certain amount of stage direction in order to work together and fulfill the purpose of the ritual. This is not only true of Pagan rituals. Catholicism is an excellent example of a religion that relies heavily on prescribed rituals and ordered worship. And even the Protestant faiths usually include a program that describes the parts of the service, hymns to be sung, and times for prayer and offering. When you are worshipping alone, however, you can choose to be a lot more flexible. Some Pagans enjoy the theater of a well-done ritual or need the focus of the various actions and objects. As you advance, however, you should begin to consider those trappings optional as opposed to necessary. You can, with some practice and focus, cast a circle, interact with the Deities, and even perform the entire ritual in your head.

The benefit to having a routine, even if you perform it alone or in your own thoughts, is that, as you repeat the structure in ritual after ritual, it begins to facilitate the correct mindset. That is, the act of speaking certain words or performing certain actions will trigger the change in consciousness you need to connect with your Deities. In addition, if you're a disorganized person, as I am, having a base structure can keep you on track. One disadvantage in having a standard ritual method that you stick to is the risk that it will become rote, without will and energy behind it, and therefore ineffective. Another disadvantage is that it might limit what rituals you can perform and when you can perform them.

Performing rituals spontaneously, on the other hand, allows you to integrate them more fully into your life. You don't have to wait until the right moon phase or travel to a sacred spot. You can connect with the Deities freely, according to need or inclination. This also allows you to keep your rituals fresh and potentially more powerful. The big negative in complete spontaneity is that it doesn't always work for a group. When you work with others, everyone will need some kind of idea as to what's going to happen next. The exception would be people who are very close and work together a great deal in a spontaneous way. Another negative is that the ritual could become disjointed or chaotic. You might leave out some necessary component of the ritual.

The best solution for most Pagans is a balance between the two. While I know people who really thrive doing spontaneous, even chaotic rituals, most of us want a certain amount of structure, even when we're working alone. Yet, as advancing Pagans, we should resist the temptation to simply pick a ritual out of a book and read it verbatim. Our Gods and Goddesses appreciate the creative effort we put into our connection with them.

WHEAT FROM CHAFF—LISTENING SKILLS

So, you've crafted a ritual to invoke a particular Goddess. You did the research to find Her correspondences, wrote an invitation, and included some lovely verse. You cleansed, cast, called . . . but nothing seems to have happened. There are times when performing a ritual feels like organizing a party that no one shows up for . . . this is to be expected. While we are all connected and the Deities continuously surround us, there are times when closer communication just isn't possible or practical. Acknowledging this and learning to recognize it are important steps in improving your rituals.

When you call but no one seems to answer, you will want to spend some time thinking about why it might have happened that way. But first, remember to complete your ritual. It's still useful to demonstrate your devotion and respect and, whether or not your chosen Deity appears, you may still have generated a lot of energy that can be put to good use. Also, don't forget your breaking procedures, like grounding out excess energy and uncasting the circle. Otherwise you may feel unbalanced and disconnected.

There are many reasons that you might not powerfully connect with a particular Deity. It could be that your state of mind or of health wasn't appropriate. If you are distracted or ill, prayer is the best way to speak with your chosen God or Goddess. The rigors of performing a more complex ritual may simply exacerbate the situation. You must be in a centered and focused state in order to hear and connect with a Divine being. This is much more difficult when you have something else on your mind or are suffering with the flu. However, if you are down—physically, emotionally, or mentally—it's better to do something than do nothing. This is when you need Divine guidance and help the most. But to invoke in an all-night ritual under those conditions might be too much.

Another reason that you may feel a lack of communication might involve the Deity or Deities you chose to call. Perhaps you picked Deities whose personalities and natures conflict. In that case, one or all may not appear. Or perhaps this is a Deity you've never worked with before, one who's not right for you. We're not going to click with every God or Goddess out there. Yes, they are fundamentally all part of the great whole, but, practically speaking, they are also distinct and individual beings. The way I figure it, if you invoke or invite a Deity who doesn't connect with you, He or She just won't show up. The response will be similar to saying "Not one of mine, sorry." I've been to numerous group rituals where I definitely felt the presence of the Divine even though I wouldn't normally connect to the Deities being called . . . but someone there does, or it wouldn't have worked. Pagan Deities tend to be tolerant and inclusive, but to call on a Deity you have to first resonate with His or Her energy.

The trouble comes when beginners aren't aware of this situation and don't know that nothing happened. When you're starting out, it can take time to even sense Divine beings when they *do* show up. But as an advancing Pagan, you will most likely have had at least one intense connective experience. Use that as the standard by which you judge all other rituals you do. Obviously, not every ritual we perform will result in the most powerful level of communication. In fact many rituals aren't designed to do so. But if communication is your goal, then keep working and improving your sensitivity and technique until you meet it.

TEMPLES: YOUR SOUL, MIND, BODY, FAMILY, HOMETOWN, COUNTRY, PLANET, UNIVERSE

Many books on Paganism talk about the home altar or magic room. These are both examples of temples. A temple is a sacred space and a place of worship, and part of the path of Paganism is to build or sustain these areas of the sacred. But temples encompass more than just physical locations or magical circles. No doubt you're familiar with the saying "Your body is a temple." Despite the subtle current of self-denial inherent in this idea, it actually is true. There are many other temples as well, including your own mind, your hometown, and the whole universe. A holistic worldview says that every place is potentially a temple. So what does this mean for the advancing Witch or Pagan?

You probably have temples where you've done a lot of work—your soul for example, or your family. But there may also be temples you've neglected—perhaps your body or your town. In fact there may be temples that seem beyond help (like our planet). But, in light of the power of magic and ritual, this is not really true. Our prayer for world peace or magic for tolerance does make a difference. Why, considering this power, do we sometimes neglect some of these temples?

I know that I sometimes get overwhelmed by all the problems out there, confused and stymied about how to deal with them. Environmental issues are an example. I want to do what I can to be environment-sensitive, but the issues are so broad and there's so much to consider that I don't know where to start or what more I can do. But doing nothing isn't the right answer either. One solution is to set small goals in a number of areas. Instead of simply deciding to be more aware of the environment, I decide to recycle more consistently or to compost my organic waste. Instead of a blanket proclamation that I will "eat better," I decide to cook at home more and try to avoid fast food.

I know these steps sound very small. But it's better to have a small goal that you can meet than a large one that you cannot accomplish. People, in the United States particularly, can be very extremist. They don't simply want to lose weight; they want to lose twenty pounds in a week. They don't want to exercise; they want to look like Mr. or Ms. Universe. They don't want to keep their house neater; they want to live in *House and Garden*.

Why am I bringing this up now? Because ritual work is all about connecting with your Deities *in order to improve yourself.* And you do that not only by listening to their lessons but by doing work in your various temples. When your mind, heart, spirit, or house is in disarray, you're building barriers that keep you from knowing your own Divine nature. And while you may never make huge changes in your town, your country, or the universe, you have an obligation as a citizen to do what you can. But for many of us, the question is Where do I start?

Large goals aren't impossible to meet, but there's the tendency to give up when we don't meet them. If you can't lose twenty pounds a week, why bother changing your eating habits at all? If you don't have the skills or wealth to make your home a showplace, who wants to even try decorating? The truth is, if you set a realistic, achievable goal, not only are you more likely to meet it, it's more likely to make a real, long-term difference in your life or the lives of others. Being realistic is really just being honest with yourself. I know I'm not going to get up every morning at 4 A.M. and go to the gym for an hour-long work-out. But with a little effort, I can start walking the dog more often.

This is the kind of inner truth-telling that we need to do if we're going to know ourselves better and make positive changes in all our different temples.

FOOD FOR THOUGHT—A PLEA
FOR MEMORIZATION

Despite being solitary, I've been to and participated in a number of rituals over the years and have even had a hand at creating group rituals myself. Some have been amazingly powerful, moving experiences; others, not so moving. You've probably experienced a few less than stellar rituals yourself: one that was boring, or too long, or inappropriate in some way. I've seen many of these mistakes, and have made some of them myself. With a group, it's not always easy to build a ritual that will please and touch everyone.

But there's one mistake I see over and over that I simply do not understand. I call it the problem of the paper-rattling ritual. So many times I see group rituals where the participants are handed a sheaf of papers at the beginning and expected to perform the ritual while reading along. These papers contain every word of the ritual, everyone's lines as well as stage direction. It's like a script for a play. Of course, in one respect a ritual *is* a play—a work of sacred theatre with the purpose of getting everyone together and connecting with the Divine. However, a ritual isn't a play performed for an audience or even for the participants; it's a play for the Divine.

In addition, for most plays the actors usually have the script in advance. Not so for these rituals. Usually the start of the ritual is the first anyone's seen of the script. I've even seen cases where someone who's not even directing wrote the ritual. That is, even the high priestess and priest have never seen this particular script before. Both the leaders and ritual participants are confused, squinting at paragraphs of text in candlelight, missing their lines and cues, mangling pronunciation, and generally losing their way.

With a little advanced preparation, this doesn't have to be the norm. We can have beautifully prepared rituals that really move the participants, without having to work through fifteen pages of script. It's going to be very difficult, if not impossible, for group members to reach the necessary state of altered consciousness when they're confused about what's going on and too busy reading. How can you help raise energy to invoke a Deity when the HP is busy mumbling "open the portal . . . we ask thee . . . light candle . . . oh, I light the candle now" because she's never seen the material before? The answer is that you can't and it will adversely affect the outcome.

The only solution is to take the time and effort to memorize the ritual in advance. What? I hear you asking. How can I memorize fifteen pages? Well, obviously that's going to be a difficult feat, but with a well-constructed ritual, you shouldn't have to. You won't have to rattle papers, everyone will know what's going on, and you can focus instead on the real work of the ritual: contacting your God and/or Goddess. Here are some suggestions for building rituals that allow you to avoid the paper-rattling problem:

- **Reduce the number of spoken words in the ritual.** Many of the written rituals I've seen are filled with bulky blocks of text. They may actually read pretty well on paper, but it's obvious that they were conceived at the keyboard and never read out loud. Ritual is about focusing the energy of the participants onto the same "wave." And that work doesn't really take any words at all. Make each word count and include fewer of them.
- **Simplify the language.** As a writer and lover of poetry, I appreciate stylized language. But there's no reason to sprinkle our rituals with "thees" and "thous." If the language of the rituals is composed in the way we speak, it will be much easier to remember. Even if some parts are stylized (such as a poetic invocation), not everything has to be in the language of the Middle Ages.
- **Share the wealth.** One person should not be doing all the work of the ritual. Sure, there might be a single creator, but he or she

should be working with and sharing ideas for the ritual throughout the process. If you have lines for others in your group, they should have these lines in advance (and not five minutes in advance; I'm talking a week or more). If you have an overall structure, you should let everyone know what it is. This is particularly true for portions of the rituals where everyone takes a turn speaking or performing some action. Sure, some rituals are more open than others, inviting people who aren't members of the group. However, the core membership should still share the effort of both creating the ritual and memorizing the lines. In addition, if you expect guests at your rituals, you should build the ritual in a way that allows them maximum participation without needing to memorize anything on short notice or read off a sheet of paper.

- **Do your own work.** Despite the necessary cooperation between group members, there's still going to be one person who's primarily in charge of the event. Typically the HP, this person invokes or invites, delivers the reading, handles much of the action, and coordinates the ritual. This person should also be instrumental in creating the ritual. She can't simply be handed some material beforehand and expected to do a good job.
- **Don't hand out every word in advance.** I've seen this problem numerous times. Even when the material has been practiced and is well delivered, the other participants end up being more involved in keeping their place and reading along than in the ritual itself. Even if you choose to use notes or cue cards for certain sections, not everyone needs to have them. Simply make sure you cue people for the parts of the ritual that are theirs. You'll have a much more focused group.
- **Consider the parts of the ritual.** Many rituals for major Sabbats include a lesson about the nature and symbolism of the holiday. Your regular group should understand the basics in advance, but you may have some new ideas you want to talk about, or you may be expecting some guests or other participants. In church, this part of the ceremony is typically called the

"reading" or "lesson." Another important part of the ritual is going to be the invocation (or invitation), where the high priestess or priest calls on the Deity or Deities to be with or enter into the participants. Which part of the ritual would be harmed less by reading, as opposed to memorizing? There's no reason that a four-page dissertation on the meaning of Imbolc can't be read aloud. Just make sure the reader is familiar with the material and has read through it before, preferably several times. But the invocation or invitation is going to be difficult to do correctly while reading from a paper. In fact, memorizing your invocation should be your highest priority.

- **Consider stage direction.** What tools are you going to be waving around? Will you need your hands free? If you have some notes to follow, where will you put them? If you give notes to the other participants, where will they put them? A bit of thought in advance will make for a much smoother ritual. Especially since the only thing worse than a group of people heads down and focused on a printed script is a group trying to juggle lit candles with the crumpled script in hand.
- **Take advantage of your group mind.** If you work regularly with the same people, you can take advantage of the fact by designing rituals around a core set of actions that always remain the same. The method for casting the circle, the calling of the quarters (if you do so), the basic sequence of events: all these can remain the same every time. Soon everyone will learn the parts and be able to cast or uncast without having to reinvent the wheel or struggle to memorize anything new.
- **Learn to use your voice.** Only peripherally related to memorization, it's still an important part of ritual work. I think that many people are so used to reading their rituals, they never have a chance to practice their delivery. If you are invoking the Goddess, don't just read your lines, *emote* them. Really resonate the power within you through your voice. Oration used to be considered an important part of the classical education. Learn to speak clearly, to enunciate well, and to breathe from the diaphragm at the correct times.

Of course, in even the most well constructed ritual, things will go wrong. Candles refuse to light, people miss cues and forget lines, the weather or nearby traffic noise can refuse to cooperate. This doesn't mean that the ritual was a failure. The Deities respect all our efforts to contact them and perfection isn't required. All that's really needed is a willing heart, the right intent, and the dedication to have the very best ritual possible.

CHAPTER 7 EXERCISES

Pagan Lent

Catholics observe Lent from Ash Wednesday to Easter Sunday, a period of forty days. During that time, they keep a personal resolution to give something up as part of their religion. Pagans aren't typically into that kind of self-denial and find the concept strange. I remember being baffled when my best friend in high school gave up chocolate for Lent. Suffering or burdening oneself for the sake of spirituality seems somehow wrong to the Pagan mindset. Our religions are about experiencing joy and appreciating beauty, not denial and deprivation.

Yet there's a long history of people making such sacrifices in order to become closer to the Divine. From Hindus' vegetarianism to Buddhist monks' celibacy, the idea behind Lent exists in many faiths beyond Christianity. The difference between true self-sacrifice and masochistic self-denial is in the reasons behind the act—no matter what faith you profess. For example, if you give something up as an exercise of Will or to improve who you are, it can be a spiritual experience. This is very different from practicing Lent as an exercise in martyrdom or because of a poor sense of self-worth. And this kind of dedicatory act doesn't *necessarily* have to involve giving something up. It might, in fact, be about taking something on.

There are some very good reasons to consciously make changes in your life in this way (whether you are breaking an old habit or establishing a new one). First, when done with the right mindset, it can be a marker of your spiritual progress. Resolving to make changes can also be a kind of long initiatory rite to help you move to a new stage. You can use these kinds of tasks to prove something important to yourself. Finally, commitment to change is fundamentally an exercise of your Will, and this can both strengthen you as a person and strengthen your connection with the Divine. In fact, exercising your Will in this way can help open the doors to magic in your life. After all, magic is causing change by the exercise of Will. The point is to pick a resolution that will act to advance you on your path and then stick to it. For example, you might resolve to meditate each evening before bed, worship outdoors, or finally finish that philosophical tome.

Of course, Pagans wouldn't be making these kinds of resolutions before Easter (unless, perhaps, they were dedicated to Eostre). In the U.S., January 1 is the traditional time for making resolutions, but many Pagans celebrate Samhain or All Hallows Eve as the end of the old year. This might be an optimal time for making a resolution to give something up. You could endeavor to give it up forever, or perhaps just until Yule (the time of new birth for many Pagans). For resolutions focused on bringing something new into your life, you could shift to the other side of the calendar, to Beltain or May Eve. Of course, depending on the calendar you work with, any time would work.

Pagan Rosary

The rosary is another good idea that is too often associated only with Christianity. In truth, many religions use prayer or meditation beads as part of their worship. For example the Muslim, Bahai, Hindu, and Buddhist faiths all use strings of beads for prayer or meditation.

You can buy beads meant for prayer at most metaphysical shops and over the Internet; however, as with most things, it's more powerful to create your own. First, decide what the purpose of your beads will be. A string of prayer beads could act as a dedication to a particular Deity, a meditation tool, or even a personal affirmation reminder. You could have a wheel-of-the-year prayer-bead string that takes you through different holidays, or a lunar string for the phases of the moon. In fact you could take this a step further and create these strings as teaching tools to help others learn about different aspects of your faith.

Once you have determined a purpose for your prayer beads, the next step is to decide on one or more prayers to connect with the beads themselves. For example, you could write short invocations to your God or Goddess, or pick meaningful sayings or poems or even mantras or meditative sounds (like *ohm* or *aum*). In the Catholic rosary, different sized beads have different prayers associated with them. You can have as many or as few different prayers in your rosary as you like; however, you will need to memorize all the items you pick.

Finally, you need to decide how many beads to include, what kinds of beads will be appropriate, and at what intervals different beads should occur. Give this some thought. Numerological symbolism is important and can connect with the deep unconscious mind. The materials, shapes, and sizes can all improve your spiritual connection or meditative state. Bead shops will commonly carry a number of different materials, including semiprecious stones and minerals. In addition, you can use natural or found objects.

For example, a lunar rosary can use silver beads shaped like full and crescent moons, and the actual pattern of waxing and waning throughout a whole year or groups of threes. A rosary to an Earth Goddess may include wood or stone. Acorns and natural holey stones would make for wonderful natural prayer beads, especially when strung in intervals of nines and fours. Beads for the Horned Lord may include antler and pinecones or amber (petrified pine resin). Let your intuition and symbolic knowledge be your guide. The final step could be to consecrate or bless the beads for their purpose.

Now you can use the prayer beads to meditate or communicate with your Deities, or hang them as part of a protective spell. Note that you could make a connection here to the witches' ladder, a braided cord strung with beads, feathers, or other objects and used as part of a spell. But the most appropriate use of prayer beads would, naturally, be to pray with.

CONCLUSION

Whether we're conducting an elaborate holiday celebration or reciting an evening prayer, any ritual we perform is part of the core of Pagan religious practice. And if we are sincere and devoted, we can be sure that our rituals are being heard. Far from considering the Divine a sideline or occasional event, the advancing Pagan will benefit from including it in all aspects of life. From asking favors to being given a task, every time we connect with our Deities we grow closer to Them and have a greater opportunity to learn from Their wisdom. And while we can learn a lot from written sources, both ancient and modern, the best knowledge comes from our own intuition and personal connection to the Divine.

With practice, this connection can move beyond the confines of ritual and into our everyday lives. We can begin honing our Wills to improve ourselves, come to see ourselves as part of the universe, and open ourselves to building the various temples in which we reside. Seeing our world and every being as sacred can begin to heal the sense of separation that afflicts us all. Beyond any faith or particular pantheon, this is the purpose and benefit of religion.

As Pagans, we have only ourselves to guide this process. Choosing the right Deities, building connections, and working toward integration—these are every Pagan's personal responsibility. Yet, without the need for formal clergy, we can connect to the Divine on an individual level, without interference and requiring no interpretation. All we need are the basic tools of ritual structure and knowledge of the Divine energy.

Whether you're practicing magic or ritual, one of the most powerful tools you have at your disposal is the ability to reach an altered state of consciousness. It can improve your ability to perform magic as well as connect you to your God or Goddess. Yet no area of Witchcraft has commonly been more veiled in secrecy. From "flying potions" and ecstatic trances to invocation and prophecy, reaching other levels of consciousness is a powerful ability that truly marks the advancing Pagan.

CHAPTER 8

Altered States of Consciousness

THE MORE I PROGRESS ON MY SPIRITUAL JOURNEY, THE MORE I REALIZE that the term "occult" is a misnomer. Far from being hidden or secret, the world is actually teeming with spiritual knowledge. The trick is to know where to look and what questions to ask . . . and to be ready for the answers. From books to dreams to places of natural beauty, the universe is ready to gift us with the keys we need to unlock the mysteries. However, there *are* still secrets. Occult knowledge does exist, waiting for the dedicated seeker to discover.

Beyond our normal, day-to-day consciousness lie completely different—or *other*—realms. These magical places are hidden from all but the most devoted aspirants to wisdom. Like the journeyman or -woman, you must travel to these destinations to discover their secrets. The trick is that the doors to these lands are within our own minds, and we have to alter our normal state of consciousness to unlock them.

The ability to unlock the door and move into the other realms is critical to many of the areas we've discussed. Beyond that, the lands of the mind, linked as they are to lands at higher planes, are filled with insights, help with problems, access to various powers, and all sorts of beings. Much can be learned and gained from exploring them.

LOSING CONTROL AND TAKING THE RISK

We live in a very rational culture. Even Pagans, believing as we do in so many nonrational things, are affected daily by the dominant mindset. It can be difficult to move past our busy brains and into more intuitive realms. If you've ever been frightened to speak in public or perform before a crowd, you know the effect your own inhibitions can have on you. It's the same when attempting a change in consciousness. Our rational mind inhibits our ability to let go and simply experience, at an instinctual level, the landscape of our own inner world. Moving from those areas to others of noninternal origin is doubly difficult. Yet, we must overcome these restraints if we're going to progress.

The first major roadblock is our need for control. Moving into a trance state is primarily a matter of experiencing each present moment, without analysis or judgment. We have to surrender control of ourselves and our rational minds. For example, if you are dancing at a ritual (whether solitary or group), do you ever have a problem just letting yourself move without interference from your conscious mind? Do you perhaps feel silly, ashamed of your body, fearful of offending others? All these are hindrances to achieving the altered state that ecstatic dance can engender. If you are meditating, can you keep your mind silent and ignore distractions? You cannot reach a deep trance level if you're worried about mundane concerns or the neighbors' dog barking.

There are ways of reducing inhibitions and overcoming our rational minds. Just as a beer or two will make people brave enough to sing Karaoke or ask someone to dance, certain practices can distract or confuse our rational brains so that we can slip past to the nonrational.

The second roadblock to altering consciousness is our fear. Releasing control, and the techniques to help us do so, can be very frightening. We may fear "losing our minds" and not being able to return. Or we might be nervous about the repercussions of the intrusion of the everyday world. What would happen, for example, if in the middle of a trance, someone came knocking on the door? Finally, there is a fundamental human tendency to fear change, the unknown, and the different. Pagans are, by their nature, less prone to this than some;

however, most of us still struggle with it. Finally, we can have legitimate fears about what we might discover about ourselves during a trance.

But if we are going to enjoy effective ritual and magic, we must take the risk and overcome our fears. Some people have a definite knack for this kind of work, while others don't . . . and very deep work can be risky. However, it is valuable to explore altering our consciousness to the limits of our ability, and to keep practicing. This is what separates the shamanic paths, including Pagan ones, from other religions. Our path is *participatory*. We are expected to act as our own guide and experience things personally, and not through an intermediary. That means we need to learn to lose ourselves in altered states, because we can't always rely on someone else to do it for us.

MOVING PAST VISUALIZATION

As imaginative creatures, we have the ability to visualize or create detailed pictures in our heads. We do this when we have ordinary dreams, when we fantasize, and when we replay a scene from our past. Changing our consciousness, however, is much more than just imagining. I've been to a number of rituals that included a guided meditation. While this kind of group meditative work can be very valuable, there's also the danger that the participants will simply picture what the guide is saying, instead of experiencing it.

It's the same when you cast a spell. You can't simply think about what you want; you have to *feel* it. You must take what you can imagine and symbolize it so that your subconscious mind can access it. When trying to alter your state of consciousness, you must still your conscious mind completely so that your experience can move directly to the subconscious, and from there to other realms.

This is why just about every beginner's book describes techniques for meditation. It's the safest and one of the most powerful ways of learning to *be in stillness*. When you learn to quiet the conscious mind, you won't simply be visualizing what you want to happen; you will experience what is actually happening in the inner realms. Sitting around creating pictures in your head is no more valuable than watching a video that you create. Your rational mind will interfere, interjecting into the script and never allowing you to move past mental playacting.

Instead you have to shut down the script writer, the internal censor, and take the risk of being irrational. As you descend into the subconscious, like Inanna's descent into the underworld, the trappings of your rational self will be stripped away. Eventually you will arrive, your ego naked, to explore your internal lands and the doors to other realms.

THE HOUSE WITHIN

The human mind can be described as a large house with many different rooms and levels. This is a common metaphor for understanding the subconscious. Ancient Greek techniques for evoking memory described building a pathway in the mind, like a large hall, to hold pictures of the things you need to recall. The house metaphor is useful for Pagan paths as well.

If you picture your mind as a house (a roomy split-level ranch for example), then the ground floor would be your conscious mind. It's the place where you spend most of your time and are no doubt the most familiar with. Friendly, useful rooms such as kitchens, bathrooms, living spaces, and bedrooms are on this level. The doors at this level are like our senses, allowing us to escape the confines of our minds to enter the everyday world and to bring our impressions there back with us. When dealing with the conscious mind, information enters through the front door and takes up residence as thoughts, memories, and ideas. Our conscious minds aren't always the most organized of places (just as our houses can be messy), but we can usually find what we need when we need it.

The floor above the ground floor contains "higher source" information. This includes artifacts from previous lives, data from our higher selves and other guardian spirits, and messages from the Gods. Like a sunny attic, stuff stored here may be a bit dusty from lack of use. And like antiques stored in a grandmother's attic, they may not make much sense to us now. But it is worthwhile to explore them.

It is here that faith resides, as well as the inklings we all have that the world is more than we can see and that this is fundamentally a good thing. When we despair and our normal perspective is limited by hardship or trial, we can benefit from spending time with the bright treasures in our attics.

The attic of the mind also includes a trapdoor that leads to the roof. It is here, under the sky and stars, that we can connect most directly with our Deities. With some practice, we can also learn to fly, launching ourselves from here into other realms such as the astral. When completing a spell by sending your energy out into the astral, you can picture yourself standing on the roof of your internal house and flinging the energy up and out.

The floor below the ground floor is our subconscious. If you thought your conscious mind was disorganized, just wait until you begin exploring here. Like the garage, storage closet, or mudroom, the subconscious mind tends to collect all those items that we aren't dealing with in the conscious right now. These can include old or painful memories, dream images, and unacknowledged hopes, fears, and desires.

Since people don't tend to spend a lot of time down there, it can be musty, dusty, and rather badly lit. While exploring in the attic can seem like a fun adventure, finding items in your subconscious is more like digging through crumbling boxes of old paperwork. For every useful record you find, you have to dig through things like old tax forms, long expired warranty cards, and faded receipts.

As in a split-level house, there are exits from this level as well. The garage door, the mudroom side entrance, and the exit to the back garden are metaphors for some of the alternate routes to our inner house. However, unlike the front door and windows, these exits don't lead to the everyday world. No, there are a host of lands beyond the day-to-day reality that we typically experience. We can access these through our subconscious mind. Paradoxically, they exist independent of us, and yet are accessible only through our own subtle perceptions. That means that the metaphors you use to describe these places will be based on both relative and archetypal symbolism.

The subconscious level of your mind also includes access to the basement . . . which is usually haunted. This is Jung's shadow realm, where all those darker impulses that we refuse to deal with reside. Bad past experiences, guilt, fear, and hate all settle into the basement of your inner house like ghosts or demons. They gain power by being ignored and are anything but helpless. Anyone who has survived a trauma of any sort knows how the memories of that event, no matter how much we try to repress them, can affect the conscious mind and our ability to cope with the day-to-day world. They are the source of Post Traumatic Stress Disorder (PTSD), which can affect soldiers (it's also known as shell shock) as well as disaster, abuse, or rape survivors.

Like dangerous chemicals that might be stored in the dank basement of an old home (no cozy finished basements here), the shadow can, if given enough power, poison the rest of the house. When we ignore them, unacknowledged thoughts or memories take on a life of their own. Calling them demons or ghosts in this context isn't at all inappropriate. These beings may be constructs of the mind, but that doesn't make them any less terrifying to deal with.

Yet, if we are to live well-balanced and healthy lives (in both the spiritual and practical sense), we must confront these creatures. We can exorcise them completely (as with the crippling memories of prior victimization) or tame them by giving them a controlled place in our consciousness (as with our own darker impulses). In either case, our efforts will be well rewarded. To really explore the lands beyond our own minds, we need to have a safe and secure base to start from. And day-to-day life will also be improved when we approach it with a fit mental state.

The interaction between the levels of our houses is a subtle and malleable thing. Items can move from level to level just as we move furniture or knick-knacks in our homes. Interaction between our conscious and subconscious minds is the most common. When things go missing from your consciousness (like the name of your new neighbor), it's usually because items you aren't dealing with at the moment are sinking into your subconscious mind. In addition, items in the subconscious may come bubbling up—in dreams or meditation or in the course of your everyday living and decision making.

Dark or negative images that you aren't able to deal with in your conscious life will sink into the basement of your mind, where they often take on lives of their own. This is because the key to coping with terrifying memories, dangerous impulses, and past hurts or guilt is not to ignore them but to acknowledge them as a part of yourself. Remember, it is through being repressed that the shadow gains the type of power it needs to be a disruptive and destructive influence in your world.

There are also connections between our lower levels and our higher ones. Items stored in our attics may end up assimilated into our conscious lives. And important mysteries we discover on our path often get stored here when we aren't actively looking at them. In addition, higher source data has an indirect effect on the other parts of our inner house. Just as a box of your grandmother's keepsakes can exert a benevolent influence (even if you never open it), the messages contained in our attics can help us cope with troubles and struggles in our lives.

THE USES OF ALTERED STATES

Many books on the occult describe methods of altering your consciousness as an end in itself. That is, once you've practiced their meditation or trance induction techniques enough, you can metaphorically leave your body (really, you are leaving the house of your mind) and travel to other realms. However, they don't talk about the reasons that you might wish to do so.

Adventure, excitement, the sheer exhilaration of mastering a new skill—the heart of an explorer knows that you don't need a reason. The climber scales a peak simply because it is there. However, if we look beyond these surface motivations, we see that the adventuring spirit often hides a deeper need to understand the world, find the meaning of life, better understand the self, or discover one's place in the world. It is the same on a spiritual level. There are numerous reasons to alter your consciousness and explore the lands beyond; much wisdom that the advancing Pagan needs is located there and every area of study or practice we've covered in this book depends on it.

As a journeyman Witch or Pagan, traveling to foreign lands to gather wisdom is, in effect, your job. Of course, when we travel in altered states, we don't really pack our bags and head out into the unknown on a physical level. But we are traveling nonetheless. When we embark on a guided meditation, practice pathworking, or cast the circle, we are narrowing the gap (or thinning the veil) between our everyday conscious world and these other realms.

Far from merely a fun adventure, this is a necessary part of advancing on your path. You have to step out of your normal routine (the little village of knowledge where you grew up) and explore the larger world. This is the literal "mind expanding" process that people in the New Age movement often talk about. Of course we expand our minds whenever we try something or go somewhere new. It's just that, internally, we aren't limited by time, finances, or other practical concerns.

Even the most cerebral and conscious adherents of our spiritual practices benefit from the application of the wisdom gained in altered states. When I sit critically reading a difficult book, it seems as if I'm only working with my conscious mind. However, I'm also making connections to both the knowledge stored in my subconscious and information from my higher realms. Remember, the goal isn't just to memorize information by rote but to connect it holistically to what we already know.

We all experience "a-ha" moments when something we read makes a relevant memory surface or connects to something we know, but forgot. Those moments mean we have accessed our subconscious minds. When we read something and suddenly know that it's *real* or *true*, or conversely, *false* or *wrong*, we have received a message from our higher self. These types of messages will prove very valuable to your research and path if you train yourself to listen and not ignore them.

The act of reading may seem mundane, but the act of understanding is always magical and therefore benefits from an altered state. If you are ever stuck on a difficult idea, free-form meditation on the idea can trigger revelations in understanding at a later time. Conversely, forgetting it and moving on to something else can achieve the same result. That's because both techniques allow your inner world to go to work on the idea while your conscious mind is distracted.

Making these connections is the core and key to symbolic thinking, which lies behind so much of what we've covered in this book. This means that to develop the kind of connected and holistic world view that is so necessary for the advancing Pagan, you must be able to place the things you "know" in the context of the unknown. That is, you need to use your knowledge to travel to the lands beyond—just as the very act of taking those journeys will enhance, connect, and solidify your knowledge.

Something you *know* is very different from something you read about, or suspect, or think you might believe. And one source for that kind of knowledge is in the confirmations we receive from testing these ideas in the laboratory of the wider, nonphysical world. I've met Pagans who profess to believe many things but admit they don't have the internal proof that brings complete knowledge. Are the Deities real? You may have your suspicions, but the only way to know is to get out there and make Their acquaintance—beyond your own mind. Once you interact with a Deity on His or Her terms, not buffered by what your conscious mind wants to think, you will never doubt again. You will have moved past the realm of belief into the hard-core field of absolute certainty.

Of course, ironically, the things you absolutely know aren't the things that others know. And neither version of truth is wrong. Yet you must be willing to embrace and seek out this knowledge and defend it . . . even while respecting the knowledge of others. This is how we build confidence in our own power and abilities. The person who believes everything but knows nothing, will always be hindered by uncertainty. On the other hand, those who have created wisdom for themselves will be strengthened by it, particularly when they remember that their truth is theirs alone.

Divination and the interpretation of omens are other areas where your experience is greatly enhanced by altering your state of consciousness. Many of the best oracles, diviners, and seers have the ability to easily slip into an altered state whenever they interpret an omen or perform a divination. Whether you are reading for yourself or others, silencing your conscious mind allows you to access useful information that you might not normally see.

If you've ever experienced or witnessed a reading where the diviner completely ignored accepted meanings or interpretations and instead seemed to speak directly from a separate source, you've experienced an altered-state oracle in action. This type of reading will usually be more accurate than normal, even more accurate than possible with the system being used. For example, Tarot cards can point to physical problems, but usually they cannot tell you the specifics of the ailment. When a diviner suddenly announces that you are suffering an illness of the stomach, he or she is accessing information that's not "in the cards."

Altering your consciousness also works for interpreting omens.

Sometimes you know that an omen has occurred, but not what it means. This is the time to take your question to a larger venue: your own subconscious, your Deities, or the lands beyond. Usually the information you need, or the help you need in interpreting it, will be found there. In addition, your own explorations may serve you much better than trying to interpret an omen through a book. Your experience will often be specific to you, and the meanings of various symbols, while guided by the archetypes, will also depend on your own experience.

For Pagans, the natural world is a source of endless knowledge and fascination. So it shouldn't be surprising to find that altered states and the wild places are connected. In fact, just being in the wilderness can open us up to other worlds. When in nature, even the most nonmagical person will often get a sense of being watched or touched by some type of nonhuman awareness. And as you may have guessed, deliberately altering your consciousness can be of immeasurable value when experiencing Mother Nature.

First, it can be easier for the rational minded to enter an altered state when in a natural setting. At least, this has always proved true for me. While sitting in my house meditating always seems near impossible, put me in an isolated or wild location and I'm halfway to Neverland already. Many of my most potent spiritual experiences have been in outdoor locations (even ones as boring as my own backyard). So whenever I have a burning question or issue to resolve, I like to try to get outside to think about it.

Second, altering our consciousness in a wild setting can attune us to beings with timescales and modes of communication very different from ours. If you've ever shared greetings with a rock, run with a river, or talked with a plant, you know that you have to be in a certain frame of mind to do it. This is why so many people recommend meditating outdoors with your back against a tree. Wild animals also can provide wisdom when we learn the skill of connecting with them.

There are other beings we can speak with as well, if we know how to change our mindset appropriately. The back garden door on the subconscious level of the house in *my* mind leads to fairy land or the hollow hills. It's one of the few of the lands beyond that, for me, can overlay the "normal" world—but only in wild places. Yet, without altering my consciousness, all I will find outdoors are breezes and bugs and allergies. Of course we can still enjoy nature for what it is, and it's valuable that we do so. But if you are a typical urban or suburban Pagan, it's worth your while to become comfortable enough in nature to let go and connect with deeper levels.

When you work magic, altering your consciousness is a mandatory part of casting your spell. As spells work not in the real world but through a connection with the astral, we need to be able to access the rooftops of our inner houses. This is the part of magic that so many spellbooks forget to mention. Without the necessary altered state, the most elaborate spell is just so much useless posturing and pomp. However, with a well-honed ability to get the energy of the spell "out there," you can work miracles with only your mind. This is why a spell that works for one person may not work for another, and why some people have little luck with their magic no matter how many correspondences they memorize.

It is the same with ritual work to connect with your Deities. Of course, you can pray to your God and Goddess, talk to Them, imagine They're watching over you. However, if you want to really *meet* Them and get answers to your questions, an altered state is necessary. In fact, the best way to connect to your Deities is to meet Them on Their own turf. This is one of the primary functions of the circle. Inside this space, the connection between the conscious world and the other realms thins. In fact, it's a great place to start from when performing a pathworking or guided meditation of any sort.

In addition, it's important to be able to hear what our Deities are telling us. Since They often speak by omens, in symbolic language, through dreams, or from our own intuition, it's a good idea to sublimate the conscious mind when trying to discern Their messages and requests. This might be accomplished during a ritual, or afterward in a post-ritual "debriefing." The second method works well for a group ritual. After everyone's gone home, take a few moments to meditate on the outcome for you. Even in the most tight-knit group, the messages of the Deities are often extremely personal. You will want to spend some time thinking about your individual experience as well as the experience of the whole group.

Far from being a sideline or fringe activity, practicing meditation and other methods of altering consciousness is absolutely essential for the advancing Witch or Pagan. Your abilities here will enhance your success in every other area of practice as well. In addition, it's only through knowing ourselves, including the deepest regions of our inner houses, that we grow spiritually. This growth goes beyond any single path or school and is the key to advancing all of humanity.

Naturally, you can use your explorations to help you in various ways. You can obtain advice, answers to problems, help for both your magical and mundane life. But beyond that, there is really only one reason for putting in all the effort, practice, and patience that's required—the understanding of your True Will.

The Pagan religions, like any true spiritual path, can help you improve yourself and your life. With a little devotion and effort on your part, you can make better decisions, take responsibility for your actions, improve your magic, get rid of old baggage, and open yourself to the wonders of the universe. However, our primary purpose and reason for existence is to know the Divine so that we can become closer to It in all Its aspects. This is what discovering our True Will is all about. The part of ourselves that still remembers our Divine source is the part that also understands what our Will is meant to be. When we begin to see this plan and purpose we have created for ourselves, from a higher state, we can flow, fearlessly and with ease, through the vagaries of the everyday world. This isn't necessarily an easy process. It can be the work of many lifetimes and take much effort and dedication. However, after getting even a glimpse of the Divine plan of the higher self, you will know the time and effort were well worth it.

Reality

When you first begin to visit the realms beyond the conscious, you might find yourself wondering whether a particular experience was "real." In this context, the question is essentially invalid. The concept of "real" means little to Pagans and Witches in general, and even less when you move past the conscious, everyday world. In my everyday life, I can trust my senses to tell me what's real and what is not. However, it doesn't quite work the same when dealing with the subconscious or other realms. The better way is to approach the question from a practical standpoint.

For example, what you may really want to know is whether the experience was "just your imagination" or whether it had an external source. The truth is, since the world is holistic and interconnected, even things that are in your imagination connect directly to experiences outside yourself. Still, we want to make sure that our experience was authentic and not just a self-induced head game. One key is to realize that imagination and visualization are still connected to the conscious mind. If you are thinking about an experience *while you are experiencing it*, your conscious mind is still involved. It may distort the actual message you receive or overanalyze the information you get.

Another way of differentiating the experiences of your conscious imagination from those in your subconscious: the two types of experiences have different textures when you undergo them as well as when you look back on them. This is similar to the quality or feeling that accompanies omens or the action of synchronicity in your life. A bit of a chill and later blurred memory are indications that you have experienced something with a source beyond your conscious self.

Finally, when you ask whether an experience was "real," you might instead be wondering whether the being or beings you encountered were real. Again, the term "real" doesn't mean much here. Whether you're exploring your subconscious mind or other realms, you should treat any other being you meet as a real entity. Because these beings, either created by you or living an independent existence, are cohesive and aware energy forms . . . just like you are. Corporeal-centrism has no place in the exploration of altered states of consciousness.

Safety Considerations

There are some risks associated with the exploration of the lands beyond our own inner house. Even your subconscious mind can be a place where frightening or upsetting things can occur. Of course, if we never did anything that made us uncomfortable we would be neither effective Pagans nor effective humans. Life is risk and living it a greater risk. The key is to be as aware as possible and take all necessary precautions beforehand.

For example, when exploring the subconscious mind, the primary risk is to your own mental health. As I mentioned earlier, parts of your inner house may be haunted by old ghosts or demons. Yes, these beings are created by your own imagination, but that doesn't mean they aren't "real." In the inner realm, they are independent energy beings—just as you are. You may have things buried in the dark basement of your subconscious house that you are not ready to deal with. Digging them up can have repercussions in your everyday life.

These old memories can be as terrifying as anything you confront outside of yourself. The fact that they are a part of you makes them potentially even more devastating. If you embark on a mission to exorcise one of your demons, be ready for a fight. Destroying the hold a past memory has on you is still destroying a part of yourself. However much you will be improved by the removal of this baggage, there may be a voice inside that places self-preservation above all else. It may complain that you won't be the same or that you are somehow losing a part of your identity. You may actually be getting a great deal of mileage out of these old injuries. But you must remember that you are working to improve yourself and be willing to let go of old wounds.

Another risk in exploring the subconscious is the symbolic nature of some of the information you find. You may see yourself in distant times and places, experience communication from various beings, or feel like you are accessing some special knowledge. Yet it's important to remember that the concepts of "real" and "literal" don't hold up under the scrutiny of the conscious mind. There's a reason that we spend most of our time in the conscious world . . . that's where the lessons are. You can't expect your subconscious to solve all your problems in the here and now. Yes, by dealing with your shadow side, including your hidden fears and old haunts, you can make great improvements in your life. But you must deliberately manifest the information you receive into your conscious life for it to make a difference. Just as when you are casting a spell, the final step is bringing it back into the world with you.

It's also important to keep in mind that you will still filter this data through your own subjective experience. You may feel like you've received a message from an alien source, angels, a favorite God or Goddess. But you must judge the validity of the message itself, and not your interpretation of the source. Is the information helpful? Useful? Healing? Does it teach you a lesson? Solve a problem? Open new doors? If not, forget it. And if it does, remember that you are still filtering the data through your personal, relative symbol set, which might not be the same for everyone.

In the lands beyond your own inner world, the risks are a little different. Yes, you can still experience things you aren't ready for, things that could perhaps harm your psyche, and you must certainly remember that any information you receive will be packaged symbolically. Beyond those two caveats, however, are other issues you must consider. First, these lands aren't created or owned by you in the way that your subconscious mind is. That means that you share these realms with other seekers of all types. In addition, the beings you encounter aren't ultimately under your control the way a wayward memory or ghost of the past is. In exploring any new place, you can't assume that everything is about you or that every being you meet will have your best interests at heart.

For me, pushing energy out into the astral (as during a spell) is a matter of standing on the roof of my inner house and tossing my symbolic energy creation out into the astral world. If properly targeted, this energy will go about the business of creating opportunities for the spell to manifest without interference. However, this is very different from taking the leap and actually heading out to explore the astral.

When you venture out yourself, you should always travel well aware and protected from harm. This means casting a circle, grounding and shielding, and perhaps leaving various protective markers on your path. Also, keep your wits about you and have an open mind about everything you see. If you meet another being, always act polite and reserved—come from a place of power and it's rare that you will be disturbed.

MEDITATION—ARE YOU REALLY PRACTICING?

In writing this book, it was important to me that I relay only the things that I have participated in or that have worked for me. Of course, not all my ideas will work for *you*, but at least they are from my own experience. That's why this particular section is challenging for me to write. One of the most common pieces of advice you've probably received as a beginner is to practice some kind of daily meditation. But taking even a short time every day to sit and let your mind empty can be difficult. It takes a lot of self-discipline to do it regularly and a lot of practice to get it right. When I ask myself honestly how well I've been practicing my meditation, I have to admit I'm not always proud of the answer.

Taking time to meditate makes me feel more centered and balanced, clearer about my path, and more able to enter a trance state when needed. It has effects similar to those that come from getting some regular exercise (and indeed, aerobic exercise like cycling is meditative for me). However, as with getting out there and working up a sweat, getting *in* there regularly and working my own brain is a challenge. This is especially true because I tend to be well anchored and not prone to trancing out easily. Here are some of the techniques that have made it easier to incorporate meditation in my life, although that remains one of my biggest challenges:

- Although many books recommend setting aside a regular time to meditate, I find that *remaining flexible* is important for me. If I try to set aside a regular time, I'm sure to miss it and feel guilty. But if I'm open to the possibility of meditating whenever and wherever it fits into my life, I end up doing more meditating than I would otherwise.

- When in a deep trance, not much can bother you. I've been in situations where I didn't register even extreme disturbances. But *minimizing distractions* as much as you can will make the transition to a deeper place easier to accomplish, especially when there's no more pressing need to meditate than simply regular practice.

- Books will also recommend a number of appropriate physical positions in which to meditate. Again, you can be in a state where you don't feel your body at all, but if that's difficult for you, I'd recommend *getting as comfortable as possible*. It's best to be in a position where the energy can flow freely through your body, but the important thing is that you can easily relax.

- *Breathing comfortably* will facilitate moving into a meditative state. As you relax, your cycle of breath will naturally lengthen. But worrying too much about how much, how long, or how deeply you're breathing is counterproductive.

- In a similar vein, you will want to put some effort into *finding the most comfortable location* to meditate. Whether outdoors or indoors, in a special room or your favorite hangout, you should feel safe and secure. I find one of the best places for me to take some regular meditation indoors is in my hot tub.

Of course these suggestions aren't going to work "in the field"—at a group ritual for example. But by arranging circumstances to be conducive to practicing, you're more likely to make time for and have success in your meditation. And with practice, you'll get more accomplished and better able to lose yourself in a more challenging or public venue.

~~~~~~

FOOD FOR THOUGHT—PAGANS AND "DRUGS"

One question that commonly comes up for debate in Pagan circles is whether Witches or other Pagan groups should use psychoactive substances. Psychoactive (literally, activating the psyche) is officially defined as "affecting the mind or behavior."[36] By this definition, meditation, drumming, dancing, chanting, fasting, and so on, are all psychoactive. So from that perspective, the answer is definitely yes.

Of course the term psychoactive is typically used to refer to various drugs, particularly ones in common use in the sixties (when the term was invented), for example lysergic acid diethylamide (LSD) and psilocybin. Individuals used these substances specifically to explore altered states of consciousness. In native shamanic cultures, ingesting or inhaling various mind-altering substances including fly agaric, datura, coca leaves, and so on, has a lot of backing in both mythology and anthropological evidence. Indeed, humans have a long history of exploring plant life and other natural substances that have interesting effects on the mind and body. This probably constitutes the beginnings of medicinal herbalism, which forms the foundation of our modern pharmacopoeia.

But however common these practices were in native cultures, they are not as common among Pagans today. Many plants used as psychoactives in ancient times are now considered deadly poisons. Some needed to be prepared in a particular way to mitigate toxic effects; however, they were and are still dangerous. In fact many, such as *datura stramonium* or jimsonweed, are potentially lethal. In addition, with our more detailed understanding of human biochemistry and physiology, we have better knowledge of the potential harmful side effects caused by various substances.

There's a second very serious set of problems associated with psychoactive substances. Beyond the physical, there are also emotional, mental, and spiritual risks. To put it bluntly, it's very hard to "blow your mind" dancing or drumming or meditating. You'll get only as disconnected from the corporeal body and conscious brain as you can handle. Taking a foreign substance into your system, however, can put you far past that point and cause lasting harm. In native cultures, there was typically a structure of training and secret knowledge that had to be learned before a student of the mysteries could use the more powerful and poisonous plants or compounds.

However, a number of substances, while not psychoactive in themselves, can be used to enhance the individual's ability to activate his own psyche. Some of these are quite tame and yet work well when combined with other methods of inducing trance. For example, a boring cup of chamomile or valerian tea can help relax you before a meditation. A double dose of caffeine before an all-night ritual can keep the dancing and drumming going longer. And a reasonable amount of alcohol can loosen the inhibitions and cloud the rational mind (which is why it's such a bad idea to drive after drinking).

The point is that plant substances can be used quite legally and safely to help you in meditation or trance. But tread cautiously. There are a number of interesting urban legends about the psychoactive effects of various odd items that have no basis in reality. Before proceeding to unfamiliar territory, always double-check your research and get as much legitimate information as possible. A solid grounding in herbalism will keep you on the right track.

CHAPTER 8 EXERCISES

By now you should know that the most meaningful exercises are those that you create for yourself. Altering your consciousness is such an individual and personal endeavor that advice on how to accomplish it is useless. But there are things you might try to improve your ability to access other realms and have the best experience possible.

Many Roads

Every occult book and teacher will have suggestions for how to meditate correctly or induce a trance state. In fact this particular topic is often presented in a very dogmatic way. Authors will warn against certain practices while recommending others . . . and their instructions often overlap or conflict. Part of the reason is that exploring the lands beyond can be very advanced work and have some inherent risks. However, as with so much in the spiritual realm, there really isn't only one true or right way of going about it.

It's tempting to take the advice of a single expert and quit worrying about what other people are suggesting. However, we all have our own way of altering consciousness. What works for one person may not work for another. So it's a good idea to try new techniques regularly to find those that best match your skills, personality, lifestyle, and unique mindset.

As you come across new ways of meditating, give them a try. If you see a description of someone inducing a trance with a certain method, attempt to emulate it. Of course, use your common sense in evaluating practices and take all the precautions you need to. Above all, mine your own intuition as to what works for you and what doesn't. If you feel clumsy and have no sense of rhythm, dancing yourself into an ecstatic trance state won't work. If the Qabalah is completely foreign to you, you probably won't be interested in pathworking based on the Tree of Life. The point is not to close yourself off to new ideas; evaluate them for usefulness and then give them a try.

Of course, it's more complicated when working with a group. In that case, everyone will want to be on the same page and agree on how the group will coordinate the trance or meditation process. The point is to remain flexible and not be afraid to experiment.

Healing the Past

One of the most powerful things you can do to access the other realms is to work at healing those past events that have a hold on your subconscious mind. It will make you not only a better "traveler" but also a better Witch or Pagan, and a better person. It's human nature to want to avoid pain, but it doesn't serve us to push our own unpleasant ghosts and demons away. If you ever find yourself facing one of these entities, don't ignore it. Instead, think about it and what it means for you. Allow yourself to get to know this old hurt, because if you do not know it, you will not be able to heal from it.

The right therapist can be helpful, of course, but you can also make great strides relying on your own intuition and objectivity. Just remember that the past cannot directly harm you here in the present. Its power is the ability to affect your emotions, decisions, and mental state. For example, phobias are powerful irrational fears that are often triggered by traumatic past experiences. Yet researchers have found that even a crippling phobia is relatively easy to conquer. By facing what they fear, people can overcome phobias surprisingly quickly.

When you face the thing that you fear, you can then move to neutralize it. This is where the healing process starts. You can release its hold over you and reclaim the energy you've been wasting while denying, hiding from, or even fearfully brooding on your fear. You can not only find healing but advance on your own spiritual path as the newly released energy you reclaim is used for beneficial purposes.

Integration

The messages we receive and lessons we learn from altering our consciousness are symbolic, metaphoric, archetypal, and all around slippery to grasp. But that doesn't mean they don't have a purpose in our everyday lives. The goal is to integrate our spirituality with our day-to-day existence. They are not wholly separate lands where the knowledge and language of one aren't relevant to the other. In fact, our inner world overlays our consciousness every moment and has a powerful, if subtle, effect on everything we do.

When you explore the lands beyond, you have to remember that the final goal is to integrate those experiences with the "mundane." At first they may not seem to go together, but with practice, you will begin to see all parts of the world as holistically connected. Far from being irrelevant or different, the keys we get from our inner exploration are *exactly* what we need to solve problems in our other world as well. When you examine these experiences relative to your whole life, they are easier to understand and take on a deeper meaning.

CONCLUSION

There are so many areas where attaining an altered state of consciousness is helpful: from assimilating knowledge, understanding the symbolic language of the universe, enjoying nature, and performing divination and magic to practicing that "old time" religion. It's also fundamentally healing and can allow us to know ourselves and potentially even our True Will.

Yet, these goals can't be attained without some practice. No matter what forms of meditation or trance induction you try, the important thing is that you keep practicing. Sometimes it seems there's no room in our everyday lives for this kind of work. However, for the advancing Witch or Pagan, the rewards are well worth the effort. No matter how rational your nature, you can learn to explore your inner house and travel to the lands beyond it. When you "tune out" the chatter of your conscious mind, the subtle harmonies of the universe can be heard. When our surface thoughts are silenced, the music of the spheres becomes a symphony that we can learn to understand.

CHAPTER 9

Specialization

THE PAGAN PATHS INCLUDE A MULTITUDE OF DIFFERENT POSSIBILITIES and options, especially for the advancing Pagan or Witch. We have the freedom to explore and determine what works for us individually, without dogma or interference by any human authority. However, once you begin branching out and learning more, this plethora of options can become confusing. There's so much to know and learn, deciding what direction to take can be a challenge. In addition, many areas that might attract the advancing Pagan require years of study and dedication to master.

Throughout this book, I've emphasized the importance of acquiring a broad base of knowledge. It's vital to our growth that we don't set arbitrary limits on the things we read, think about, and explore. This is how we build the language of symbolic connections that prove so useful in our magic and in our lives. But there comes a point, too, for the journeyman or -woman Pagan, where we must pick areas within our knowledge base to focus on. It is in this way that we become masters at a particular skill.

PICKING YOUR FOCUS

I used to envy the kids in school who knew exactly what they wanted to be when they grew up. I'm not sure even now! But I have learned a lot more about what I like and what I'm good at since I was young. It's the same when deciding on an area to focus on in your spiritual life. Often, the challenge is narrowing it down to a reasonable set of expectations. After all, you practice Paganism because you want to, because you love it. Therefore the odds are that many topics may fascinate you. Fortunately, unlike picking a major in college, you aren't limited to just one. While it would be impossible to learn everything at the same time, you can easily take on several subjects and master them. And once you do, you can pick new ones.

Twelve years or more of school can take the fun out of learning for just about anyone. But learning for learning's sake, to fulfill our souls or bring us closer to the Divine, *should* be fun. Remember, when you are studying for your own growth, there are no limits. You can proceed as fast or as slowly as you prefer, you can dedicate any amount of time, you can spend as much or as little as you choose. When you're stressed about learning, it's hard to retain the knowledge you acquire. That's why, after cramming for a test, most people forget the information they learned as soon as the exam is over. If you enjoy what you're learning, however, it's more likely to stick with you for a lifetime.

Perhaps you will need a change in mindset, but learning can become enjoyable again by simply considering those areas you love as well as your strengths and weaknesses. If you hate a topic, there's no reason to subject yourself to learning more about it. If you have a particular strength, augmenting it will feel easy. But even challenging topics can be fun. Picking an area of weakness to focus on can be difficult, but the results are usually worth the work. You will feel more confident having gained proficiency in something you previously thought impossible. No matter what you choose, you should always endeavor to do your best.

EXCELLENCE

In everything you do as a Pagan, it's important to manifest excellence. That doesn't mean that we're always, or even frequently, perfect. It doesn't mean that we attempt to do only those things that we are already skilled at. It means that we recognize our talents and always strive to do as good a job as possible. When we put the effort in to do our best, it furthers us on our path and pleases the Deities. They don't care about faultlessness, but They do care about our effort and intent. When we take the time to thoroughly study and practice, our abilities in that area will improve. This is beneficial not only to our relationship with the Divine (who appreciates our dedication) but also to our own development of will. In addition, these efforts can manifest themselves in other, completely unrelated areas of our lives.

Practicing Paganism is not like being in high school or college; there are no rules to tell you when your study is complete. Indeed, while you may become *a* master at some particular arcane skill, you may never completely master it. There will always be more to learn, and when you're interested in a topic, you should keep learning and growing. Because of this, there's often no one to judge our progress in any objective way. How do we know when we've reached a point of mastery or excellence?

One way is by taking advantage of those structured programs that already exist. For example, you might enroll in a course on herbalism. You can follow the curriculum, learn from tests whether you've assimilated the material, and receive a certificate at the end of the course. But not everything you might want to study will come in such a convenient, prepackaged format. For those topics that don't, you will have to set your own goals.

The thing to remember is that you should set your goals in attainable steps and determine an end point that is challenging, but one that you can reach in a given time. For example, you might decide that to become an expert at divination you will: (1) spend three months researching divination methods from around the world, (2) pick two methods that you are familiar with and two that are completely foreign, (3) spend eight months studying those methods through both education and practical means, and (4) invent your own, completely different method of divination based on what you've learned.

For each major step, you can set attainable subgoals. Perhaps for step one, you can decide to: find books on divination in various cultures, read a certain number of them, keep notes on different methods you discover, and turn your notes into a section in your personal writings or book of shadows. At the end of the year, you might give yourself a challenge to test your knowledge. For example, you could have a get-together where you divine for all your friends, or offer free readings at a local fair or public ritual. In any case, the point is not what goals you set, it's that you make the effort to attain them. It's through this kind of self-determined will and dedication that we earn the right to call ourselves experts, masters, or authorities.

Still, many of us have felt hampered by having too many interests and options to pursue. Perhaps the easiest way to begin thinking about where to focus your efforts is by looking at some of the various "jobs" that Pagans can hold. While we're antihierarchal and nondogmatic as a rule, there are roles that you can fulfill, for yourself and your community, which lend themselves to certain related skills. This way, you can pick a set of topics you want to excel at that have an inherent interrelationship. The following are some of the jobs that you might aspire to:

HEALER

From mainstream medical professionals to alternative health practioners, there are many Healers in our Pagan communities. Some are Healers who also happen to be Pagan (a Wiccan nurse for example). Others are Pagans who are specifically called to the healing arts. In either case, they provide valuable services to other Pagans in their communities. Whether practicing physical, mental, emotional, or spiritual healing, these dedicated individuals are called to serve others in a very practical sense.

From my friends who are Healers, I know that the call to help others is something they feel very strongly. Many have mundane careers in medical or alternative health fields as well as an interest in healing for the Pagan community. They might be counselors or spiritual advisors in addition to herbalists, massage therapists, Reiki healers, or more everyday nurses, doctors, and psychologists. Those who specialize in healing are the most likely to also make a living from their art.

Physical Healers can often be found in the first aid tents at festivals. They are available to treat the many ailments that can occur when a large group of Pagans get together to celebrate. They always seem to suggest the right herbal concoction for any problem. Perhaps they practice massage, acupressure, or Reiki and can help when you're ill or injured. Or they have good advice for improving your lifestyle through diet, exercise, and medication before you become sick.

Mental healers are likely to be found counseling the troubled. They have open ears and closed mouths, taking patient confidentiality very seriously. They know the right questions to ask to help someone who's suffering from depression and can determine when more serious treatment is necessary. At rituals, you often find such a Healer huddled in a corner helping someone work through a personal crisis.

Emotional or spiritual Healers are literally the ministers of our communities. They can help when you're stuck on a problem, working through a moral quandary, or trying to decipher a message from your Deities. They may be involved in prison outreach programs for incarcerated Pagans or act as mediators in disputes between different groups. They are tolerant of multiple paths but have a good sense of when people are fooling themselves. You might find them giving gentle advice and guidance to the newer members of our Pagan religions.

When you work with Pagan Healers, there are a number of things you can do to help honor the work they do:

- **Remember that healing takes energy.** Even Pagan Healers who use modern medicine often augment their skills with their personal energy. And Healers who practice energy healing such as Reiki or aura sensing obviously put a great deal of themselves into their work. When you are on the receiving end of this kind of healing, try to give some of that energy back when you are well enough to spare it. Something as simple as a back or foot rub can be a great treat for those who sometimes give more than they receive. If you are lucky enough to have a retreat spot (a hot tub, meditation room, soothing garden, or cabin in the woods), allow your Healer to enjoy it as a way of refreshing her- or himself.

- **Honor the value of the Healer's work.** Many Healers have spent a great deal of time and money obtaining the skills and training they need to offer their help to the Pagan community. In addition, some rely on proceeds from their healing work to support themselves on either an occasional or full-time basis. If a Healer charges for her services, respect and understand her point of view and pay promptly. If she does not routinely charge, consider offering a payment anyway. While she may feel uncomfortable accepting cash, you can still barter a service or give a useful gift. Treating her to lunch, arriving with a home baked goodie, or supporting her when she needs help are all subtle ways of offering compensation.

- **Keep in mind that Healers need a break too.** There's an old joke about how doctors are always being approached at parties by people asking about "that mysterious lump on my neck." I'm sure that psychologists get a lot of "I've been depressed since my divorce" when they mingle. It's the same for Pagan Healers. There's a time and place for everything. It's much better to ask when a Healer is available to talk about your issue than to simply offload it. Even if you don't have a specific complaint, discussing health related issues all the time gets tiresome.

- **Sometimes Healers need you to say no for them.** The strong calling to help others can mean that Healers stretch themselves too thin. If you know a Healer who's always offering to help, sometimes the best way to support him is to help him conserve energy by refusing. Let him enjoy the festival for once instead of treating twenty cases of heatstroke. Allow him to nurture himself as well as others.

- **Take responsibility for your own health.** If a Healer recommends an herbal mix, make sure you're not allergic. If you receive advice on improving your health, make every effort to take it before returning with the same issue. If you are unsure about anything, get a second opinion. The most gifted Healer in the world can't help you unless you are willing to help yourself.

The primary thing you need to become a Pagan Healer is to truly feel the call to heal and let it permeate all aspects of your life. You cannot be effective if you only feel the need to help others through a craving for power or self-gratification. In fact, healing is a very demanding and difficult path. If you do not feel a strong altruistic urge to help others for their sake and not your own, you will never be an effective Healer and may actually do harm.

As specialties go, healing is one of the more structured ones. To become a master herbalist, licensed therapist, or registered nurse typically takes enrollment in an official course of study. The modern medical professions will definitely require a college education. However, if you're interested in healing and don't have the resources to attend school full-time, there are still areas that can be explored.

If you are called to physical healing but aren't ready to make a full-time career of it, you can still learn the skills and responsibilities necessary to help others. You could study massage therapy, apprentice yourself to a Reiki master, or take a first aid course from the Red Cross. Don't forget to get certified in CPR. For those with more time, many EMT courses are weekend and night affairs that you could take while holding down a day job. You can also learn more about healthy living in order to advise others. This means a study of diet and exercise (and practicing healthy living yourself). Finally, while becoming a master herbalist might be beyond your time and means, you can still learn some of the basics by sticking to simple remedies for common ailments. Who knows, your cough-and-cold concoction might make you famous among your friends.

If you aspire to mental or spiritual healing, you can be a little more flexible. Of course becoming a registered therapist will take training and certification. But if you find you have a gift for soothing troubled breasts (and no time for a full course of study), you can still learn what you need to help others. For example, you can be a self-taught spiritual advisor by making a study of sociology, psychology, mythology, and comparative religions. Or you could volunteer at a local crisis center or hotline. These places offer free training that has applications beyond your volunteer work. You may also decide to take a course in psychology or sociology to help you become a better spiritual counselor, without intending to receive your degree. Finally, there are correspondence courses in counseling that you may be interested in pursuing.

When you wish to heal others, it's best to be in good health yourself. Practice what you preach in regard to diet and exercise. Meditate and learn to relax and recharge your batteries after you've given up energy to help others. Learn to love others no matter who they are or what they believe. Finally, cultivate a good relationship with healing Deities. While your skills and willingness to help can be beneficial, They are the ones who perform literal healing miracles.

Healing is one of the least solitary of Pagan paths. To be a Healer, you must first have someone to heal. This means interacting with your local community. In fact, most Healers seem to attract people who need help. The concept of the lonely old wise woman or medicine man living on the outskirts of town, whom everyone approaches for help, doesn't really work in the modern world. To heal others, they have to know you, and you must have a solid reputation in your community. In addition, healing another person involves a certain level of intimacy. When you heal another, you share a bond with that person.

It's an axiom among Pagans that when you help someone else, you take on a connection to their karma and become partially responsible for their future progress. Give bad or ill-thought-out advice, and you could slow or impede another's spiritual, emotional, mental, and even physical healing process. Of course, in time, we are all called on to give advice to our friends, even for issues that are completely mundane. And we shouldn't stop doing that for fear of karmic repercussions. Instead, the key is to remain objective, analyze your own motives, and give the best advice you can based on what you know. And if you don't feel comfortable giving advice, don't! Our good intentions don't mean anything if we are also not honest about our limitations. When a friend needs advice with a spiritual dilemma, I do attempt to help, but when someone is suffering from mysterious pain or some other physical symptoms, I suggest going to a doctor.

Healers can face two related problems. First, when your tool is a hammer, sometimes everything looks like a nail. That is, because Healers have a passion for helping others, it can be hard to remember that not everyone wants or needs their help. In fact, people often suffer through challenges for reasons that have to do with their spiritual growth. It's not always appropriate or even possible to "cure" everything. Another problem Healers commonly have is in not being able to say no. Healers have a giving spirit; they truly want to help others, but that means they can become overwhelmed with demands on their time and resources. This is true whether they practice physical healing, spiritual healing, or a combination of both. If you have the will to help that marks the healer, make sure you take care of yourself too.

Healing is not a specialty to be taken lightly. Most of the Healers I know have decades of experience in both the spiritual and physical sides of their practice. Yes, there are people who have a particular gift for counseling or energy healing, but on the physical end of things (herbalism, massage, acupuncture) most people have put in a lot of work and effort to get through the appropriate training. From the master acupressure practitioner to the nurse who treated your poison ivy at the last Pagan gathering, these people give of their time and energy to help others. It's a challenging but rewarding job for the advancing Pagan.

Areas that someone interested in healing might explore include:

- First aid, emergency medical, nursing, and other standard healing techniques
- Psychology, counseling, sociology, crisis or intervention work, and other therapy-based healing practices
- Reiki, acupuncture, massage, healing touch, aura sensing, and other "alternative" healing arts
- Herbalism, aromatherapy, magical herbalism for healing, and other skills based on plants and oils

WARRIOR

Many Pagans think of themselves as pacifists and would find the concept of the Pagan Warrior odd or a contradiction in terms. On the contrary, Warriors can be a valuable asset to the Pagan community. The key is to understand that Pagan Warriors don't love war, they love peace. They are motivated by a sense of justice and fairness, honor and courage, as well as a forthright and honest approach in all their dealings.

Many pre-Christian societies had their Warriors as well as their Priests and Healers, and being a Warrior in these societies wasn't always a purely mundane role. Japanese Samurai are an excellent example of a path that combined spiritual and material concerns. In addition, the Norse society focused on courage in battle and a fighting spirit. Yet they also had a strong spiritual path that many Pagans follow today. In their society, to die in battle was the highest spiritual honor, guaranteeing a place in Valhalla.

In the past, unfortunately, war was a part of life for many people. Today we still have wars to fight, but typically they are in the realm of freedom, ideology, or internal conflict. The task of today's Pagan Warrior is not to attack but to fight the good fight for peace, tolerance, and justice.

Pagan Warriors can literally be fighters or protectors. For example, they may be employed as police officers or members of the armed forces. They might be skilled martial artists who teach others to defend themselves. In addition, they can fight for those who can't defend themselves. They might be associated with the justice system as lawyers, judges, mediators, or advocates. For all the flaws that we might find with these bastions of bureaucracy, we have to admire the Pagan working within the system to ensure fair treatment and equality for all.

Even part-time, Warriors fight legal battles, stand up for victims, root out and battle against prejudice, and act as mediators or peacekeepers. Warriors might advocate for Pagan rights, protest against or for causes that they feel strongly about, or coordinate petitions. They can also fight with words, through the media or by writing letters to our elected officials.

Warriors are the ones we call on to act as fire keepers and arbitrators at public rituals. In addition, they frequently use diplomatic skills and a calm presence to handle conflicts between different groups of Pagans as well as with non-Pagan observers. They sometimes take the role of liaison to the non-Pagan public.

In addition to these external skills, the Pagan Warrior may also be called on to battle or protect on a spiritual level. These types of tasks can include lending powerful shielding to a circle, acting as a steady ground for those in deep trance, and battling inner demons. They can be a protective presence in any working where the participants feel uncertain or insecure. The calm presence of a Warrior in a circle, watching your back, can make challenging works go much more smoothly. They can also imbue others with a fighting spirit when things are tough and we need a dose of courage and fortitude.

When working with or meeting Pagan Warriors, it's a good idea to remember a few things:

- **Don't assume that Warriors are violent.** Even the ones who fight physical battles will usually prefer not to have to fight. Unfortunately, using force to defend your home, family, or friends can sometimes be necessary. Most Pagans realize that from a broad perspective, war and violence are always foolish. However, we have to keep in mind that not everyone shares our ideals. Those who put their lives on the line to protect us from people with less enlightened views deserve our respect.

- **Remember that the Pagan Warrior is tolerant.** The most physically forceful people are often the ones most likely to live and let live. The honorable Warrior won't be interested in fighting against people who simply have a different perspective. This means that while they are often the perfect people to act as mediators, they should never be drawn into a conflict between equal, but different, sides.

- **Warriors are energetic, within limits.** They are the individuals behind coordinated protests, letter writing campaigns, and organizations for justice—but they can't do everything. Without help and support they can become jaded and burn out, abandoning their most inspired projects. Lend a hand and, by working together, real change becomes possible.

- **Take responsibility for your own safety and protection.** Warriors can really improve the energy of a Pagan group. They help keep people in line and cooperating, which benefits everyone. However, it's the responsibility of each of us to insure our own security as much as possible. To keep yourself safe, learn about defense, protect your valuables at a ritual or festival, and avoid trouble before it starts. In addition, practice moderation and try to keep your personal affairs or disputes personal.

If you are interested in being a Warrior, you have to look within yourself. Without the Will and discipline to battle your own demons, keep peace within, and marshal your own emotions, you will never be able to do so outside of yourself. You have to learn to control your responses in emotional situations and remain calm in a crisis. When dealing with others in the capacity of peace keeper, you can't allow them to push your buttons. You must keep your temper if you are to win the day and help others. This might mean counseling or therapy to work through your issues. In particular, you must deal with internal anger and feelings of aggression before you can be an effective Warrior.

Fear is the biggest enemy of the Warrior. We're all afraid sometimes, but when you allow your fear to control you, then you become ineffective in any situation involving conflict. Start small, building your own courage and fostering honesty, and you will begin to find the Warrior spirit growing within. Perhaps you suffer from a phobia or irrational fear. Most people have minor ones (bugs are a common culprit). If you have a more serious fear, facing it will build your courage. Courage means confidence, which can do more to avoid a fight than the world's largest set of biceps.

Other skills you may want to cultivate include oration, mediation, and public speaking. A commanding voice can come in very handy. The ability to express yourself clearly and calmly is very important in resolving conflicts or mediating discussions. You might learn to write a compelling opinion piece or a moving letter of protest, and skills in dealing with the press can come in handy if you act as your group's liaison.

In addition, it's important to be able to back up your words with actions when necessary. While actual force is always the last recourse of a Pagan Warrior, if you need to subdue someone (for example, a drunk and dangerous ritual participant), you need to be able to do so without causing any undue harm. Building your strength is one way of accomplishing this. Another useful way of training is to study and practice martial arts. Many schools are specifically designed for people who aren't six feet tall and built like Superman. Women can particularly benefit from studying martial arts or taking a serious course in self-defense. You might also parlay your Warrior's instincts into volunteering for a local fire or search-and-rescue group. This would require a course of training in the necessary skills, but the work can be very rewarding.

Finally, work on building your Warrior's esoteric skills. Practice shielding, grounding, and protection spells. Learn to sense auras so you can tell what emotions others are feeling. If you are asked to be a fire keeper at a ritual, spend some time communing with the blaze. Work on becoming metaphorically invisible ("don't notice me" magic) as well as projecting a strong presence when needed. Make offerings to Warrior Deities in order to learn Their lessons.

People called to serve and protect are usually social and gregarious Pagans. They are typically involved in both the local Pagan community and the community at large. Some do practice a solitary spiritual path but are typically more than happy when called on to lend a helping hand. Particularly at public gatherings, Warriors are an excellent asset in keeping things running smoothly, both within the gathering and with the outside world. The Pagan Warrior has a strong urge to help others as well as a natural distaste for deceit, ego, unfairness, and injustice.

The Pagan Warrior acts more like a knight than a soldier. They are often called to act as emissaries, mediators, diplomats, and counselors. And while they might occasionally have the need to be authoritarian, typically the goal is to avoid conflict at all costs. Because they take on this role, their own motivations and actions must be above reproach. Hypocrisy and prejudice erode the respect they need to do their jobs.

One major challenge that Warriors face is in being objective and calm in the face of strong emotion. Because they are motivated by the urge to help others, it's temping for the Warrior to sympathize too much with one side of the debate. Yet, to be effective, a Warrior needs to step back and be a nonbiased presence and authority. Warriors can't allow themselves to become too emotionally involved. In addition, because Warriors project an aura of trust, their company is often sought after. But a large ego is a detriment to their role and they need to avoid this particular pitfall as well. Above all, Warriors must control their tempers and remember that their primary role is one of peace.

Warriors are often misunderstood in the Pagan community. Just because some are called to fight doesn't mean they don't appreciate peace. Violence is always the last resort for a Pagan Warrior, but we will always need those who are willing to stand up and fight for tolerance, freedom, and liberty. If you feel the call to take up the banner for worthy causes and to help people resolve their differences, the role of the Pagan Warrior could be for you.

Areas that someone interested in being a Warrior might explore include:

- Psychology, sociology, and group dynamics in order to understand people and, in particular, crowds
- Diplomacy, debate, and constructive criticism in order to communicate effectively
- Oration and diction for a commanding voice
- Martial arts, defense, confidence, and discipline
- Advanced shielding, grounding, and other spiritually protective techniques
- Empathy and aura sensing to help analyze a potentially difficult situation

BARD

Unfortunately, students of the bardic arts are rather rare in modern Paganism. It's unusual that a circle will include a skilled musician or singer, and this is very unfortunate. The power and focus that a well-trained musician can bring to a ritual or magic working is tremendous. Part of the lack is the fact that it takes a certain level of skill and training to be effective in a ritual setting. However, another problem is that many Pagans are simply unaware of how to handle a trained Bard in their circles.

The original Bard was primarily a storyteller, passing on the oral lore of a community, specifically through music. In addition to the traditional musical storyteller, there are several other areas of musicianship that can be considered bardic in the right context. For example, a ritual drummer can keep even large groups of people synched or move them to a trance state. And a skilled instrumentalist can weave the story of a ritual through the group and keep the energy tuned correctly.

Many Pagans are creative types and may have some musical skill. But to become a Bard, you have to take that ability much further. Bards don't just create background music; they direct and modulate energy, induce trance, and teach stories or emotional lessons through music.

Like many artistic types, Bards often operate on instinct to a much higher degree than even the average Pagan. They can be irrational, but this can serve them well in their work. And they often work very hard indeed. Unlike some specialists, a half-trained Bard can be worse than none at all. This is another reason Bards are atypical in modern practice. The circle drummer *must* have perfect rhythm and the stamina never to falter, or a trance state cannot be induced. The storyteller must be a superb orator, or the story falls flat. The music must be well executed as well as appropriate for the ritual.

Like the Healer, the typical Bard is a person for whom music permeates all aspects of life. Bards are often audiophiles and may have other mundane musical careers or practices. Music for them isn't just a hobby; it's an all-encompassing passion that colors every area of their existence. They must play or sing to be whole.

By the way, if you ever have the opportunity to include a Bard in your circle, here are some ways of maximizing the experience:

- **Confer in advance on how the Bard likes to work.** Some may want to take the focus at a certain point to tell a story, while others wish to remain in the background working throughout the ritual. A drummer skilled in inducing trance should only play during parts of the ritual where that is your purpose.

- **Discuss the parts of the ritual ahead of time.** The Bard should understand how best to serve the purpose and energy of the event. If you want to increase or decrease the energy at any point, induce a trance state, or change the mood of the ritual, let the Bard know. If you have a lesson or reading that you want to include, the Bard might be the perfect person to deliver it, but he or she should have time beforehand to rehearse and become familiar with the material.

- **Include the Bard in the circle.** This would seem obvious, but I've seen people forget to bless the Bard, neglect to offer entrance into the circle, or even exclude the Bard from the casting. If you are in a situation where a Bard will play throughout the ritual, get him or her settled in advance and don't forget to cast around that area as well. Treat the Bard like any other participant, but one whose hands are literally full. If you are smudging or cleansing the ritual participants, also do this for the Bard. Determine beforehand how much distraction he or she can handle.

- **Allow the Bard's instincts to come into play.** Skilled musicians typically have an excellent sense of their audience's needs. Pagan Bards should also be highly skilled at sensing magical or spiritual energy. They often instinctively know how long to keep a trance beat going, or how best to play to meditative silence.

- **Appreciate the Bard's energy expenditure.** Because they must be tuned into the group while remaining detached enough to continue playing, Bards can become drained by the end of a ritual. I've seen Bards keep people warm during cold night rituals or induce heavy trance states, but not be able to adequately tap into the energy and still weave the music appropriately. It's important to make sure that the Bard is part of the feedback loop so that he or she benefits from the energy in the circle. In addition, make sure the Bard who wants to achieve trance state feels comfortable and not distracted. Again, confer with the Bard to determine how best to accomplish this.

First and foremost, being a Bard means having a talent for music and/or storytelling. If you are tone deaf or have no sense of rhythm, the bardic arts are probably not for you. In addition, Bards must have the ability to sense energy and manipulate it through their music. While all advancing Pagans should be well attuned to energy work, Bards must have the additional ability to meld that knowledge with their own musical knowledge.

Fortunately, if you are interested in being a Bard, there are a number of mundane teachers who can get you started. Pick an instrument (voice, drums, guitar, etc.) and take lessons to learn the rudiments of how to play. As you learn, work at sensing the energy flows around you and connecting them to your music. Some knowledge of musical theory can also be very helpful. As your basic abilities grow, make sure to nurture the creative side of your musicality. Then practice incorporating your talents into magic and ritual work. Skilled Bards may have worked many decades on their craft, but if you enjoy it, if music makes your heart sing and your spirit move, it will be worth the effort.

While making an excellent addition to group work, the bardic arts are also well practiced as a solitary. For the solitary Bard, music can increase magical potency or help connect with the Deities. In addition, there's a strong connection between music and the natural world. While most people are only instinctively aware of the links, a study of sacred geometry can help us consciously identify the way that the architecture of Nature reflects the music of the Divine. And bardic arts can be incorporated into other areas such as healing and oracular abilities.

One problem common to Bards is in communicating with others

on a nonmusical level. The metaphor of music colors so much of what Bards experience that it can be difficult for them to convey their thoughts without relying on it. In the circle, they are eloquent beyond mere words, but they will struggle to describe exactly what it is they do or how they work. This is one reason it's so important to communicate clearly with a Bard before a ritual begins. Excessively intuitive, Bards sometimes find describing their own process a challenge.

Just as in ancient times, Bards are responsible for keeping the lineage of a group or tradition alive. Their energy fortifies and focuses the circle and keeps everyone together. Their music can be used for many purposes and their stories contain lessons that we need to hear. For advancing Pagans who hear the music of the spheres in their dreams and feel the rhythm of the Earth in their bones, the path of the Bard is their calling.

Areas that someone interested in bardic arts might explore include:

- Singing, voice, and other vocal training
- Oration, storytelling, and mythology for bardic delivery in ritual
- Drumming, trance, and rhythm for moving into altered states
- Guitar, pipes, flute, and any other instrumental skills
- Musical theory, audience energy sensing, and performance

SCRIBE / RESEARCHER

As we've learned, there are a number of great books that include information relevant to the advancing Pagan. However, finding the good tidbits in a morass of less useful data can be a challenge. Old books can be difficult to read and assimilate and are often couched in metaphor or allegory. In addition, to make the most of what you find, you must then connect it to the rest of the world. The Pagan Scribe has a talent for making these connections and an ability to share them in an understandable way with others.

The Pagan Scribe is a thinker, a reader, and above all a researcher. Scribes enjoy poring over old books, finding hints of Pagan practice in folklore or fairytales, and connecting seemingly disparate ideas into cohesive wholes. One may work with a group, acting as a kind of coven librarian and source of information, or a Scribe may be solitary, seeking knowledge for himself and his own spiritual growth. In either case, the pursuit of knowledge both frustrates and fascinates. It frustrates because it often seems that the key or right connection is out of reach. But it also fascinates. The Scribe will spend countless hours seeking that spark of connection, that "a-ha" moment.

In group settings, Scribes often play a role in constructing rituals. They may have a new perspective on a Sabbat or be able to find obscure symbols for the various Deities. They can use their research skills to discover and adjust ancient invocations or poetry for a modern use. In addition, they are often great historians, understanding the truth of our Pagan past from the earliest sources available. Finally, the Scribe should have the ability to take what he or she has discovered and lay it out in a form that others can understand. This means taking on the role of author or teacher of arcane knowledge.

These skills require a logical and analytical mind, excellent vocabulary and reading comprehension, and a good memory. However, the skills of the Scribe go beyond these everyday abilities. The Scribe's most important talent is the ability to think symbolically and make connections between disparate ideas. This is a nonrational or intuitive ability, and it can create the web of connections that facilitate true understanding. In addition, that ability allows the Scribe to connect ancient knowledge to the modern world in a way that's understandable and relevant to today's Pagans.

If you have the opportunity to work with Scribes, here are a few points to keep in mind:

- **Give them enough time for inspiration to strike.** Writing a good ritual can take time. Finding obscure information requires research. If you need help of any kind from a Scribe, make sure there's enough time in advance for them to do their work. This includes time to ask questions and get the sense of the material you want.

- **Remember that reading the writing of others takes time and energy.** Writers are often requested to read and critique the work of others. It can be a challenge to do a good job. If you get useful feedback on your own writing or poetry, you could consider thanking the Scribe with a small gift (I prefer chocolate). But the thing that most writers want the most is honest, objective feedback on their own work.

- **Respect Scribes' original material.** If you have a great chant, invocation, or poem provided by your group's Scribe, make sure to keep his or her name attached. While most Scribes are happy to share their work with others, it's an insult to their hard work when it ends up on the Internet as an anonymous piece. Also, if you want to use a Scribe's work in a ritual, request permission first and credit the Scribe afterwards.

- **Make your Scribe feel comfortable.** Some Scribes are very introverted, feeling more comfortable with books than people. These individuals have a wealth of knowledge to share if you approach them with some patience. Others are most articulate in writing, less so in person. Never make Scribes feel embarrassed about the myriad facts wandering around in their brains. No one likes to feel ostracized because he or she can quote Chaucer or make three obscure connections between any two random facts.

To become a Scribe, you must find joy in reading and thinking about a broad range of topics. While particular Scribes may have areas of interest or expertise, some basic background in anthropology, sociology, and comparative mythology makes a great starting point. In addition, the ability to read critically and write well is very helpful. Fortunately, you don't need a college degree to come by this knowledge. Your library or local bookstore will have everything you need to become an expert Scribe—if you have the inclination and patience.

If you're just starting out, it can take some time to begin making new symbolic connections. At first it may seem that ideas don't relate to anything at all. As time passes, however, you will discover that new material will "click," forming a link with something you already know. The more you learn, the more this feeling will increase in frequency and power.

One problem that Scribes struggle with is simply letting go and experiencing the moment. They tend to want to analyze everything, which can have a detrimental effect on their ability to meditate or reach an ecstatic state. Their highly trained conscious minds may become fixated on symbolism, connections to other issues, and criticism. It can be difficult to shut that off when it's not needed.

Being typical bookworms, Scribes are often quiet and perhaps shy. However, many are eventually called to share what they know with others. This is where communication skills come in. To share the results of your research, you must have the ability to frame your knowledge in a way that others can understand. This means learning to write or speak clearly and directly, and at a level your audience will understand. If you have a passion for reading, a broad range of interests, and a good sense of symbolism, the work of a Scribe might be your specialty.

Areas that someone interested in being a Scribe might explore include:

- Anthropology, archeology, comparative mythology, and other ways of understanding ancient cultures
- Psychology, sociology, and tools for comprehending people
- A laundry list of magical correspondences such as colors, herbs, and planetary aspects, as well as forms of divination

- Symbolic and critical thinking skills
- Mystery schools from other cultures, such as the Kabbalah, Western occult traditions, Sufi, Taoism, and so on
- Literary criticism, reading comprehension, and writing skills

ORACLE / SEER

History is filled with stories of oracles, prophets, and seers who have the ability to tap into the future, access hidden wisdom, or communicate directly with the Deities. Often, these people were chosen by the Gods. Some had visions or the ability to leave their bodies from an early age. In tribal societies, children with these talents were marked and trained from childhood. Today, modern Oracles are often on their own, being in a position to have to train themselves.

In my experience, Oracles are usually intuitively skilled at divination, can enter trance states very easily, have a rich symbolic dream life, and are experts at invocation. They may have experienced visions. They often have the ability to disconnect and speak with the voice of Divinity, even while seeming completely conscious. They can also be highly tuned to the thoughts and feelings of others, or they can sense or see auras and other energy forms.

Their own practice is often highly intuitive and perhaps even chaotic. Many find rigid forms of ritual work tedious or irrelevant. But when it comes time to look into the future or call on the Goddess, these are the participants you rely on. Oracles can work within a group setting, however many are solitary by choice. They may have difficulty relating well to large crowds or unfamiliar people. Or they may prefer to work with a small circle of close friends. This is in part because the work they do requires a strong sense of trust and safety. No matter who you are, attaining a trance state requires that you be very comfortable in your surroundings.

Oracles are only loosely connected to their bodies. They may have health issues that come from a certain level of self-neglect and are more prone to dependency on drugs or alcohol. More commonly, they simply have trouble dealing with day-to-day concerns. For example, they may lack the ability to focus on things they find uninteresting (although, conversely, they have a supreme ability to focus on things they find fascinating). The Oracle's checkbook is rarely balanced.

There are definitely some important rules to remember when working with Oracles:

- **Prepare for a certain amount of chaos.** Oracles can sometimes be difficult to deal with in circle because they follow their own instincts as opposed to predetermined ritual. Remember that instinctual understanding is the provenance of the Oracle and allow for some flexibility.
- **Be sympathetic to the energy expenditure involved.** Entering a trance state can take a great deal of energy. Even basic readings require the Oracle to focus and reach inward to provide good information. Because they can be physically a bit disconnected, they may not notice when they're doing too much. It's important to make sure that the requests of a large group of people don't inadvertently drain the Oracle's energy.
- **Don't treat the Oracle like Cassandra.** Poor Cassandra was cursed to be a completely accurate Oracle . . . whom no one believed. But even without a curse, too many people are apt to request an honest reading and then ignore, or even scoff at, the advice they get. If you ask a skilled Oracle for a reading, make sure you're ready to hear the truth.
- **Don't compromise the Oracle's objectivity.** In a trance state, Oracles may not remember the things they say. Make sure you don't put words in their mouths or ask leading questions. One great way of ensuring that the message remains as clear as possible is to record the trance. That way, the Oracle can listen later.

If you have the gift, training as an Oracle will be beneficial to both your mundane and your spiritual life. The right training can help you confine your experiences to the appropriate time and place instead of allowing them to intrude into the rest of your life. In addition, it can focus your skills and improve your accuracy when you do practice. The best way to obtain this training is through an ethical and skilled teacher. Easier said than done. They can be difficult to find. Alternately, you can find good books on the subject of basic energy techniques such as grounding and shielding. Make a habit of deliberately and completely shielding yourself and your home on a regular basis.

Other important skills for the Oracle are meditation and development of techniques to focus attention. The kind of meditation you practice is irrelevant. Use what feels right and natural for you. One excellent method of focusing your energy is to meditate on an item you use for divination. You should also get to know many methods of divining, from the very structured (e.g., astrology, Tarot, or runes) to the very unstructured (e.g., scrying).

Focusing on your physical body can help ground you. Meditation can be useful; however, the best way to be "in your body" is to get some good old fashioned exercise. Optimally, exercise will work your body and encourage the balance you need to find your physical as well as your spiritual center. Tai chi is excellent and low impact. Almost anyone should be able to practice it.

Other areas that someone interested in being an Oracle might explore include:

- All types of divination
- Trance work and methods of altering states of consciousness
- Symbolic thinking, mythology, and intuitive metaphor analysis
- Grounding and shielding techniques
- Invocation methods for connecting directly with the Deities

HIGH PRIEST/PRIESTESS

It's a Pagan axiom that each person is his or her own priest or priestess. From the nonhierarchal viewpoint, this is certainly true—in a sense. We are all tasked with guiding our own spiritual progress and interacting with the Divine directly. At the same time, there are people who dedicate themselves to being High Priests or Priestesses on a different level. These people are called to be teachers, leaders, or devotees of a particular Deity and devote themselves to that calling.

When we think of High Priests and Priestesses (HPs) we commonly picture coven leaders or teachers of 101-type classes. And in fact most HPs are public figures who work within the broader community in some kind of leadership or teaching capacity. However, it is also possible to be an HP and be solitary. This is more a case of being dedicated or devoted to a single Deity to the point where you can be considered a Priest or Priestess of that Deity. You might never lead a group of your own, but you have a formal commitment to a God or Goddess and focus your efforts and energy on working with Him or Her.

In the public sense, HPs are typically the elders of the community, and may have many different roles—counselor, peacekeeper, coven leader, ritual director, and so on—that cross all boundary lines. They are frequently called on to give advice or direction to others, lead rituals, or perform magic.

HPs may or may not have gone through formal training within a coven or group structure, but most people will recognize their experience and wisdom. The title of High Priest or Priestess is best bestowed by others, as it is an honor. HPs must be calm and evenhanded, objective, and without ulterior motive, and they need to have a strong sense of ethics. To lead a ritual, they must be skilled at sensing and manipulating energy and working in a group. To advise others, they must have some knowledge of human nature as well as their own limitations. The calling of a public HP is "to know in order to serve." They organize, focus, assist, and direct circles and rituals and gently guide those who come to them for help. They may also end up in a formal teaching position, helping those less experienced get started on their path.

A slightly different use of the title High Priest or Priestess applies to those who are called to serve and dedicate themselves to a particular Deity. In this case, it is the Deity who bestows the title, frequently after many years. While these HPs can be solitary, their positions as representatives of a Deity may still lead them to teach or share what they have learned. It is the Deities they serve who place strictures on them or give them tasks to accomplish, and their primary focus will always be on those Gods or Goddesses.

We should honor our High Priests and Priestesses. A few things to remember:

- **HPs give of their time.** Unlike some religions, the Pagan paths do not support full-time paid clergy. That means that HPs already have jobs and homes to care for. The time and effort they devote to the community are given on a volunteer basis, a gift. Always keep this in mind when asking an HP for help.

- **They can't do it all.** No matter how much they'd like to, HPs need help to organize rituals or events and work magic. Lend a hand in whatever way you can. This includes volunteering to do the boring work like cleaning up after circle.

- **An HP with information to share has every right to charge for his or her time.** This is a touchy subject within the Pagan community, but there's validity to the statement that students will attach more value to something they have to pay for. While gouging those with less experience is not ethical, charging reasonable fees to cover time and costs is appropriate. If you don't choose to charge or pay for this kind of service, so be it. But if you wish to learn from someone who does charge, respect that person and the way he or she works, and pay on time.

- **Your HP is not a baby-sitter.** Most HPs will be there for you, even in the middle of the night, to talk you through a tough time. But that kind of dedication takes its toll. Take responsibility for your own life and try to solve your own problems first. That way, when you really need help, your HP will be there for you and won't be burned out or low on energy.

While some Pagans will embark on specific training programs (whether solitary or group-based) in order to become a High Priest or Priestess, others simply end up in that position as time passes and they learn more about their craft. They may be called on to help others or take a lead role. In addition, Gods and Goddesses may call on certain individuals to work with Them. In any case, it's the person's calling that initiates him or her on the path to becoming an HP.

In many ways, HPs are the renaissance men and women in our communities. To be effective, you need to have a broad range of skills both internal and external. You will be called on to act as counselor and mediator, so psychology, sociology, oration, mediation, and public speaking will all come in handy. You will also be asked to create and run rituals, so you should know how to write and direct them. During ritual you will need to control and direct the energy. This means general energy work in addition to grounding, shielding, and meditation. If you invoke, you will need to be able to enter and maintain a trance.

If you are called on by a particular Deity, that Deity must be your guide. You may be directed in certain practices or asked to learn something new. This can range from the very mundane-seeming to the highly esoteric. The most powerful skill you can cultivate when you work with a particular Deity is learning to listen to that Deity. Sometimes Deities communicate very directly, but often the messages are cryptic, subtle, or intuitive. Learn to listen and you will soon grow into your position and power.

The major issue that High Priests and Priestesses have to contend with is ego. As people begin to rely on you, or as you are called to lead or help others, it can make you feel very special. However, it's important (for everyone actually, but doubly so for an HP) that you not succumb to hubris or pride. As I said in the introduction, the journey we take is infinite, so we're all already halfway there—and *only* halfway there. As you advance, there may be people, some of them still beginners, who look to you for guidance. However, there are equally as many people ahead of you to whom you might look. When we keep this in mind, it keeps us humble and objective about our own motivations.

No one person has all the answers. This is also important for HPs who have been called to follow or represent a particular Deity. As powerful and valid as their experiences might be, they don't necessarily apply to everyone. Even as we seek guidance from those we consider wise, and give guidance to those who consider us wise, each person's path is individual. In the end, we must find our own unique ways of growing.

While the titles of High Priest and Priestess are typically conferred on people with a great deal of experience, you can still choose to work toward that end no matter where you currently are. Begin learning now so that, when and if you earn the title of HP, you will be well prepared for your role.

Areas that someone interested in being a High Priest or Priestess might explore include:

- Psychology, sociology, and other ways of understanding human nature
- Meditation for introspective purposes
- Diplomacy and mediation for dealing with group dynamics
- Energy sensing and manipulation
- Highly tuned empathy

FOOD FOR THOUGHT—HIERARCHY AND DEMOCRACY

While the primary focus of this book is on solitary practice, at one point or another, most Pagans and Witches are called to work or interact with others. This is particularly true of those advancing Pagans who decide to take on a particular job or role (like healing). However, this brings up questions of hierarchy and democracy within the Pagan community.

Pagan paths are *so* nondogmatic as a rule that many believe issues of hierarchy don't apply to or really affect us. This is not the case. In particular, advancing solitaries within the larger community have certain challenges to overcome. For example, without the ability to claim lineage or position within a particular group, solitaries lose legitimacy in some Pagans' eyes. In addition, there's the sense that the solitary is always a beginner. Many groups will only take you into their 101 or basics program of study, considering you a rank amateur and discounting what may be years of independent study and work.

From the other end of things, advancing solitaries are often inundated with requests by solitary beginners for training or leadership. While that is flattering, it may not be the direction the person in question wants to take. When you spend much of your time working alone, it may be discussion and work with peers and experts that you crave. Finally, claiming to be an expert within the community raises significant issues. Again, if you've gone through your group's three-ring training program, you may legitimately claim to be an HP in your tradition. But what about claims of adepthood for skills like divination, sacred poetry, healing, etc?

Many Pagans regard all claims of expertise with suspicion. On the one hand, we are an independent lot, prone to judging for ourselves. On the other hand, most of us do respect certain levels of authority. A person who has studied with someone we respect or completed a certification course we trust may have more clout. As you advance, you have to strike a balance between honest assessment and acceptance of your skills, and the understanding that not everyone will see you in the same way. I've known many Pagans who struggle with issues of democracy and hierarchy individually. Who are they, they wonder, to fault or question the claims of others? At the same time, how do we handle someone who can't back up his claims?

This clash between hierarchy and democracy comes into play most clearly in the group dynamics of a coven or circle. Some groups have a strict hierarchy where everyone knows who's in charge. Others have no stated leader and run everything completely democratically. While moderation and balance probably are the best solution to this particular issue, it's a vivid lesson for all Pagans, whether solitary or group-based.

Currently, the trend in Pagan thinking is toward a very democratic model. Eclectic practice is considered completely acceptable and there's hesitance to judge the beliefs and practices of others. In most respects, this is a very positive occurrence. However, one of our goals as Pagans is to attempt to see ourselves and the rest of the world clearly and objectively. There are things we may consider to be wrong. In those cases we have the right, and perhaps even the duty, to voice our objections—as long as we do it respectfully. Too much democracy is as stifling to open debate and competing ideas as rigid hierarchy. Neither is healthy. The sense that we cannot legitimately question other practices, beliefs, and ideas for fear of being labeled non-PC (Paganly Correct) is dangerous. Of course, we will never all agree on everything. However, one of our keys to understanding and growing is to *question* the information that we are given. Only when we feel free to do so are we really learning.

CHAPTER 9 EXERCISES

What Color Is Your Pentagram?

As you advance and your learning increases, it's a good idea to commit some time to reviewing where you are now. This is particularly important when trying to decide on an area of specialty where you may want to focus. All the things you've discovered and practiced up to this point will affect the decisions you make in the future. Of course this is true of life in general. However, since many of the spiritual lessons we learn are intuitive, internal, or difficult to isolate as part of the whole, it's vitally important to give some thought to those lessons we've learned.

Your introspection can be used to make an honest assessment of where you were, where you are, and where you would like to be. This in turn will begin to suggest areas where you need to grow on your future path. You may accomplish this self-analysis using whatever tools make sense for you: writing, divination, dream work, altered states, or a combination of techniques. This will allow you to approach the issue from different directions. What are some of the questions you should be asking yourself? In relation to your study and practice as a Witch or Pagan, you may want to ask:

- What are some of your greatest spiritual successes? Spectacular past failures? The places where you rocked and the ones where you screwed up big time—both can help you analyze your innate talents and areas where you struggle.
- Which lessons were the hardest for you to learn? Which were easy? Things that are easy for you point to your natural strengths. Those areas that are a challenge may also indicate an area of importance—one where you have a lesson to learn.
- What are some of your best "ah hah!" spiritual moments and how did they come about? Those little tidbits that can seem so mundane but really "blew your mind" when they first occurred to you are powerful lessons that you should remember. Recalling how they occurred to you will help you understand your own learning style.
- In all your reading and exploration, what topics interested you the most? The least? While we typically follow our interests,

there may have been times when we thought something sounded really fascinating, but we didn't pursue it at the time.

- How comfortable are you working with others? Are you primarily solitary or group-focused? Knowing your own comfort level with others can help you decide on a future "Pagan specialty."

- What everyday interests and hobbies do you enjoy that may be tied into your spiritual practice? In the interests of integrating our lives as fully as possible, it's a good idea to review the ways that nonspiritual hobbies mesh or mix with our spiritual path. For example, gardening can lead to herbalism and knitting to knot magic.

Keep a list of your answers to any of these questions that seem relevant and any others that you think of. Also note any revelations that come from your introspection (divination results or relevant dreams for example). Eventually, you will have a much more complete view of your own path and skill level which you can use to decide where to go next.

Play to Your Strengths, Follow Your Heart, Focus on Your Weaknesses

After giving some thought to your past knowledge and current position, decide where to put your efforts next. Despite your new level of self-understanding, this can still be difficult. How do we decide which doors we want to open now? One way is to play to our strengths, follow our hearts, and focus on our weaknesses. For example:

Amber is an advancing Pagan with a love for reading and writing. She's always had a gift for discovering hidden nuggets of wisdom in the strangest places and can make her ideas understood to a broad audience. She can definitely see herself in the role of a Scribe. She also has a strong love of music, but little training. Her main weakness is in meditation and altering her consciousness.

What might Amber choose to study? First, she decides to "play to her strength" as a Scribe. She chooses to improve her understanding of Far Eastern mythology and religious systems by studying and analyzing the connections between those paths and the ones she currently knows. Her goals include reading certain books, learning the I Ching, and immersing herself as much as possible in the cultures of China and Japan.

Next she resolves to "follow her heart" by studying music. Of course, she may not have the talent or dedication necessary to become a Bard, and this isn't even her goal, but her love of music will only be enhanced by practicing it. In addition, she'll find that her magic and ritual work will improve, even if she never becomes a virtuoso. She chooses voice lessons and begins reading books about musical theory.

Finally, she elects to "focus on her weakness" in the area of meditation. Far from ignoring her lack of skill, she takes the challenge to overcome her weakness as much as possible. She decides to take a Tai Chi class (which ties in neatly with her interest in the Far East) and resolves to practice regularly.

Stone, on the other hand, is a skilled Oracle. Although somewhat ungrounded, he is an expert diviner and can invoke Deities very easily. He also loves to cook and bake food from around the world. His main weakness is in dealing with groups of people. He's shy and feels tongue-tied unless he knows a person well.

Stone chooses to "play to his strength" by expanding his repertoire of divination skills. He picks those forms that are more associated with the Earth and nature (geomancy, runes, and one that he will invent for himself). He also decides to spend more time outdoors meditating.

Stone decides to "follow his heart" by turning his love of cooking into herbal/magical potion brewing. Cultivating some of his own herbs will give him the opportunity to relax outdoors and commune with growing things. In addition, it will be a grounding experience, helping to balance his inherent "airy" nature.

Finally, he is determined to broaden his circle of friends and overcome his shyness. He decides that an open Pagan discussion group at one of the local bookstores will give him a good start and also looks into taking a course on local plant life at the community college. This will help him in his quest to connect more fully with nature as well as meet some new people with similar interests.

From these examples you can begin to see how advancing Pagans might pick activities to study that will help them integrate their lives and give them a well-rounded set of skills, without ignoring their inherent talents. This is one way of viewing what might seem like an infinite array of possibilities, then narrowing your focus.

CONCLUSION

No matter what your goals are, the four tools needed for spiritual growth remain the same: *learn, think, question, and do.* Throughout this book, we've focused on finding the information we need to advance, thinking about what we've learned, questioning how the data fits into our worldview, and then making it real by using it. Whether you choose to work as a solitary, as part of the larger community, or with a group, your path will always remain unique to you.

The goal of this book isn't to tell you everything you need to know to advance; it is to point you in the right direction for your own study. I hope that some of the ideas here have proved useful. However, if there's one lesson you should remember, it's that only you can determine what works for you. Your instincts, wisdom, and intuition are your guides, and no book or teacher can replace that.

These hints are intended to provide a bit of practical advice and direction to make the transition from beginner to advancing Pagan as smooth as possible. I can't stress enough that the world is already literally bursting with amazing and mysterious information. These keys are occult only by virtue of being hidden to others. Dedicated seekers can find a web of connected knowledge from books and teachers, the natural world, and their own minds. Limited only by the limits we place on ourselves, the universe has provided us with a complete curriculum for spiritual growth.

As you stand on the cusp of the next part of your journey, may your search for knowledge and wisdom be fruitful and fulfilling.

Notes

1. De Shong Meador, Betty. *Inanna, Lady of Largest Heart: Poems of the Sumerian High Priestess Enheduanna.* Austin: University of Texas Press, 2000.
2. *The Internet Sacred Text Archive.* www.sacred-texts.com.
3. *Bartleby.com: Great Books Online.* www.bartleby.com.
4. *Amazon.com.* www.amazon.com.
5. *Powells.com.* www.powells.com/.
6. Agrippa, Henry Cornelius. *Three Books of Occult Pholosophy.* Trans. James Freake. Ed. Donald Tyson. St. Paul, MN: Llewellyn Publications, 1994.
7. Graves, Robert. *The White Goddess.* New York: Noonday Press, 1997.
8. Gimbutas, Marija. *The Goddesses and Gods of Old Europe: Myths and Cult Images.* New and Updated Edition. London: Thames and Hudson Ltd., 1982.
9. Hawking, Steven W. *A Brief History of Time: From the Big Bang to Black Holes.* New York: Bantam Books, 1988.
10. Stephenson, Neal. *Snow Crash.* New York: Bantam Books, 1993.
11. *Merriam-Webster's Collegiate Dictionary.* Electronic ed. www.m-w.com.
12. Guerin, Wilfred L., et al. *A Handbook of Critical Approaches to Literature.* Oxford: Oxford University Press, 1992.
13. Jung, Carl G., et al. *Man and His Symbols.* New York: Dell, 1964.
14. Grasse, Ray. *The Waking Dream: Unlocking the Symbolic Language of Our Lives.* Wheaton, IL: Quest Books, 1996. XIII.
15. Jung, 226
16. *Merriam-Webster's Collegiate Dictionary.* Electronic ed. www.m-w.com.
17. Jung, 58
18. Campbell, Joseph. *The Hero with a Thousand Faces.* 2nd ed. Princeton, NJ: Princeton University Press, 1968.
19. *Star Wars.* Dir. George Lucas. Perf. Mark Hamill, Harrison Ford, Carrie Fisher. 20th Century-Fox, 1977.
20. *Joseph Campbell and the Power of Myth with Bill Moyers.* DVD. Mystic Fire Video, 1998.
21. Whitcomb, Bill. *The Magician's Companion: A Practical and Encyclopedic Guide to Magical and Religious Symbolism.* St. Paul, MN: Llewellyn Publications, 1993.

22. Paxson, Diana L. *The White Raven*. New York: Avon Books, 1988.

23. Sahtouris, Elisabet, and James E. Lovelock. "Earthdance: Living Systems in Evolution." iUniverse.com, 2000.

24. Wolfe, Tom. *The Painted Word*. New York: Bantam Doubleday Dell, 1975. 4.

25. Cranston, Maurice. *The Noble Savage: Jean-Jacques Rousseau 1754–1762*. Chicago: University of Chicago Press, 1999.

26. Holman, C. Hugh, et al. *A Handbook to Literature*, 9th ed. Englewood Cliffs, NJ: Prentice-Hall, 2002.

27. Tennyson, Alfred Lord. "On Mortality," part LVI. 1850.

28. Hobbes, Thomas. *Leviathan* (Oxford World's Classics). London: Oxford University Press, 1998.

29. Shakespeare, William. *Macbeth*, Act IV, Scene I.

30. Crowley, Aleister. *Magic in Theory and Practice*. Thame, England: I-H-O Books, 1999.

31. Thompson, Lady Gwen (Gwynne). *Green Egg* magazine vol. III. no. 69 (Ostara 1975).

32. Doreen Valiente.

33. *Encyclopedia Mythica*. www.pantheon.org.

34. Ibid.

35. *Merriam-Webster's Collegiate Dictionary*. Electronic ed. www.m-w.com.

36. Ibid.

Bibliography

A truly comprehensive list of references would comprise a book of its own. In gathering these titles, I've tried to avoid the obvious (*The White Goddess*) and instead included more off-the-beaten-path selections. Here is just a small sampling of those books that I feel are a cut above the rest in innovation or usability.

Non-Pagan Books

The I Ching or Book of Changes. Richard Wilhelm. New York: Bollingen Foundation, 1950.

Wilhelm's German translation (translated into English by Cary F. Baynes) is one excellent translation of this ancient book of Chinese wisdom. In fact, Carl Jung wrote the foreword. While commonly used for divination, the book also contains a complete discussion of the philosophy behind the 64 hexagrams.

This isn't the type of book you read cover to cover. Instead, approach the book in sections. Try your hand at coin-toss divination or bibliomancy, read the background material (in book II) in small sections, and explore each hexagram as it appears.

The Waking Dream: Unlocking the Symbolic Language of Our Lives. Ray Grasse. Wheaton, IL: Quest Books, 1996.

One of my favorite books, *The Waking Dream* taught me the keys to symbolic thinking. It was the first book I ever read that described what it really means to view the world in an interconnected way and gives both the theory behind symbolism as well as lots of practical examples. Chapter topics include omens, Karma, and ritual.

The correspondences that can be made through a synchronistic and wholistic world view are always surprising. For example, Grasse manages to combine such disparate systems as Western astrology and Eastern chakras into a logical and useful system of personal examination.

A Beginner's Guide to Constructing the Universe: The Mathematical Archetypes of Nature, Art, and Science. Michael S. Schneider. New York: Harper Perennial, 1994.

Geometry was never this much fun! This excellent review of sacred geometry makes a strong case that the underlying truth of the universe is based on proportion, angle, and harmony of shape. I thought I was familiar with numerology, but I found something new on every page. My understanding of what numbers really mean in terms of spirituality was greatly enhanced through this book.

The book is divided into chapters by number, one through ten. Each section describes the shapes associated with that number, gives instructions for drawing it with compass and straightedge, and discusses its meaning. The examples are excellent. Schneider discusses how the principles and proportions behind each number have appeared (and continue to appear) in art, architecture, and design throughout the world.

The Return of the Goddess. Edward C. Whimont. New York: Crossroad Publishing, 1982.

A book that I am continually absorbing and revisiting. This is one of those books that stands at the crossroads of philosophy/psychology and mysticism/ Paganism. Far from strange bedfellows, the combination of psychological self-examination, archetypal understanding, and Pagan practice has always resonated strongly with me.

While I believe that Deities do exist outside ourselves (as opposed to being purely mental constructs), the goal in working with them is still, in large part, to clear out our own minds in order to understand more of our True Will. It may take some adjustment to read psychological texts as religious ones, but the results are worth it. And the size of the "metaphysical" section of your local bookstore will double once you do.

Primitive Mythology: The Masks of God (Volume One). Joseph Campbell. New York: Penguin, 1958.

Of course, I wholeheartedly recommend anything by Joseph Campbell; the man was one of the great thinkers of our time. Not an easy read, but a worthwhile one, the book is Campbell's attempt to prove the existence of a single spiritual history for all humankind that spans both culture and time.

This is the first volume of a four-volume set. In fact, Campbell was quite prolific, so there are lots of great places to start reading. If you're new to comparative mythology, you might check out his interviews with Bill Moyers as an introduction to both the man and his method of thinking.

Inanna: Lady of Largest Heart / Poems of the Sumerian High Priestess Enheduanna. Betty De Shong Meador. Austin: University of Texas Press, 2000.

Civilization's first poet was a woman and high priestess, and her subject of choice was one of the Great Goddesses of history. Moving, powerful, and above all poetic, Meador's translations from the Sumerian lose none of their Pagan power. And because she works as a scholar, not as a Pagan, I feel more comfortable about the accuracy of her translation. Not only did I learn about Inanna from the most reliable of sources, I also learned a lot about what makes for good spiritual or religious poetry.

The Book of Divination. Ann Fiery. San Francisco: Chronicle Books, 1999.

A smart, no-nonsense review of Western divination techniques. While this book gives only a taste of each school or method, it can be a great starting point for further exploration. The book is particularly useful because it is divorced from any one religious or philosophical worldview while keeping a nonskeptical tone. In fact, it's a bit of a coffee-table book of divination techniques, filled with pictures and interesting tidbits about the various arts.

Irish Cures, Mystic Charms, and Superstitions. Lady Wilde (compiled by Sheila Ann Barry). New York: Sterling, 1991.

From the back cover: "Over 100 years ago, Lady Wilde, mother of famed author Oscar Wilde and an excellent writer herself, collected these hundreds of ancient cures, spells, homespun proverbs, visionary omens and prophecies."

This book is a fascinating look at Irish folklore. Peel away a thin veneer of Christianity and get a real sense of what Irish Pagan thinking was really like. If your entire experience with Celtic religion is through the interpretation of modern Pagan authors, you might be surprised at what you find here.

Pagan Books

Unlike the bad old days, when you were lucky to find a copy of *The Spiral Dance* in your local library, there are a huge number of Pagan books on the market. The problem for the advancing Pagan is separating the useful wheat from the chaff. These books go beyond the standard introductory or Pagan 101 material.

Circles, Groves, and Sanctuaries: Sacred Spaces of Today's Pagans. Dan and Pauline Campanelli. St. Paul, MN: Llewellyn, 1992.

Not your typical Pagan book, this is a compendium of the ways that real Pagans worship and create their sacred spaces. From the most traditional to the most eclectic, this book covers both indoor and outdoor spaces. Fascinating as an overview, it can also prove inspiring to your own practice.

The book includes lots of photos as well as personal stories of how modern neo-Pagans worship. I found the rituals described less useful than seeing what people did with their own sacred spaces—from tiny traveling altars to stone circles on farms.

Earth Time Moon Time: Rediscovering the Sacred Lunar Year. Annette Hinshaw. St. Paul, MN: Llewellyn, 1999.

A respite from the standard discussions of the calendar and astrology typically found in modern Pagan publishing. This book discusses a completely lunar model for viewing the personality, one based on the moon when you were born. While written to be accessible to Pagans of any experience level, the content is innovative enough to be on the advancing Pagan's shelf.

Advanced Wicca: Exploring Deeper Levels of Spiritual Skills and Masterful Magick. Patricia Telesco. New York: Kensington, 2000.

One of only a few other advanced Pagan books. This book has a primarily Wiccan and group-oriented focus, but there is still a lot of great material that moves past the basics. Telesco relies on her extensive experience to describe more complex workings as well as giving sound advice for advanced Pagans working in groups.

The Complete Book of Incense Oils and Brews. Scott Cunningham. St. Paul, MN: Llewellyn, 1989.

A great reference source from one of the Pagan community's most well known and respected authors. This book includes instructions for actually making things like bath salts, oils, and incense as well as a ton of recipes for most magical purposes. I usually skip the pre-made spells and go straight to the section on substitutions. I formulate a list of ingredients that have the properties and uses I need, then cross-reference to what I already have on hand or growing nearby. A book of this type cannot be all things to all people, but I have had excellent success with spells, using this book as a resource.

Resources

The Internet is an invaluable resource for the advancing Pagan. Once again, I've focused on sites that are useful, but less well known than the large Pagan sites (like www.witchvox.com).

Sacred Texts
www.sacred-texts.com/index.htm
This easy-to-use site includes a broad array of religious and spiritual writings. The complete texts have been converted to HTML and are easy to read online. Or you can choose to support the site by buying a copy of all the material on CD-ROM. Texts include public domain and expired copyright (U.S.) items only, so you can feel confident that you're reading on the sunny side of the law. Read the Copyrights page for more details. One caveat: For ease of use, you should open your browser to full screen.

Areas include: Alchemy, Book of Shadows, Buddhism, Celtic, Egyptian, Esoteric & Occult, Goddesses, Grimoires, I Ching, Legends and Sagas, Neopaganism/Wicca, Shamanism, Tarot, Theosophy, and many others. Each section contains one or more relevant texts and the site is always expanding its list.

Encyclopedia Mythica
www.pantheon.org/mythica
This extensive site includes essays or descriptions based on keywords (deity name, mythological location, group of beings, and so on). While some of the descriptions are short, the encyclopedia covers an amazing amount of ground, including information from every corner of the globe. The mythology section is arranged geographically, dividing the world into five major sections. In addition, the articles are cross-referenced so that clicking on a keyword in one description will take you directly to the relevant topic.

The site also includes a search engine, punctuation guide, folklore section, bestiary, image gallery, and genealogy tables. You can even submit your own articles for possible inclusion in the site.

Myths and Legends
www.myths.com/pub/myths/myth.html
The ultimate Web directory for mythology, this site lists links to numerous other sites. Updated pretty regularly, it also includes sections for horror, fantasy,

science fiction, and medieval and renaissance. The mythology section is organized by geographical location as well as area of interest.

A barebones and primarily text-based design means that this site is easy to access over slower connections. An excellent place to start your online research on topics related to deities, folklore, mythology, and the like.

The SurLaLune Fairytales Page
www.surlalunefairytales.com

Includes the texts of over twenty familiar European fairy tales. Each tale has annotations, multicultural comparisons, and commentary. Also lists other versions of the tale online as well as places to purchase a hard copy.

Bibliomania
www.bibliomania.com

This site boasts "Free Online Literature with More than 2000 Classic Texts." Also includes tools to help with comprehension, including book notes, summaries, reference works, and study guides. The front page might look a little unfriendly (or give you a headache), but simply click on a main header for a list of available sections and topics: "Read" for fiction, poetry, and essays; "Study" for study guides and teacher resources; and "Research" for nonfiction and reference works. There's a good search engine included as well. Of particular note, the study guides section includes a good introduction to literary criticism and the full online text of Nicholas Culpeper's Herbal.

Bartleby
www.bartleby.com

Reference material, poetry, fiction, and nonfiction—this site includes a ton of classic material. The poetry section alone is well worth the visit. In addition, there are several encyclopedias, *Brewer's Dictionary of Phrase and Fable*, *Bulfinch's Mythology*, and an abridged version of *The Golden Bough*.

The site includes indexes by author, subject, and title as well as an excellent search engine that allows you to search either the entire site, individual areas (such as All Reference), or specific works.

Perseus Digital Library
www.perseus.tufts.edu

This site includes a very extensive collection of online classical texts, with lots of material on classical Greek and Roman writings. Each article includes extensive cross-references to other relevant material.

The volume of material on the site makes it a valuable resource, but unfortunately, it's difficult to find what you need. Start by clicking "Help Library" at the top of the main page and reading the "Frequently Asked Questions" section. Also, see the "Tools" link for ways to access the material.

The Endicott Studio
www.endicott-studio.com
The Internet home of "an interdisciplinary arts organization for Mythic and Interstitial Arts," this site is dedicated to a group of writers and artists who are interested in combining myth, folklore, and fairy tales with contemporary art. Members include Charles de Lint, the Frouds, and Terri Windling.

The group publishes newsletters and the site includes links to other artists as well as books, conferences, and so forth. This beautiful site includes Terri Windling's amazing artwork and lots of great, thought-provoking material.

The Second Circle
www.thesecondcircle.org
My website, with tools for the advancing Pagan, articles and essays from and for Pagans who've moved past the beginner stage.

Index

Academic books, 20, 31, 32
Accuracy
    in books, 27–29
    in divination, 67–68
Actualization, 13
Acupressure, 188
Aerobic exercise, 89–90, 146
Agriculture, wheel of the year and, 82–84
Agrippa, 20
"Ah hah" moments, 169, 215
Air, xiv, 99–100
Akashic Record, 43
Alcohol use, 180
Altars, 150
Altered consciousness, 161–83. *See also*
    Meditation
    drug use, 179–80
    exercises, 181–83
    human mind and, 164–67
    losing control and risk taking, 161–63
    safety considerations, 175–77
    uses of, 167–77
    visualization, 163–64, 174
American Indians, 16–17, 42, 79, 128
American Theosophical Society, 18
Animal companions, 93
Animals, Deity correspondences and, 131
Animal totems, 17
Aphrodite, 127, 130–31
Apotheosis, hero's journey and, 51
Appearance of Deities, 131–32
Apprentices (apprentice stage), 1–12
Archaeology books, 16
Archetypes, 35, 41–43
    hero's journey, 43–53
    myths and, 22
Art books, 18
"As above, so below," 37, 63–64

Astarte, 131
Astral plane, 99–100, 102–3
Astrology, 18, 63–64
Athena, 42
Atonement with the Father, hero's
    journey and, 50–51
Attainable goals, 151–52, 186–87
Attractive spells, 99, 121
Augury, 63–67. *See also* Omens; Portents
Auras (aura sensing), 188–89, 197
Author biases, 27–29
Authority, questioning, 3–4
Avatars, 130–31

Bacchus, 129
Baneful magic, 98
Bards, 198–202, 217
Bartleby, 19, 228
Beads, for prayer or meditation, 157–59
Beginners (beginner stage), xi–xii,
    xiii–xiv, 2. *See also* Apprentices
Belly of the Whale, hero's journey and,
    47–48
Beltane, 82, 83
Bias, in books, 27–29
Bibliography, 223–26
Biodegradables, 81
Blessings, 112–14, 146
Bloduwedd, 42
Body as temple, 150
Book of Shadows, 117–18
Books, 15–33
    about dreams, 68–69
    applying ideas from, 30–31
    for beginners, xi–xii, xiii–xiv
    bias in, 27–29
    bibliography, 223–26
    for covens, 10–11
    Deities and, 130–32

Books (continued)
    exercises, 31–33
    finding hero's journey in, 57
    hard to read, 20, 23, 31
    historical versus intuitive knowledge,
        27–29
    Scribes, 202–6, 216–17
    study tips for reading and
        understanding, 23–27
    where to find, 15–19
Bookstores, 15–19
Brain indigestion, 25
Breaking circles, 145, 149
Breathing, 178
Bride, 129, 131, 135
Brief History of Time, A (Hawking), 31
Brownies, 86

Cabala, 18, 181
Calling Deities, 140–42, 144
Call to Adventure, hero's journey and, 45
Campbell, Joseph, 224
    hero's journey and, 43–53, 57
Camping, 17, 78, 81, 85
Candle magic, 103–4
Capitalism, 119–20
Cassandra, 207
Casting circles, 144
Catholicism, 147, 156–57, 158
Cause and effect, 60
Celts, 29
Changing your mind, 34–58. See also
    Altered consciousness
    archetypes and, 41–43
    exercises, 54–58
    hero's journey, 43–53
    Jung and, 35
    relativism and, 40–41
    symbolic thinking and, 35–38
    synchronicity and, 38–39
Charging, in rituals, 144–45
Charms, 112–14
Christmas, 83–84
Circles
    breaking, 145, 149
    casting, 144
    drummers, 199–201
    logic of, 97–98

Clairvoyant dreams, 70, 71
Cleansing, in rituals, 143–44
Coincidences, meaningful, 38–39, 66–67
Collective unconscious, 35, 39, 43
Color(s), 122
    correspondences, 55–56
Comparative religion, books about,
        15–16, 18
Concordances, 55–57
Cone of power, 144–45
Conscious mind, 161–67, 168–69,
        174–75, 176. See also Altered
        consciousness
Correspondences (connections), 37,
        40–41
    symbol diary for, 55–57
Covens, 10–11, 124, 143–45
Critical thinking, 31–33
Crossing the First Threshold, hero's
        journey and, 47
Crossing the Return Threshold, hero's
        journey and, 53
Cross-quarter days, 82–84
Cultural biases, 27–29
Cultural conditioning. See Changing your
        mind

D&D Syndrome, 114–15
Daring
    inward, 102
    outward, 100–102
Dark side, 42–43, 166–67, 175–76
Darwin, Charles, 88
Deconstruction, 21, 32
Deities (Gods and Goddesses), 125–38.
        See also Myths; specific deities
    altered states for, 172–73
    archetypes versus, 42
    books about, 15–16
    direct contact with, 132–33
    discovering your, 127–33
    inviting and invoking, 140–42, 144
    journeyman period and, 2–3, 4–5
    listening skills, 148–50
    mixing of, 125–27, 128
    patron, 128–30
    relationship with, 135–38

requests from, 133–35, 136–37
researching, 130–32
rewards and responsibilities of, 133–35
teaching styles of, 136–37
Demeter, 21–23, 131
Democracy, hierarchy and, 213–14
Departure, hero's journey and, 44–48
Destiny, 59–60
Devotions, 146
Diary, symbol, 55–57
Difficult (hard to read) books, 20, 23, 31
Dionysus, 136
Discrimination, against Pagans, 116
"Dishes of life," 114–15
Distractions, 178
Divination, 59–75, 170
  accuracy in, 67–68
  augury compared with, 63–64
  books about, 18, 225
  Deity selection and, 129
  exercises, 73–75
  free will and, 59–61
  nature of time and, 61–63
  pitfalls of, 64–67
Dreams (dream work), 68–71, 117, 118, 129
Drugs (drug use), 179–80
Druids, 29
Drummers, 199–201
Dryads, 130

Earth, xv, 99–100. See also Nature
Emotional baggage, 8–9, 182
Emotional healers, 188–89, 191
Energy
  raising and targeting, 102, 144–45
  sending out, 103–4
Energy healing, 188–89
Enheduanna, 19, 224–25
Environment. See Nature
Environmental laws, 81
Environmental protest, 85, 150–51
Equinoxes, 82–84
Ethics, 105–12
Everyday magic, 113–15, 118–20
Evoking, in rituals, 140–42
Exercise (aerobic), 89–90, 146

Exercises
  altered consciousness (Chapter 8), 181–83
  books (Chapter 2), 26–27, 31–33
  changing your mind (Chapter 3), 54–58
  divination (Chapter 4), 73–75
  journeyman period (Chapter 1), 11–14
  magic (Chapter 6), 120–23
  nature (Chapter 5), 89–93
  rituals (Chapter 7), 156–59
  specialization (Chapter 9), 214–18

Fairies, 86–87
Fairy tales, 16
Familiars, 93
Fantasy, reality versus, 4, 8
Fate, 59–60
Fear, overcoming, 162–63, 182
  Warriors and, 196
Feminist criticism, 32
Feng shui, 18, 119
Fire, xiv–xv, 99–100, 101
Fire keepers, 197
Folklore, 74–75
  books about, 16
  fairies, 86–87
Folk (kitchen) magic, 112–14, 146
Foretelling. See also Augury; Divination
  pitfalls of, 64–67
Forgiveness, in journeyman period, 3
Four powers, 99–105
Frau Holda, 129
Frazer, James George, 27
Freedom to Live, hero's journey and, 53
Free will, 59–61
Freud, Sigmund, 35, 67
Friday, 101, 103–4
Friendships, 6–7, 10

Gaia (Gaia Theory), 76–79
Gardening (gardens), 78–79, 92–93
  books about, 17–18
Gardner, Gerald, 125
Geas, 134
Gimbutas, Marija, 27, 29
Goals, 150–52, 186–87

Gods and Goddesses. *See* Deities; *and specific gods and goddesses*
Grasse, Ray, 36, 37, 223
Graves, Robert, 25, 26, 27
"Great global matriarchy" dispute, 27, 29
Great Mothers, 37, 42, 77
Greek and Roman deities, 126, 130, 136
Green, 37
Greenhouses, 79
Guardians, 84–87
Guilds, 12

Handbook of Critical Approaches to Literature, 33
Harm none, 106–7
Hawking, Stephen, 31
Healers, 187–93
Healing circles, 98
Healing spells, 97
Health books, 17–18
Heart, following your, 216–18
Hecate, 136
Hera, 126
Herbalism, 17–18, 179–80, 190–91
Hero's journey, 43–53
    finding in books, 57
    stage one: departure, 44–48
    stage two: initiation, 48–51
    stage three: return, 52–53
    your life as, 57–58
Hero with a Thousand Faces (Campbell), 44
Hierarchy, democracy and, 213–14
High Priest/Priestess (HPs), 209–12
Hiking, 17, 80, 81, 90
Hindsight, 54
Historians, 203
History books, 16
Holidays, 82–84, 131, 141, 154–55
Home altars, 150
Honesty, in love spells, 110–11
Honesty, keeping secrets and, 115–17
Horus, 135
House sprites, 86
Human mind, 164–67
Humor, in journeyman period, 3
Hysteria (mass hallucinations), 8

I Ching, 18, 65–66, 119, 223
Imagination, 174–75

Imbolc, 82, 83, 131
Inanna, 131
Inhibitions, reducing your, 161–63
Initiation, hero's journey and, 48–51
Inner house, 165–67, 174–77
Inner peace, in journeyman period, 5
Instincts (physiological urges), 41–42, 54, 72–73
Integration, 182–83
Interconnectivity. *See* Divination
Internet resources, 19, 227–29
Introspection, 214–16
Invoking Deities, 140–42, 144
Inward daring, 102
Inward knowledge, 102
Inward silence, 102–3
Inward will, 103–4
Irrational thinking, 36, 161–62
ISBN (International Standard Book Number), 19

Jehovah, 128, 135
Jesus Christ, 84
Job spells, 108, 123
    ethical considerations, 111
    four powers and, 99–105
    symbol creation, 121, 122
Journeyman/woman (journeyman period), 1–14
    changing your mind, 6–7, 34–58
    covens and solitaries, 10–11
    exercises, 11–14
    lessons of, 3–5
    reading books, 15–33
    risks involved in, 6–10
Jung, Carl Gustav, 35, 68, 166
    archetypes and, 41–43
    relativism and, 40–41
    synchronicity and, 38–39
Jupiter, 122

Kali, 129
Kitchen (folk) magic, 112–14, 146
Knowledge
    historical versus intuitive, 27–29
    inward, 102
    outward, 100

"Know thine enemy," 31–32
"Know thyself," 102

Labyrinth, time as, 62–63
Land spirits, 84–87
Lent, 156–57
Lessons. *See* Exercises
Librarians, 203. *See also* Scribes
Libraries, 15–19
Lines of power, 79–80
Literary criticism, 32–33
Loki, 131
Lord and Lady, 125, 137
Losing control, 161–63
Love spells, 110–12
    best day for, 101, 103–4
Lucas, George, 44
Lughnasadh, 82, 83

Magic, 95–123
    balancing checkbook as act of, 118–20
    building book of symbols, 117–18
    charms and blessings, 112–14
    Deity selection and, 129
    ethics of, 105–12
    everyday, 113–15, 118–20
    exercises, 120–23
    how it works, 98–105
    logic of the circle, 97–98
    ritual compared with, 96–97
    symbol creation, 120–23
    truth, honesty, and keeping secrets,
        115–17
Magic Flight, hero's journey and, 52
Magician's Companion, The (Whitcomb),
    56
Magic words, 121–22
Man and His Symbols (Jung), 35, 38
Martial arts, 196–97
Massage, 188–89
Mass hallucinations (hysteria), 8
Master of Two Worlds, hero's journey
    and, 53
Material wealth, 119–20
Meaningful coincidences, 38–39, 66–67
Meditation, 163–64, 177–79, 181, 208
    beads for, 157–59
    techniques for, 178–79

Meeting the Goddess, hero's journey and,
    49–50
Memorization, in rituals, 152–56
Mental skills, in journeyman period, 5
Midden heaps, 29
Mind, 164–67
    changing your. *See* Altered
        consciousness; Changing your mind
    clearing your, 102–3
Money, 119–20
Monotheistic religions, 34, 40, 126, 147.
    See also Catholicism
Morals. *See* Ethics
Morrigan, 127
Murder, 106, 107
Murray, Margaret, 27
Musicians, 198–202
Myths (mythology)
    books about, 15–16, 20
    extracting meaning from, 20–23
    hero's journey, 43–53
    Internet resource, 227–28

Native Americans, 16–17, 42, 79, 128
Nature (natural world), 74–75, 76–94
    agriculture and the wheel of the year,
        82–84
    altering consciousness and, 171–72
    exercises, 89–93
    Gaia Theory of, 76–79
    journeyman period and, 7
    land spirits and guardians, 84–87
    one-sided view of, 87–89
    power spots in, 79–81
9–11 terrorist attacks (2001), 67–68
Nondogmatism, 10, 213
Note taking. *See also* Book of Shadows;
        Symbol diary
    finding synchronicity and, 54–55
    reading books and, 25, 26
Nyads, 130

Objectivity trap, 64–66
Offerings, 142–43, 145
Omens, 63–64, 74
    altering consciousness and, 170–71
    Deity selection and, 129
    synchronicity and, 39, 66–67

Oracles, 206–8, 217
Oration, 196, 198
Outing Pagans, 104–5, 116
Outward daring, 100–102
Outward knowledge, 100
Outward silence, 104–5
Outward will, 104
Overuse pitfall, 66–67
Owls, 42

Pagan Bards, 198–202, 217
Pagan Healers, 187–93
Pagan Lent, 156–57
Pagan Rosary, 157–59
Pagan Scribes, 202–6, 216–17
Pagan Standard Time, 61
Pagan Warriors, 193–98
Palmistry, 18
Pan, 135
Parks and gardens, 78–79
Passage of time, 61–63
Patron Deities, 128–30
Paxson, Diana L., 57
Peace keepers, 195, 196
Pentagrams, 214–16
Persephone, 21–23
Personal correspondences, 55–57
Personal ethics, 105–12
Personal goals, 150–52, 186–87
Personal relationships. See also Love spells
    with Deities, 135–38
    friendship, 6–7, 10
Personal responsibility, 138–40
Personal symbols, 40–41, 42
    diary for, 55–57
Philosophy books, 16, 18
Phobias, 182, 196
Physical exercise, 89–90, 146
Plants, 179–80
    Deity correspondences and, 131
Poetry books, 18
Portents, 39, 63–64
Powells Bookstore, 19
Power spots, 79–81
Prayer beads, 157–59
Prayers, 97
    Deities and, 129–30, 143, 149

Prediction. See also Augury; Divination; Dreams
    pitfalls of, 64–67
Prometheus, 130
Prophecy, 142
Prosperity spells, 109
Protection spells, 158–59, 197
Psychoactive substances, 179–80
Psychology, 35
    books about, 16, 18
Public libraries, 15–19
Public speaking, 196, 198

Quan Yin, 135
Quid pro quo, 133–34

Rational thinking, 35–36, 161–62, 171
Reading. See Bibliography; Books
Realistic goals, 151–52, 186–87
Reality (real), 174–75
    fantasy versus, 4, 8
Rede, 106–7
Refusal of the Call, hero's journey and, 45–46
Refusal of the Return, hero's journey and, 52
Regalia of Deities, 131–32
Reiki massage, 188–89
Reincarnation, Deities and, 128
Relationships. See Personal relationships
Relativism, 39, 40–41
Religion
    books about, 15–16, 18
    ethical behavior and, 105–6
Renaissance Festivals, 83
Repression, 8–9, 42–43, 166–67, 175–76, 182
Repulsive spells, 99, 121
Rescue from Without, hero's journey and, 52–53
Researchers, 202–6
Resolutions, 156–57
Resources, 223–26
    Internet, 19, 227–29
Responsibilities, 138–40
    of Deities, 133–35
Return, hero's journey and, 52–53
Risk taking, 161–63

Rituals, 13, 124–60
  creating, 140–43
  Deities and, 125–38, 141–42
  devotions, 146
  Drummers for, 199–201
  exercises, 156–59
  goals of, 150–52
  listening skills, 148–50
  magic compared with, 96–97
  memorization in, 152–56
  parts of, 143–45, 154–55
  personal responsibility and, 138–40
  routine and spontaneity of, 145–48
  Scribes for, 203–4
  search for "God," 127–33
Road of Trials, hero's journey and, 48–49
Romanticism, 88–89
Rosary, 157–59
Runes, 65, 73–74

Sabbats. *See* Holidays
Sacred geometry, 79–81, 201, 223–24
Sacred spaces. *See* Circles
Sacred Texts, 19, 227
Samhain, 82, 83
Sanity, 4, 8
Santa Claus, 84
Scribes, 202–6, 216–17
Scripted rituals, 152–53
Scrying, 65–66
Secrets, keeping of, 115–17
Seers, 206–8
Self-assessment, 214–16
Self-confidence, 112
Self-dedications, 13
Self-sacrifice, 156–57
September 11 terrorist attacks (2001),
  67–68
Shadow, 42–43, 166–67, 175–76
Shrines, 146
Silence
  inward, 102–3
  outward, 104–5
Singers, 198–202
Solitaries (solitary study), 10–11
Solstices, 82–84
Specialization, 184–219

Bards, 198–202
  excellence in, 185–87
  exercises, 214–18
  Healers, 187–93
  High Priest/Priestess, 209–12
  Oracles, 206–8
  picking your focus, 184–85
  Scribes, 202–6
  Warriors, 193–98
Spells, 96
  altered states for, 172–73
  building book of symbols, 117–18
  charms and blessings, 112–14
  Deity selection and, 129
  four powers and, 99–105
  personal ethics and, 105–12
  symbol creation, 120–23
Spiral, time as, 62–63
Spirits, 130–31
Spiritual epiphanies, 70–71
Spiritual healers, 188–89, 191
Stage direction of rituals, 155
Star Wars (movie), 44–53
Stealing, 107, 108
Stone circles, 79, 86
Storytellers, 199, 201
Strengths, playing to your, 216–18
Subconscious mind, 163, 164–67,
  174–77, 182
Supernatural Aid, hero's journey and, 46
Symbol(s). *See also* Archetypes; Personal
  symbols
  building book of, 117–18
  creating, 100–102, 120–23
Symbol chits, 73–74
Symbol diary, 55–57
Symbolic thinking, 35–38, 40–41, 169
Synchronicity, 35, 38–39, 40
  finding (exercise), 54–55
  overuse pitfall, 66–67

Tarot, 63–64, 71–73
  pitfalls of, 64–67
Teachers, 10–11
  Deities as, 136–37
Tea leaves, 65
Technology (technological advances),
  118–20

Temples, 150–52
Temptation, hero's journey and, 50
Terrorist attacks of September 11 (2001), 67–68
Therapists (therapy), 9–10, 182, 191
Thinking
    critical, 31–33
    rational versus irrational, 35–36, 161–62, 171
    symbolic, 35–38, 40–41, 169
Thor, 135
Three Books of Occult Philosophy (Agrippa), 20
Time, nature of, 61–63
To Dare, 99–105
To Keep Silent, 99–105
To Know, 99–105
Tools
    for learning, xiv–xv
    making from natural world, 91–92
Topographical (trail) maps, 17
To Will, 99–105
Trance state, 162–63, 177–78
Trauma, 8–9, 166–67, 175–76, 182
Travel books, 17
Trees, observation of, 91
Trials, hero's journey and, 48–49
True Will, 173–74, 183
Truth, keeping secrets and the, 115–17

Ultimate Boon, hero's journey and, 51
University bookstores, 19

University libraries, 19
Urban life, 77–79

Venus, 37, 103–4, 130–31
Visualization, 11–12, 163–64, 174
Voice, 155, 196, 198
Von Franz, M.-L., 38

Waking Dream, The (Grasse), 36, 37, 223
Walker, Barbara, 27
Warriors, 193–98
Water, xiv, 99–100
Weaknesses, focusing on your, 216–18
Wheel of the year, 82–84
White Goddess (Graves), 25, 26
White Raven, The (Paxson), 57
Wiccan Rede, 106–7
Wilderness survival classes, 17
Wildlife rescue groups, 79
Will. *See also* Free will
    discovering True, 173–74, 183
    inward, 103–4
    outward, 104
"Wise woman," 11–12
Wolfe, Tom, 87
Women's studies books, 16

Yule, 83–84

Zeus, 126, 136
Zoos, 78–79